REDISCOVER THE

MAGICK

| OF THE |

GODS

| AND |

GODDESSES

About the Author

Jean-Louis de Biasi is a author, lecturer, and Hermetic philosopher who has studied the various topics of the tradition since the 1970s, and who has been initiated into the highest degrees of several Western initiatic traditions. Introduced very early into the Ordo Aurum Solis, in 2003 de Biasi became the tenth Lifetime Grand Master. He is also in charge as Reverend of the religious expression of the Hermetic tradition called Ecclesia Ogdoadica.

De Biasi's philosophical and spiritual tradition is rooted in Neoplatonic and Hermetic affiliations, and includes masters of the tradition such as Plato, Proclus, Iamblicus, the Emperor Julian, Pletho, and Ficino, to name a few. He is also the Grand Patriarch in charge of the Ordre Kabbalistique de la Rose-Croix (the Kabbalistic Order of the Rose-Cross, O.K.R.C.).

He was initiated into Freemasonry and raised in 1992. He is a 32° Scottish Rite Freemason, Southern Jurisdiction, U.S., F.G.C.R., Royal Arch Mason. He is a specialist of Masonic Rituals and Esoteric Freemasonry.

He is invited regularly to various countries where he gives workshops, seminars, trainings, and conferences on philosophical and traditional subjects and expounds on his writings.

He is the author of several books in French, which have been translated into several languages, and he is now writing in English for Llewellyn Publications.

To read more about Jean-Louis de Biasi, please visit him online:
https://www.facebook.com/jeanlouis.debiasi
http://www.debiasi.org
http://www.aurumsolis.info

revealing the mysteries of theurgy

REDISCOVER THE
MAGICK
OF THE
GODS
AND
GODDESSES

Jean-Louis de Biasi

Llewellyn Publications
Woodbury, Minnesota

First English-Language Edition, North America
First Printing, 2014

Originally published in French as *ABC de la Magie Sacrée*
Copyright Editions Grancher, 2010
Translated and upgraded by Jean-Louis de Biasi

Cover art: iStockphoto.com/12363556/©ShutterWorx
Cover design by Kevin R. Brown
Edited by Patti Frazee
Interior art provided by Jean-Louis de Biasi

The Seal of the Aurum Solis and its Star are used with permission from the author, Jean-Louis de Biasi, who is the Grand Master of the Aurum Solis.

Llewellyn Publications is a registered trademark of Llewellyn Worldwide Ltd.

Library of Congress Cataloging-in-Publication Data
Biasi, Jean-Louis de.
 [ABC de la magie sacrée. English]
 Rediscover the magick of the gods and goddesses : revealing the mysteries of theurgy / Jean-Louis de Biasi. — First English-Language Edition.
   pages cm
 Includes bibliographical references and index.
 ISBN 978-0-7387-3997-7
 1. Theurgy—History. 2. Magic—Egypt—History. 3. Hermetism—History. I. Title.
 BF1623.T56B5313 2014
 135'.45—dc23   2014008763

Llewellyn Worldwide Ltd. does not participate in, endorse, or have any authority or responsibility concerning private business transactions between our authors and the public.
 All mail addressed to the author is forwarded but the publisher cannot, unless specifically instructed by the author, give out an address or phone number.
 Any Internet references contained in this work are current at publication time, but the publisher cannot guarantee that a specific location will continue to be maintained. Please refer to the publisher's website for links to authors' websites and other sources.

Llewellyn Publications
A Division of Llewellyn Worldwide Ltd.
2143 Wooddale Drive
Woodbury, MN 55125-2989
www.llewellyn.com

Printed in the United States of America

Other Books by Jean-Louis de Biasi

The Divine Arcana of the Aurum Solis

Secrets and Practices of the Freemasons

The Order of the Sacred Word

ORDO AURUM SOLIS

Anno MDCCXCVII Condito Constat

By Authority,
P∴B∴, Administrator General, A.S.—O.S.V.

"The Theurgists are not counted in the herd
of men who are subject to Fate."
—*Chaldaean Oracles*, Fragment 153

"O blissful Goddess, I am your initiate.
Awaken in me the memory of the Sacred Mysteries,
and take away forgetfulness forever."
—Excerpt from the *Orphic Hymn to Mnemozyne*

Acknowledgments

I would like to offer my grateful thanks to Martin Parrot, Mario Basile, and Waleed for their expertise and help with different parts of this book. As it is always difficult in our daily lives to find the time to investigate the specific subjects I have written about in this book, their support was very much appreciated.

I also thank the initiates of the Aurum Solis who participate regularly and actively share their experience and ideas in the forums of the Order.

I also want to thank Carl Weschcke for his foreword and his deep understanding of what is at stake on the spiritual, philosophical, and social levels. In the Western tradition, few people can be considered to be founders and builders. Undoubtedly Carl, former Grand Master of the Aurum Solis, is one of them, and his work manifests it.

I am very grateful to Don Kraig, who reviewed this book and shared with me his expertise as an author. Don passed away few months after this book was achieved. In December 2013, Don sent me an e-mail saying: "Your book is no longer just a good book ... it is fantastic. You have made the topic, including the history—and many people are bored with history—fascinating to any reader and practical for anyone who wants to start using the system. Congratulations." I will cherish his personal advice the rest of my life as an author. Thank you, Don, and I wish you the best in the afterlife!

Finally, there aren't enough words and this space is too limited to show my gratitude and appreciation for my wife, Patricia, for her essential and continuous support. Her presence is a real power that helps me continue the work I am doing as an author and as Grand Master of the Aurum Solis.

For
Eric Ronteix

Contents

Figures

How to Use This Book

This book is intended to be a real initiation into the magical and Theurgic tradition. For this reason, it has been organized in a very precise way. Each part has a specific function and will help you unveil the Western Mysteries, which have been hidden for many centuries.

When you open this book, you must understand an essential point: *Each part of this book is important and has a special role to play.* Even so, you can read these chapters in any order that appeals to you. You are free to read the last part before the second part, or the fourth after the fifth.

Your reading should be guided by your interest. If you want to begin the exercises first, start there. When you feel the need to understand where these rituals came from, you can read the chapter on history in Part One. There is no problem with this strategy at all.

Below I have summarized the purpose of each part in order for you to clearly see the progression of the book. You will find a short introduction at the beginning of each chapter. At the end of each chapter you will find a review with eight questions. These questions will help you develop your understanding and memory.

The Seven Steps of This Book
Part 1—*Knowing Your Roots Is Essential*

Theurgy is a Pagan tradition: Nothing can exist without roots. Knowing the origin and the history of a family helps us to understand its specific attributes. To understand Theurgy (sometimes called High Magick), you must know that this is a Pagan tradition that appeared at the beginning of the Western spiritual tradition.

The chain of the initiates: From the time of the Egyptian Empire to our current time you can follow this chain of initiates down through centuries. Dogmatic and political religions tried to kill these masters and destroy their work. Initiates of the magick of the Gods and Goddesses succeeded in keeping this inheritance alive.

History is a keystone: All traditions are not strictly equivalent and history is the key to understanding why this is so.

Part 2—Constructing a Healthy and Safe Life as a High Magician and Theurgist

The two major pillars of the Theurgic tradition: The Theurgic tradition has two major pillars that support and delimit the healthy life of the student: philosophy and ritual.

The first pillar, philosophy, is not a sterile and useless intellectual discourse. Philosophy is a real spiritual exercise that helps you to develop three essential parts of your magical personality: 1) it helps you develop a healthy and rational mind; 2) it helps you discover how to enjoy your life here and now; 3) it helps you understand and prepare for the process of your death.

The latter of these two pillars, ritual, is different than magick. When you understand that Theurgy is a ritual work focused on raising your soul with the help of divinities, you can begin this path without any risks.

Part 3—Discovering the Presence of the Divinities in the World and Understanding Why Monotheistic Religions Separated the Divine from Our World

A disconnected world: We are living today in a world that has become disconnected from the sacred and the divine. Monotheistic religions have severed the direct relationship that existed in the Pagan world between believers and their Gods. The monotheist chiefs used their dogmas as weapons to gain supremacy over Pagans and their world.

A Pagan world full of divinities: In the pre-monotheistic world, Gods and Goddesses were present everywhere. Worshippers and Theurgists used many ways to reach the Gods. The existence of a divine principle above this spiritual ladder (which is impossible to define) was accepted, but without rejecting the notion of sacredness in the world.

This part is intended to clearly explain how this spontaneous and original relationship to the divine was distorted in order to take it from you.

Part 4—Recognizing a True Sacred Book and Understanding Its Role

The revelations: From the beginning of humanity, Gods and Goddesses have spoken with people who were trained to receive their messages. This was the birth of what is known today as "sacred books."

Sacred books are not equivalent: Paganism, including Theurgy, has teachings that offer the student fundamental information about the philosophical and ritual processes. However, you must learn why all sacred books are not equivalent, and why some of them are even dangerous. To do that, you must first learn how to recognize the validity of divine revelations.

This chapter will also provide you with an original translation of the first book of the *Corpus Hermeticum*.

Part 5—Understanding the Macrocosm

Life is enjoyable: Once we have become aware of the roots of this Theurgic tradition—know that our body and our physical life should be enjoyable, understand how the rituals must be used, and feel the divine presence all around us—we are ready to unveil the cosmic order.

Structure of the cosmos: The first step that is unveiled in this part is the simple structure of the cosmos. This is the first structure you have to use in your Theurgic journey. There are no complicated or unrealistic notions here. The pre-Christian Theurgists always used those elements that are well-known to everyone who practices Theurgy: four elements, seven divine spheres, the Aether, and twelve divine powers.

Part 6—Understanding the Microcosm and Revealing Your Destiny

The microcosm: In the Western tradition there is a well-known concept: the macrocosm (the cosmos) and the microcosm (us). The previous chapter unveiled the traditional structure of the macrocosm. The present part unveils the microcosm. You must learn how you are constituted in order to understand how your occult structure works, and what its purpose is.

The temple blueprint: The Theurgic tradition uses the representation of a traditional Greek temple to highlight the five principles of human beings: Body, Body of Light, Soul, Spirit, and the Divine.

From this point you will be able to understand the purpose of Theurgy and safely begin your Theurgic Great Work.

Part 7—Clear Fundamental Rituals Enable You to Eventually Rise to the Highest Levels of Consciousness

The three cosmic principles: You can now fully begin to practice and use the three cosmic principles: 1) *Elements* (Theurgic Ritual of the Pentalpha); 2) *Planets* (Ritual of the Seven Gates); 3) *Signs* (Ritual of the Celestial Temenos).

The planetary days unveiled: Be aware that this part will clearly unveil ritual principles that have never previously been explained, such as the true way to calculate the planetary days and hours.

This Celestial Ladder provides the clear steps we need to use Theurgy in order to ascend to the highest levels of consciousness we can reach.

foreword

Where to start?

That's a writer's challenge whenever asked to contribute a foreword to a new book.

The Magick of the Gods and Goddesses is premised on the antiquity of the Western esoteric tradition, and of the Aurum Solis (A.S.) within that tradition. It's specifically about particular magical principles and certain techniques with elements specific to the A.S. tradition. It would be easy for someone to say, "Well, just start at the beginning."

Everything has some kind of beginning, but in a case like this, a beginning point is hard to establish in historical fact. Many of the original resources that a historian uses were lost through time and ignorance and then by the deliberate destruction of writings deemed "heretical" in the early history of Christianity. This was particularly so at the time of its *political* union with the Roman Empire under the Emperor Constantine in the year 313, when thousands of sacred and esoteric writings were gathered and destroyed in order to create the single approved public text we know today as the Bible. The goal was to create a theocracy through control of a rigid theology and institution to manipulate the people. The agents of the Emperor and the "Church Fathers" were very successful in this.

In the centuries that followed, more declared *heretical* writings were discovered and destroyed and their practitioners driven underground or executed. Even with the advent of Protestant Christianity in 1517, such persecution continued into modern times. In 1600, astronomer Giordano Bruno was condemned by the Catholic Inquisition and burned to death for stating the sun was a star among many.

Along with the establishment of the imperial Roman Catholic Church as a religious monopoly in Europe came the belief and intention of world domination, just as now proclaimed as the right and goal of some sects of Islam and as once proclaimed by the Jewish Moses: "This is what the LORD, the God of Israel, says, 'Every man put his sword on his thigh, and go back and forth from gate to gate in the camp, and each of you kill his brother and friend and neighbor.'" (International Standard Version ©2012.)

Blind faith in God as interpreted by proclaimed prophets, messengers, priests, and preachers leads to abuse and inevitable conflict. Surely no God asks you to murder in "His Name," nor to abuse women or hide their beauty. In seeing beauty in women and in all of creation we awaken to beauty within and add to beauty without. No God or Goddess requires you to deny sensual pleasures or to call sex other than for procreation "sin." There is no sin, no evil, no crime other than that executed by humans motivated by greed, hate, and blind obedience.

Two thousand years ago there were no universities in the Roman Empire, which extended over most of Europe and into Egypt and parts of the Mediterranean Middle East. After the Empire's collapse, the first European university appeared in 1088 in Bologna, followed by the Universities of Paris and Oxford in 1096 and of Cambridge in 1209. With scholars and students now doing research, some of those early esoteric writings, literally hidden underground, were uncovered and students and scholars alike began to explore alternate views of the Universe and of the spiritual nature of life, existence, and of the person. Knowledge began the long journey to replace blind faith and required obedience to ignorance and brutality.

But it was only with the advent of the printed book that the back of the religious "Thought Police" was finally broken. (I have an original copy of the *Nuremberg Chronicle* printed in 1493.) As "mass produced" printed books became increasingly affordable and available, so came public access to knowledge and its increasing spread beyond the limits of authoritarian "academia." Still, it was not until the Europeans came to America to escape religious domination that the first free public school was founded in 1634—free to the students and free from religious domination. True education became a reality. Here were the beginnings of the modern era when practical knowledge for everyday living enabled ordinary people to climb the economic and social ladder. Today, free public education and its requirement for all is nearly worldwide except in very strict and isolated Islamic communities.

Freedom from domination by the Church and the increasing access to information and knowledge through books and education marked the transition in human consciousness that is the "New Age." Astrologically, it is described as the passing from the Piscean Age of blind faith to the Age of Aquarius and inspired spiritual knowledge formulated in rational thought. It is also the passing from the age of proclaimed authority in which "teacher knows best" to one in which the student becomes his own best teacher, able to utilize the tremendous information and knowledge resources of this New Age. Good teachers today serve as helpful guides to the student's personal study and practice. We learn by doing, not just by listening.

It was the appearance of "phenomena" at the home of the Fox sisters in 1848 in rural New York State that gave birth to the modern religion of Spiritualism and, in turn, to the scientific investigation of psychic phenomena and the now-recognized science of parapsychology. Spiritualism focused on survival after physical death. Parapsychology's main focus was on the physical demonstration and measurement of non-physical phenomena. Esoterics know that the cosmos is far greater than the physical universe and that most psychic phenomena occur in higher non-physical dimensions and only reflect downward into physical manifestation.

During this same period, the widespread news of psychic phenomena created the atmosphere in which esoteric knowledge moved from secrecy to accessibility. The old esoteric adage: *When the Student is ready, the Teacher will appear* is exactly correct. Learning, growth, development, and attainment are all your responsibility. Even with the benefit of good "teacher-guides," you learn through self-study, and by doing it yourself. You must practice and apply what you learn knowing that <u>practice does perfect</u> your initial knowledge through personal observation, followed by testing and new practice. Don't blindly accept what others tell you: use your mind and apply your developing intuition. All esoteric teachings have the same message: "Ye are Gods in the making." Your destiny is to become more than you are, and your obligation in these critical times is to "Do it now!"

If we are the progeny of a divine creator, then *nothing of our nature can be other than divine.* But becoming more than you are requires work and self-transformation. The body grows and becomes transformed through care, training, and physical exercise; the mind grows and becomes transformed though education, training, and mental exercise; and soul and spirit likewise grow and become transformed through study, training, and exercise. That is the system available to Aurum Solis students.

The author quotes Nietzsche—"If you want peace of mind, just believe. If you want the truth, you must search for it." The system of training mind and imagination makes the search practical and real. Truth is not given to you despite the claims of priests and preachers that truth is within their faith. Through ritual and systematic meditation upon proven viable symbols, truth is progressively experienced and understood in personal context.

It is time for you to take the next step forward in your own growth and development, and in so doing you are taking the next step in human evolution that is the essence of the Great Plan from the "Beginning." Even if we can't point to a historic beginning in ancient times, we do know that the <u>concept</u> for this magical tradition is very old. Regardless of age and place of origin, it is intrinsic to your very being. Some call it the "Path of Return," knowing that our origin lies before, and "above" physical manifestation, and that our purpose in life—our very real "assignment"—is to grow, develop, and to become all that we can be.

As students of the Aurum Solis system, you become part of a band of independent workers participating in the "Great Work" that is the purpose of our being. You are <u>not</u> part of any band or congregation of *disciples, guru followers, acolytes, chosen people,* or any other kind of dependent on any external teacher, master, or authority. Your responsibility is to your own High Self, to all of humanity, to the health of the planet, and to the greater cosmos in which we all have our being, whether we prefer to call it (not Him, or Her) God or Goddess, Divinity, Creator, or Source.

It's a great adventure, a wonderful journey, and I thank you and wish you *bon voyage.*

Carl Llewellyn Weschcke
Chairman, Llewellyn Worldwide, Ltd.
7th Past Grandmaster Ordo Aurum Solis

Co-author with Joe H. Slate, Ph.D
Astral Projection for Psychic Empowerment
Clairvoyance for Psychic Empowerment
Doors to Past Lives & Lives Between Lives
Llewellyn Complete Book of Psychic Empowerment
Psychic Empowerment for Everyone
Self-Empowerment through Self-Hypnosis
Self-Empowerment & Your Subconscious Mind
Astral Projection for Psychic Empowerment meditation guide,
Audio CD
Self-Empowerment through Self-Hypnosis meditation guide,
Audio CD
Vibratory Astral Projection & Clairvoyance meditation guide,
Audio CD

Introduction

Many years ago, when I was still young, I had three strange encounters. Even if they appeared to be different, each one had an impact that echoed at the deepest levels of my memory. Behind what I perceived, I felt that each of the encounters was connected to a common source.

The first encounter happened when I was walking on a beach. The sun was high in the sky. The sounds of the waves and the calls of the birds were the only noises around me. Then I saw her, naked, stepping into the sea. When the sea was at the level of her hips, she stopped and performed a strange ritual, declaiming texts in a language I was not able to understand. As she threw water up to the blue sky, I saw the water shimmering in the rays of the sun before it flowed back down onto her body. Drops of water were scattered about on her hair, which shone in the sun. Her body seemed to be totally immersed in the natural elements, deeply united with the sun and the sea, balancing the whole cosmos in a ritual I didn't understand.

Another time, I was walking in the country under a grey, cloudy sky and I saw a woman at the edge of a wood. Facing the direction of the rising sun, it seemed to me that she was talking to creatures I was not able to see. She raised her arms to the sky and I saw a ball of light, bright as the sun, whirling just under the dark clouds. Then the sky opened and rays of the sun lit up the place, warming the wet land. A light mist began to rise as a sweet breeze stirred.

The last encounter occurred while on a long journey in Egypt, during the astrological sign of Leo. I was visiting a little temple far from any tourist group. It was the beginning of the afternoon. The sand and the stones were scorching. I saw a man. He was moving in silence in the ruins, sometimes touching parts of the walls, praying in a language I had never heard before. He was invoking the ancient divinities who lived in this temple. I felt a powerful presence around him, and progressively, the reality of a living chain of initiates became clear to me. I felt deeply that if divinities are immortal, they cannot ever die or be killed out. They are still there now, listening to the voices of their initiates, waiting for the time when they will be welcomed again by the people of the world.

These encounters echoed deeply in me. They were a part of what removed the veils that still cloaked my memory at that time.

There is an official history and a forgotten history. Even if we are unaware of that, we have become accustomed to the idea that history and religions form progressively. Consequently, the newest religions will often present themselves as the best and final accomplishment. Even if we can talk about progress in science, progress on the spiritual level is not the same thing.

For a little more than 1500 years Christianity has spread, first in the Western world, and then all over the world. It is historically clear that a large and essential part of what comprises this religion has its origin in the ancient philosophies, spiritualities, and initiations. This new religion was not built out of nothing, on virgin territory. For thousands of years, powerful civilizations, including the Chaldean, Egyptian, Greek, and Roman civilizations, have really been the foundation of the Western world as we know it today.

The pre-Christian religions were not as organized and coherent as Christianity. In fact every tribe, every race, and every city had its own major divinity or group of divinities. Paganism, as we know it today, didn't exist in the ancient world. The word "Paganism" was coined to characterize peasants who did not give up on their beliefs and traditional rituals fast enough to suit Christians who were trying to convert them. In Paganism, everyone was free to choose one or more divinities that suited them, and free to continue to worship the divinities of their own family. Everyone was able to change divinities and to welcome a new divinity brought to locals from a foreign city by relatives who travelled abroad. Temples were also scattered everywhere and pilgrims travelled from one to another, always worshipping different Gods and Goddesses.[1] In opposition to the modern monotheistic religions, these ancient religions were inclusive instead being exclusive.

Figure 1: The symbol of the Sun God Shamash, being a form of the eight-pointed star, was widely employed all throughout Mesopotamia.

In every period of history, there were people who were eager to unveil the mysteries and have something more than simple prayers. Just as you are searching today, they were looking for a real and direct

---

1. As a matter of fact, the convention of capitalizing the name "God" (singular) and not capitalizing "Gods" or "Goddesses" comes from a religious influence that has been consistently trying to minimize the importance of the Immortal Divinities. This book is about the Hermetic and Theurgic traditions, and I have always been tolerant and respectful of all beliefs. For this reason, I will use capitals in this book for "God," "Gods," and "Goddesses."

contact with the divine world in order to accomplish several purposes; some related to their daily lives, others related to the afterlife. Various systems were progressively developed in order to achieve these inner experiences. In the Western tradition, "schools of Mysteries" and High Magick (Theurgy) were the main systems utilized by those who were not satisfied being simple believers. In parallel with the development of these secret ceremonies, several philosophies emerged. Some of them were more focused on the study of nature, but most of them explored the universe and the divinities.

The Neoplatonic and Hermetic traditions (Plotinus, Iamblichus, Proclus, for example, are part of this school) developed essential concepts to understand the cosmos, the nature and destiny of the soul. Understanding the world was an essential step, but just as today, initiates were eager to really act and change their lives. They reasoned that if the divinities are all around us it would be necessary to understand how to contact them and how they can help us achieve our goals as humans. This purpose is far higher than popular religion or magic. It originated with a deep desire to understand what we are, but, at the same time, to have a clear and progressive method that is able to help us in life and after death. These concerns were the same for the first philosophers. In the Mediterranean world they developed a very powerful initiatic and magical tradition called the Theurgic tradition, sometimes known as "High Magick."

This Western tradition provided real and effective Theurgic rituals. Marks of these rituals can be found here and there in different modern initiatic Orders, though they are sometimes deformed or fragmented. Fortunately, these teachings were preserved in different ways and were reenacted during the Italian Renaissance. Eventually, they were handed down to modern times through the links of what is called the "Golden Chain." These processes (visualization, lucid dreams, individual Theurgic rituals, etc.) enable us to harmonize the different levels of our being, in order to return to a good internal balance and to the serenity we once possessed. Once this is accomplished, we will be able to restore our place in the cosmos, and to act freely, having a positive effect on our life and destiny.

Magical and Theurgic rituals use the human inner powers to increase or enhance beauty, love, and pleasure. Balance and harmony are the main points of this esoteric and spiritual approach.

This is the tradition I will teach you about in this book. The exercises and rituals provided in this book come from the same pre-Christian and pre-Qabalistic sources. I will explain the historical and philosophical markers, but also the main rituals you must use in order to make progress on this path.

Gods and Goddesses speak to everyone, and no ideology can pretend to impose its divinities on anyone else without restraining personal freedom.

Take the time to really enjoy your studies. You should revel in them. Every time we learn and read sacred texts, we are really praying. Our studies are like a perfume rising up to the divine. As you will see when you read the text of the *Corpus Hermeticum*: "The virtue of the soul is Gnosis, because the one who knows is good, pious, and already divine." (C.H. 10:9)

When I open a book that was written by a Theurgist such as Iamblichus, I am always amazed at how eternal his words are. Some questions, some mysteries, are the same today as they were centuries ago. It has always been strange and fascinating for me to feel such a personal contact with this Chain. Theurgy and Hermetism[2] are vehicles of pure light, which is far different from what we see today in most magic orders. They are replete with an abundance of symbols, medals, seals, degrees, honors, etc. A Hermetist or Theurgist is looking for simplicity. Men and women are both looking for the same thing. When I was

---

2. In 1997, a scholar proposed a change in the spelling of Hermetism in order to distinguish the period before and after the Renaissance. For the period before the Renaissance, he proposed that the spelling remain "Hermetism." But for the period after the Renaissance (up to and including today) he proposed the use of a new term: Hermeticism.

Hermetism refers to the period up to the Renaissance and Hermeticism refers to the period after the Renaissance, up to and including today. Even though this distinction is an artificial one, it can be quite useful. For example, since I am writing about the period prior to the Renaissance in this book, I chose to use the term "Hermetism" throughout this entire book.

first placed in direct contact with this Ogdoadic Chain, I realized and deeply felt the worthlessness of the initiatic charts, degrees, and the exciting clothing that was used in other orders. I saw that if a tradition is true and luminous it must be simple and without any anger or violence. Initiation cannot be an intellectual game used by magicians who sit around arguing for their power or pleasure. When you feel this light, when you feel the Golden Chain, you feel the responsibility that comes with this power. At that moment, your vision of the world changes. This can happen in an instant, perhaps during an initiation, or even while reading. This Theurgic tradition is the heart of the Western heritage. By unveiling it, we accomplish the first step in bringing light to ourselves, after we have been stuck in the shadows that are created by various dangerous spiritual traditions. Searching for beauty in our body, as well as in the intellectual and spiritual aspects of our being, will manifest this teaching for us. It is easy to tell you to focus on your body in our contemporary world. This is nothing new, even to the excesses that include the adoration of the physical body. The body is the manifestation of divine beauty. That is why a respect for the body and the quest for beauty are deeply religious and spiritual behaviors. When we behave this way, it helps us penetrate the surface meaning of the things around us, and ascend to the ideal of beauty.

May the words of Proclus be yours: "O Gods, by the understanding of the holy books and by dispelling the obscurity which surrounds me, grant me a pure and holy light that I may know the incorruptible God and being that I am."

Part 1
Mysteries of the Golden Chain

Knowing Your Roots Is Essential

Theurgy is a Pagan tradition: Nothing can exist without roots. Knowing the origin and the history of a family helps us to understand its specific attributes. To understand Theurgy (sometimes called High Magick), you must know that this is a Pagan tradition that appeared at the beginning of the Western spiritual tradition.

The chain of the initiates: From the time of the Egyptian Empire to our current time you can follow this chain of initiates down through centuries. Dogmatic and political religions tried to kill these masters and destroy their work. Initiates of the magick of the Gods and Goddesses succeeded in keeping this inheritance alive.

History is a keystone: All traditions are not strictly equivalent and history is the key to understanding why this is so.

Mesopotamia—The Mother of Civilization

The roots of Western esotericism are to be found in Mesopotamia, which is the birthplace of Western civilization. This is the place where very ancient cities were conceived and built (ca 5300 Before Common Era). This is the place where writing first appeared and also the place where the first structured religions, spiritual beliefs, and systems of magick were developed. Astrology (the most ancient manifestation of astronomy) was invented and used both for organizing calendars and for magical-religious purposes. Later, and progressively, this knowledge spread all over the world, beginning in the Far East, in the countries known today as Egypt, Greece, and the Mediterranean world. It is possible to frankly state that the ancient traditions, which have their roots in Mesopotamia, are the origins of the most ancient and authentic sources of knowledge.

Even if Egypt had developed its knowledge of astronomy from the time of its earliest history (5000–3000 BCE), we can see a real connection between the Old Kingdom of Egypt and the Akkadian Empire (3rd Millennium). This was the time when Egyptian architects created the first pyramids. Some of the same esoteric principles that unify religion and astronomy can be found in both Egypt and Mesopotamia. It was in the Neo-Assyrian Empire (700 BCE) that some aspects of astronomy and religion were united in what is known as astrology. Later, during the Ptolemaic Period (305–30 BCE), Egypt became the place of an extraordinary fusion between their own knowledge and the knowledge of the two other most-advanced civilizations in the world: Babylonia and Greece. It is quite obvious that these contacts, which existed from the beginning of their civilization, were not limited to astrology but involved many sorts of superstitions, different kinds of magic, and more advanced spiritual practices.

The God Thoth and the Goddess Isis were the founders of this specific lineage of magicians. Their light shone for thousands of years upon the entire Western world. The "Sacred Mysteries" and the "Cult of Isis" became better known than the Theurgic and Hermetic traditions that were derived from the teachings of Thoth, which remained more discreet and veiled. It is obvious that this part of the heritage constituted the roots of the tradition of magick, or, more precisely what is called "Theurgy." I will have the opportunity later in the book to speak more extensively about Hermetism, but it is good to know that this word has become a designation of a tradition that came from the practical and theoretical teachings of Thoth (who became Hermes for the Greeks). Knowing the most significant historical and symbolic markers, it is possible to see the manifestation of this tradition all throughout history and with research to uncover the most essential and immortal parts of this doctrine.

The description of how this divinity revealed itself in Egypt is not a fairy tale. It is a description of the world that the ancient Egyptians believed in. This is the place where the Theurgic tradition appeared for the first time.

Egypt—Birth of the Theurgic Tradition

First it is important to explain that the radical difference that exists today between what is considered to be real (the visible and measurable world) and what we believe to be unreal or fantasy (the invisible world) didn't exist in the ancient world. The ancient people instinctively knew how to overlay different levels of perception without rejecting one in favor of the other. In other words, when a pre-Christian scientist explained that the earth was a sphere and was able to measure it very accurately, he was performing a great rational work. At the same time he was able to go into a temple and worship Thoth or Isis, listening to the reading of these sacred myths with an intelligent understanding of the symbolic and moral message in it. If we consider it from our inner being, we will realize that myths tell stories about an absolute reality and they convey a powerful message. Yet, at the same time, this divine story was not understood by the priest or scientist of that time as a real description of a material phenomenon. This is also true for magick and ritual ceremonies, because this art involves other energies that are invisible.

However, the way that the leaders of what is known today as "revealed religions" explain their origins has changed. Today in the major religions, many believe that if they chose to admit their creation story had a mythological character, such an admission would decrease the power, efficacy, or veracity of their religion. In spite of their stance, stating the story of their origins is real and historic is becoming less and less believable today, because of the scientific progress we have achieved.

What can be surprising is to understand that myths and physical reality can both be true at the same time, because they do not describe the same thing. The traditional attitude of a Hermetist was, and still is, that these founding stories are powerful symbolic narratives capable of adding rich depth and meaning to our existence. Such affirmations do not justify the use of any kind of text in a religious context. Some texts can be dangerous because of what they explain or teach. As you will see in the part about the "sacred books," this is the reason you cannot honestly say that any text is sacred. If we are willing to put our rational mind on hold for a while, being eager to know the origin of these mysteries, we can make even more progress. This is the mental attitude we must adopt, though perhaps this is more true for an examination of the beliefs of Egypt than those of Greece. For modern humans, affirmations are "true" because they can be outwardly or inwardly verified by experience. When we read a myth, we are crossing a threshold into a sacred place. For a while, our reality must change. Like a child, we will accept as real this "true" story, which took place on the "black earth" of Egyptian soil. This story tells of the birth of the world and constitutes the first step of the Hermetic and Theurgic tradition. It is essential to state that, even if you believe some of the elements employed here are similar to those provided in biblical mythology, they predate the Hebrew sacred texts.

There was a time when the Gods had not yet manifested themselves. Only chaos filled the universe, like a vast primordial ocean. (Several different symbolic representations could have been chosen to represent this time, but many civilizations have used the image of a large ocean.)

Within this ocean were powerful primeval deities. They were composed of four pairs of personified deities. Each pair represented the male and female.

These deities were: Nun and Naunet, who were the personification of the primeval seas and the world in the space before creation; Kuk and Kauket were the personification of the infinite darkness that reigned in the primeval space before the birth of the sun; Hu and Hauhet personified the infinite; and Amun and Amaunet personified that which is hidden.

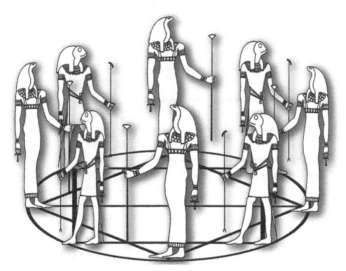

Figure 2: These four pairs of deities, male and female, were the personification of the powerful primeval deities; the first manifestation of the Sacred Ogdoad.

Each deity had a human body. The Gods had frog heads, and the Goddesses had snake heads. The number four is not unintentional. Egyptians knew the cardinal points. The Heliopolitan myth describes the four children of the Goddess Nut. During the process of embalming, the viscera were protected by the four "sons of Horus," who were protected by four Goddesses. In the "Coffin Texts,"[3] it is written that the

---

3. The "Coffin Texts" are a collection of magical texts written into the coffins of the dead during the Middle Kingdom (2000 BCE).

God Shu created eight unlimited beings to help him hold Nut's body. The number four is the symbol of balance, which can be symbolized by a square.

As you can see in this myth, the number four is in fact a number that can be organized into pairs. This tradition left us with several symbols that represent this primordial activation. One of these symbols is the intertwined double square. Here the number eight is manifested from the number four in order to symbolize the activation or manifestation of something that had no shape until that moment.

This Ogdoad[4] precedes the manifestation of the Ennead[5] (worshipped in Heliopolis) and, as you will see below, it was the Ogdoad that was the origin of the sun.

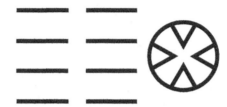

Figure 3: Egyptian writing of "Kemenu, the City of the Eight."

The divine Ogdoad began to organize, to equilibrate, and to bring order out of chaos.

An intense concentration of energy manifested at the center of the primeval ocean, which was the result of the activation emerging from the Ogdoad.

This fantastic, dynamic push shook the primitive matter and caused the first hill to emerge. A lake formed on the island that had been created.

Then an ibis (or a goose according to some versions) appeared, gliding above this blazing island of light. It alighted at the top of the hill and laid an egg. This was the first manifestation of the union between the celestial divine principles and the primeval Ogdoadic principles, which had just made the manifested world emerge.

---

4. Group of eight divinities. (For more, see the glossary.)
5. Group of nine divinities. (For more, see the glossary.)

The egg cracked and Ra, the Sun God, appeared in a blaze of light. He rose up into the sky to irradiate the world with his beneficent rays. The blaze of this first rising sun illuminated the whole of the cosmos.

Next, the members of the Ogdoad manifested themselves in their visible shape and these eight deities approached the lake. They worked a magical rite together, making a lotus flower gush up out from the water. The flower opened up in a dazzling light and gave birth to a feminine being. This Goddess rose up to the heavens and united with Ra. From their union Thoth was born. He was the first divine offspring and founder of the Hermetic tradition. For this reason the Ogdoad has sometimes been called the "souls of Thoth."

The Ogdoad put the earth in order, and the earth knew a golden age. Three of these divine couples retired from the visible world, remaining the guardians of equilibrium. Amon and Amaunet left Hermopolis for Thebes.

In this first sacred monticule, which became the center of the world, a city was built that ancient Egyptians called Khemenou, or the "city of the Eight" or "the Eight Towns." It was afterward known by the Greek word "Hermopolis." Since then, Thoth has also been called the "Lord of Khemenou." It is also there that fragments of the original sacred cosmic egg were conserved, in the most sacred part of the temple. Few pilgrims in antiquity had the immense privilege of getting a glimpse of these fragments, and being permitted to bathe in their intense aura. Tradition tells us that a few of these fragments were set in a stone, and this created the matrix of the magical chain.

The Temple of Hermopolis became the place where all magical rites were performed, retaining the presence of the eight divinities of the Ogdoad under the presidency of Thoth, to whom the city was dedicated. The Ogdoadic tradition tells us that the first primeval Ogdoad was later associated with eight major divinities who became the tutelary powers, wardens of the Theurgic tradition. This presence was maintained for many centuries on the actual physical locus where the original creation was first manifested. An assembly of priests and Theurgists was created there, under the protection of Thoth.

The main information about the Ogdoad comes from a large book written by the German Egyptologist Kurt Sethe called *Amun und die acht Urgötter von Hermopolis*, published in 1929.

Several centuries after the temples in Hermopolis were built, they were damaged during the second Persian invasion in 343 BCE. In the twentieth century, a tomb was discovered in a city called Touna el-Gebel (a necropolis situated in the middle of the desert, near El-Ashmounein, which is the current name of Hermopolis), and this discovery offered us the extraordinary opportunity of reading the story of Petosiris, one of the Grand Priests of Thoth in Hermopolis. He was also called the "Priest of the Ogdoad." He lived in a period following the conquest of Egypt by Alexander the Great (332 BCE).[6] The engravings on the walls tell how he reenacted the rituals of the temple, how he decided to organize the priests, and how he ensured the perpetuation of the tradition. He consecrated the first stone of a limestone temple dedicated to the God Ra, God of the Sun, "the son of the island of flames."

Figure 4: The Egyptian name of "Thoth."

Petosiris built a wall around the temple and named the place: "the birthplace of all Gods." This temple was the place where the relics of the cosmic egg were preserved, and from which the Sun God had emerged.

---

6. Most modern scholars believe that Petosiris was High Priest of Thoth during the second period of Persian rule in Egypt (which was before Alexander). Nevertheless, it has also been mentioned that he probably continued as High Priest in the years after Alexander the Great's conquest of Egypt.

Thoth became the central God "surrounded" by the sacred Og-doad. Usually his written name is composed by drawing a hieroglyphic symbol of an ibis perched at the top of a pole. Sometimes we can find his name written with the drawing of a baboon or composed just with phonetic symbols.

It is not surprising to see his written name using the animals that were associated with him. Surprisingly, to those who are not familiar with these ancient writings, the phonetic symbols that comprise his name do not constitute his name as Thoth, but DHwtj (Djehuti).[7] The name Thoth was used by the Greeks, because it was the way the modern Egyptians pronounced his name. It is also possible that the name in use today (Thoth) has always been just the exoteric version of a more magical and invocatory pronunciation.

Figure 5: The symbolic presence of Thoth in his baboon shape as it is in the Mojave Desert, southwest USA.

Modern Egyptologists proposed several etymologies that help us to understand the meaning of his name. "Djehu" could be the name of

---

7. The famous, modern magician Aleister Crowley was aware of this, so he used the spelling "Tehuti." Modern magicians, following Crowley's path, generally continue to use the same spelling. The linguistic characteristics of the ancient Egyptian language allow these differences, consequently there are difficulties knowing exactly how words in ancient Egyptian should be pronounced.

a city in Egypt and Djehuti the name of the God of this city. His name could also express the meaning of "messenger" or "chosen one."

It is difficult in modern times to know whether these different names or pronunciations came from symbolic attributions associated with the divinity, or from a simple phonetic evolution. I could argue that, since everything is related to the divine, this evolution did not occur by chance and it corresponds to a different level of the divine reality of this God. In an attempt to keep this simple, in this book I will continue to use the usual name of Thoth instead of Djehuti (or Tehuti).

It is important to say a few words about the way the Egyptians depicted this God. Traditionally, Thoth is shown with three possible shapes: a baboon, an ibis, or a human with an ibis head. He is often portrayed as carrying the palette of a scribe. In the ancient texts, such as the *Pyramid Texts*, Thoth is the one who guided the King through the river of the skies. This is one of the representations of this God as the "guide of the dead." This function of Thoth has been more and more associated with him, and he is currently equated with Anubis under the Greek form of Hermanubis. From the most ancient times, Thoth was considered to be a lunar God. The hooked shape of his beak and the two-tone feathers (black and white) are the main symbolic explanation of this association.

The tradition says that the symbol of the baboon was chosen because the baboon shouts when the sun rises in the morning. As the moon obtains its light from the sun, Thoth obtains a large part of his power from his role as the secretary and counselor of his father, Ra. The importance of the moon phases in Egyptian life and the annual festivals in the temples can easily explain why Thoth was considered to be the founder of the cosmic order, as well as all the religious and civil institutions. He was the one who chaired rituals in the temples, and presided over sacred ceremonies as well as the writing of sacred texts and magic formulas, which were used during these celebrations. In this way, he became the master of all the magic arts. Thoth was considered to be the original source of the occult powers that are present in the different aspects of the divine rituals. Esoteric wisdom was attributed to him and some of the names used to describe him included "the Mysterious" and "the Unknown."

Other aspects of Thoth have been developed in the history of the Western esoteric tradition, including those functions associated with magick and justice.

Figure 6: Egyptian writings of Thoth as the "Lord of Divine Words."

The first of these, magick, is a consequence of Thoth's role as the God who revealed writing to humanity: Thoth is the God of writing and scribes. This function may not seem significant if we think about writing as it is today, but we must remember that Egypt used a form of hieroglyphic writing. From the earliest times, this kind of sacred writing was conceived as a specific kind of magical invocation. I don't want to develop this concept too extensively at this point, but it is important to explain that hieroglyphs are not an arbitrary representation of something visible, nor of an idea. Each visual symbol is directly connected to its spiritual or divine counterpart. This invisible part is an archetype. In a way, hieroglyphs are talismans that manifest the invisible power in our world. This writing manifests the invisible in the visible and allows a manifestation to come from the divine plane. In modern linguistics, this kind of writing is called "performative writing." It is considered as "performative" because it is a kind of writing that is not limited to a description, but in some way really is an active process that results in manifestation.

Now you can understand why this writing is considered to be magical. This is the reason scribes chose Thoth as their God. They were not priests, but they knew the correct words to write, and, as such, they were able to understand the rules of magick. The complexity of this knowledge and their expertise was used on the invisible planes and on the visible plane for administrative purposes.

Scribes were known as "disciples of Thoth." They constituted a privileged class of society. Several sculptures or paintings associated a scribe with the representation of a baboon or an ibis. A herald is also one of the functions of a scribe. It is his duty to announce what the King, or the God, decides. The Greek God Hermes inherited this function of being a messenger.

Thoth is the God who knows everything. He was the inventor of mathematics, astronomy, and the sciences. His potential seems limitless. He created spells and taught Isis all magical formulas. With this knowledge, Isis was able to raise her husband Osiris from the dead. Thoth also taught her the specific magical words that enabled her to cure and protect her son Horus. Several magical books that probably contained all the knowledge of the world were granted to her.

The idea of justice is also related to Thoth. We can see this connection in many representations of the *Book of the Dead* when he is accompanied by the Goddess Maat. She is the one who manifests cosmic order and justice. Thoth is sometimes called the "Supreme Judge" and "the One who judges." Consequently, he is the one who establishes peace among the Gods.

Figure 7: Thoth being named the Thrice Great (Trismegistos).

Thoth will develop his function as a judge in .the afterlife as the Judge of the Dead and the psychopomp. In mythology, it is he who declares that Isis has received the power of language or of the "Word." He is the one who wrote down the result when Anubis weighed the souls of the departed. He is depicted with different shapes in these episodes, often being portrayed as a scribe with an ibis head, or a ba-boon seated at the top of a scale.

As the one who knows the secret formulas of rebirth, Thoth helps the initiate as he completes the passage between life and death, and vice versa. In some texts he is known as the one who is "small on the second day of the month and tall on the fifteenth." He is the one who can remember the cycles of the cosmos and consequently the lunar phases. He is the one who treats the "eye of the moon." With the help of Shu, God of the sky, he protects Osiris.

Figure 8: The Greek God Hermes as the Messenger of the Gods, carrying the Ogdoadic Light.

All these descriptions of the divine founder of the Hermetic tradi-tion give a good explanation of Thoth's character and functions. As I just said, the Greek God Hermes is the symbolic successor of Thoth. We can see him as Thoth's cousin and maybe this is the reason why we can see that there is very little connection between their iconography.

It is important to emphasize three principal steps in this historical evolution, which are:

• The Original Thoth (Egyptian)—The Original Hermes (Greek)
• The Hermanubis
• Hermes as a Magus

At first glance, you might suppose that the ancient representation of Thoth has been lost or absorbed into other systems over time. This figure may have been totally absorbed initially by the Greek iconography of Hermes, then by the character of the Magus. You will soon discover that this is inaccurate. The tradition of the divine magick I am talking about maintained the essential symbol of the Ogdoad as a living presence. This is why the Theurgic and Hermetic traditions have been called the "Ogdoadic tradition" by initiates.

Archaeologists and historians know very little about the knowledge, rituals, and ceremonies performed by the Grand Priests of Thoth. It is important to emphasize once again that the divine magick, which is also called Theurgy by Iamblichus, is totally different than popular magic. Their rituals and the goals were different. For people, the magic they used and knew comprised a set of formulas that were used to obtain what they needed in their daily life. For the Priests of Thoth, the divine magick was a way to keep the divinities alive and present in the temple. It was a way to communicate with them and to receive knowledge and power from them. (I will speak more about this later in this book.)

This tradition was passed from master to initiate, in complete secrecy. None of the explanations about the sacred texts or the rituals were unveiled. Several witnesses confirmed the existence of these secret teachings. The link, which was formed when the tradition was passed from master to initiate, was called "diadoche" by the Greeks, meaning "succession." We can find the same idea in the "Golden Chain of the Initiates." The direct teachings involved the communication of the sacred texts, which was known as "the sacred discourses." The traditional communication of these texts, and the fact that they were taught in secret, increased the relationship of trust among the initiates of this circle. This is the way in which the tradition was perpetuated and developed in Egypt over the centuries.

Such famous lineage of masters and initiates became the living manifestation of the initiatic Mysteries. They are the real and visible founders of this tradition.

Figure 9: Pythagoras was the first famous figure to travel to Egypt to learn the secrets of this ancient religious and magical tradition. (House of the Temple, AASR-SJ, USA)

As you will very quickly discover as you read this book, many of the Greeks eager to be initiated into this secret wisdom went to Egypt. It was during the Ptolemaic[8] period that a real cultural exchange between the two cultures eventually developed. This bridge was perceptible on several levels, but here I have chosen the levels that are most closely connected to our subjects, which are: philosophy, religion, initiation, and

---

8. (305–30 BCE)

Theurgy. Later in the book, I will explain more clearly about what "philosophy" is when seen from the point of view of a Hermetist. Meanwhile, it is essential to realize that what has been defined as "Hermetism" is not an isolated elaboration. It is a special attitude of the mind that allows a true initiate to build into himself a real balance between various aspects that most people generally cannot reconcile. Philosophy was developed as a quest for wisdom and something we might call "rational thinking." Religion is understood to be a unique series of rituals that welcome the divinities and build a strong relationship with them so that we can ascend to their realm. Initiation was established in order to really activate different centers of power within the initiate, and to open their perception of the invisible worlds.

Of course, different parts of this wisdom were already known here and there. Geographically, Alexandria was the unique place in which these aspects coexisted in peace for a long time, protected by the Ptolemaic Dynasty. Moreover, some initiates were, simultaneously, erudites, scholars, and physicians who succeeded in building a strong and clear knowledge of the physical world while keeping their inner vision of the divine levels open and active. Reason and intelligence were associated for the good of science and humanity.

At the same time, this tradition was always very cautious regarding the eagerness of more dogmatic religions to convert them, and to impose those religions' unique point of view on them. The Hermetic approach is rooted in having an open mind, which allows criticism and challenges to its beliefs. In this way, philosophy and science can make progress. The Hermetic and Theurgic teachings do not demand a unique and absolute view of the universe. It is for this reason that the development of Christianity and its will to impose its vision on others was so catastrophic for the entire society. Don't forget that most of the time honest people from both religions, both traditional and monotheistic, were not violent. It was the desire to gain power over the people that led these religious activists to violently impose their views.

The peaceful views of the initiates gave long life to a tradition that has been characterized differently at different periods in history. I have written extensively about this topic in my book *The Divine Arcana of the*

Aurum Solis,[9] especially about the "schools of the Mysteries" and the specifics of Hermetism.

I will now explain more precisely how this tradition was perpetuated. As this is not an historical essay, I will simply highlight what is suitable for our purpose, leaving open the opportunity to write more precisely about some of these periods at a later date.

The Transmission of the Theurgic Heritage

We can plainly see how old the Egyptian civilization is and how the sacred place called Hermopolis appeared. It was there that the Hermetic tradition had its foundation and roots. It is essential to remember that Egypt was a country with many myths and sacred places. Each of them was founded as a result of a specific mythology, and they were managed by a specific clerical organization. Of course, they were not all in contradiction. As with other mythologies, there was an exchange of the elements of various myths. The divinities were actors in many different myths, even if, in general, each myth put the focus on one specific divinity. Such was the case in Heliopolis for the God Atum, in Memphis for the God Ptah, in Thebes for the God Amun, and, as I mentioned above, it was also true in Hermopolis for the God Thoth.

It is not necessary to look for a coherent picture that is able to unify these different myths, because there is no such thing. Generally, if we consider the myths separately, a kind of coherence may be found, but this is not the case if we try to find a general and unique vision for all the myths. Egypt was not monotheistic and never has been, from the time of its origin. Each sacred place was the center of temples and clergy of the local divinity. As usual, some of these priests and priestesses were more focused on the magical and ritual planes and others on the political level. There is not something we can identify as an "initiation" per se [10] in the period of time up to the Ptolemaic period, even if it is easy to see that some of the rituals and teachings were restricted to specific

---

9. Jean-Louis de Biasi, *The Divine Arcana of the Aurum Solis* (Woodbury, MN: Llewellyn Publications, 2011).

10. I am talking here about "initiations" as they were developed in the Hellenistic schools of Mysteries.

priests. This was the basis of what would eventually be established and structured as an initiatic tradition.

It is necessary to highlight a point that is both true and very important no matter what period of history we are discussing: not everyone is curious. Some, like you who have chosen to read my book, are more attracted to and concerned with metaphysical, spiritual, and esoteric subjects. In this little group you are a part of, there is another, even smaller group that is eager to take another step forward, to find a school, a master, and a spiritual family. You might also consider that there is another group of people who are willing to travel, sometimes even in dangerous circumstances, to faraway places in order to find this hidden light. In the past, a very few students from Greece, Italy, and Syria did just that. They constituted a web of philosophers, adepts, and initiates who maintain a close link with us. It is possible to trace the primary lines of the tradition in order to understand how this tradition, and ultimately this lineage, were constituted.

The first famous figure to travel to Egypt in order to learn the secrets of this ancient religious and magical tradition was Pythagoras, in the fifth century. He spent a long time in Egypt and obviously received the teachings and training that were available in the temples of this country. He travelled to several countries, probably even to India, in order to understand the world and the Gods. Ultimately, he founded a school in the south of Italy, which was open to both genders and organized in two essential parts: the exoteric and the esoteric. Each student was required to progress from the outer aspect to the inner aspect. This organization survived his death and Plato received these teachings and initiation from Philolaos, who was the chief of this school.

Just as Pythagoras had done, Plato travelled to Egypt in order to receive the teachings from priests who were part of the clergy of Heliopolis (near modern Cairo). It appears that his mentor was the priest Sechnuphis. Plato then founded the first Academy in Athens. Today scholars agree on the fact that this Academy maintained the organization of the Pythagorean School by the publication of books and with oral and private teachings. It is startling to realize that this Academy was active from the fifth century BCE until the sixth century CE (with an interruption of two centuries). We are talking here about a tradition that has remained active for over ten centuries! Even if the different heads of the Platonic Academy developed personal philosophical views, all of them were working on the basis and the interpretation of the books from the Master Plato, in addition to the teachings that came from Pythagoras. It is obvious that other teachings and practices from Chaldea, Egypt, etc., were well-known and openly discussed. Even if we cannot find many teachings about ritual practices in the Academy, undoubtedly the traditional rituals devoted to the divinities were performed regularly. We find some indications of that kind of activity here and there in the literature. Do not forget that the teachings were founded on a specific kind of discourse, which Pythagoras called "philosophy"—the "Love of Wisdom."

Figure 10: Plato, the founder of the famous school the "Academy," which endured for over ten centuries. (House of the Temple, AASR-SJ, USA)

We find several sacred myths in the writings of Plato, including very interesting hymns, like those at the end of Phaedrus: "Beloved Pan, and all ye other Gods of this place, grant me inner beauty; and may the external be in harmony with the internal; May I always reckon the wise to be wealthy, and may I have only such a quantity of gold as a temperate man can bear and carry."

This school was working, teaching, and worshipping the muses and the Gods all throughout the centuries. As I said, the school was still active during the second century CE. It was at this time that three different books appeared in Egypt, which were used to found the famous tradition discussed here. (I will explain more about the two first books in the chapter about the "sacred books.") The three books are:

1. The *Chaldaean Oracles*.
2. The *Corpus Hermeticum*, also referred to as the *Hermetica*.
3. According to Iamblichus, the third text, which is lost to us today, was a book written by a prophet (priest) named Bitys. He translated this text from hieroglyphics found in the Temple of Sais in Egypt. Iamblichus said this text was about the ascent of the soul by the use of Theurgic rituals. Authors, such as Zosimos of Panopolis, also mentioned this book in their writings.

Earlier I mentioned that there were people in that period who were eager to make progress in attaining knowledge of these religious Mysteries. Even if the details of their doctrine were occasionally different, they were brothers and sisters in the spirit of Plato and Pythagoras. It is possible to see that they knew each other and that their doctrines were a constant subject of discussion and development. There is no doubt that their spiritual practices were part of a traditional religion, in addition to what secrets they received in the Egyptian Temple.

When the *Hermetica* was composed, it was a corpus that was always associated with specific philosophical studies. The *Hermetica* echoed the voice of Thoth-Hermes, which was put into a book for the benefit of their initiates. For their part, the *Chaldaean Oracles* described a series of precise and more specific practical rituals that they called "Theurgy." It is essential to understand that this association among the Pythagorean, Hermetic, and Neoplatonic traditions created a strong identity, which can be clearly identified in the "history of ideas." Even if a large number of books have been lost, a few survived.

These books offer us evidence of the existence of this spiritual family. The situation of a modern student is far easier, but presents several challenges and frustrations. As I just stated, a large number of books were destroyed and parts of this heritage are missing. Fortunately, inner rituals and essential teachings were preserved. If you want to learn magick today, there are a large number of books available, including all the epochs of the history. Most of the time, they were written in the period of time between the Middle Ages and the nineteenth century. They are deeply influenced by the Hebrew and Christian Qabalah. The challenge is to understand that we have to be guided in our study and rituals in the same way we were taught at school. Sometimes we have to learn foreign languages and philosophy, other times we must do gymnastics.

When I received my teachings in this tradition, it became obvious that a line through the past exists. The doctrine and teachings were always in direct relation to the rituals. The goal was clear. It is the same for every student who has the real desire to progress and to master the Theurgic tradition. When I read daily reports of the studies and ritual exercises that are sent in to me by Aurum Solis students from different cultures (American, Brazilian, African, Russian, Asian, etc.), I realize that our teachings provide a reliable structure to the spiritual path. No matter the student's origin, the results of studying these lessons and reading these sacred texts really changed their lives. This deep experience is only possible by the use of a coherent tradition. It is impossible to achieve such results by using tools that come everywhere and are sometimes in opposition. When we perform Theurgic rituals we use very precise laws and energies. Of course you can read anything you want, but it is better and safer to do it when you have found your own axis. This is a kind of discipline that is really effective.

It is important not to confuse the Hermetic tradition with the Ancient Mysteries. There were several very special places in the ancient world. These places were associated with certain divinities, and specific ceremonies were designed to enable a candidate to really undergo an inner experience during these sacred ceremonial plays. An esoteric message was generally revealed, which was associated with secret signs and specific items that were given to the new initiate. At the same time the initiate was offered the opportunity to really feel and experience specific states of consciousness, sometimes including the experience of death and the afterlife. There were numerous "Mysteries," but I might mention the Mysteries of Orpheus, Dionysus, Isis, Eleusis, Samothrace, etc. The elaboration of the concept of initiation is clearly related to these ceremonies of the Mysteries.

At this time it was the custom for both the masters and students of the Hermetic tradition to be initiated into several Mysteries. For example, we see evidence of this in the writings of Apuleius (125–180 CE), who wrote: "I was initiated in Greece into a large number of cults. Symbols and souvenirs were given to me by the priests and I keep them carefully with me. . . . You initiates of the God Liber, you know what you keep hidden in your home and worship in silence, away from the profane. Is there someone who would be surprised that someone initiated into several divine Mysteries keeps at home special signs or items wrapped in linen, the purest fabric which can be used to veil sacred items?"

Figure 11: Iamblichus of Chalcis, Head of the Theurgic tradition.
(TU Delft Library)

It is very difficult to know whether or not they were specifically "Hermetic" initiations. In fact, it is important for us to know that the reading of the three books I just mentioned was considered to be an invocation and an initiation. We believe that these adept philosophers were able to provide their students with a deep interpretation of the revelations they received from the Mysteries. These specific Mysteries were not a construction of the Hermetists. They remain external to this Pythagorean/Neoplatonician lineage.

There now appears in the history of Hermetism someone who will play an exceptional role: Iamblichus of Chalcis[11] (245–325 CE). He was taught by Porphyry of Tyre (233–305 CE) who was the scholarch (chief) of the Platonic Academy of Athens. Porphyry travelled a lot and was one of the masters of Iamblichus. It is very likely that Porphyry passed on his philosophical heritage and initiations (from Plato and Pythagoras) to Iamblichus. Iamblichus additionally learned all the Platonic texts, en-acted several ancient Mysteries, and ultimately received what became a real revelation, the full revelation of the *Chaldaean Oracles*.

Figure 12: Apamea, the place where Iamblichus developed his famous Theurgic school.

---

11. Iamblichus of Chalcis, also known as Iamblichus Chalcidensis or Iamblichus of Apamea.

Figure 13: The tombs in Palmyra; Iamblichus's tomb is on the right.
(TU Delft Library)

Iamblichus became one of the most famous figures who defined Theurgy. Of course as I explained, magick existed prior to this period, but Iamblichus created a powerful and comprehensive system. It was really at this moment that this spiritual family found its axis and homeland. Iamblichus taught in Apamea, Syria throughout the entire first quarter of the fourth century. Of the numerous books written by Iamblichus, only a few of them survived. The most famous is *De Mysteriis* (*On the Mysteries*). As most of the books that were related to Theurgy have disappeared, this book must be considered to be the heart of this tradition.

The voice of Iamblichus can still be heard today, just as if we were still in his Syrian school at Apamea. I cannot talk about him and his school without remembering the "Theurgic pilgrimage" I did in Syria several years ago. Walking in the ruins of Apamea at sunrise is an amazing experience. The ancient city covers a large area. A long avenue surrounded by high columns cuts through the ruins. Here, we do not feel as if we are at the center of a noisy modern city such as Athens. We are in a silent place where we can feel the ghosts of the inhabitants who lived here. The pavement of this long avenue is still intact, and so are the sidewalks. I remember looking at the separation between the blocks that constitute the sidewalk and finding numerous pieces of broken Roman glasses. Our eyes and our fingers are really touching artifacts of the daily life that could have been used by Iamblichus. Walking along this axis brings us to the place where he taught his lessons about Neoplatonism and Theurgy. Even today, we can see this square classroom surrounded with a few stone rows. The place is not too large, but is large enough to accommodate a group of students. When we sit in a place like that, the communion is intense and unforgettable. If you are working in this tradition, as I am, the impact is even more powerful. While we live we carry this light with us forever. This school is not a place of martyr and does not exalt anger. This is a place of luminous life and we can feel that when we stand here and salute the rising sun.

Figure 14: Sculpture on the tomb of Iamblichus in Palmyra (Syria).

All throughout his long life, Iamblichus would teach this tradition and train many disciples. His school was perpetuated after his death under the direction of four successors. This is not the place that Iamblichus was eventually buried. His burial place is further to the east of the country, in a place called Palmyra. It was, of course, another stop on my pilgrimage in Syria.

Palmyra is an oasis in the heart of the Syrian Desert, where a rich and complex civilization developed. Even the writing was different there. Outside the ruins of the large ancient city, to the south, we find the different tombs of the previous inhabitants. They buried their dead both underground and in towers. The tomb of Iamblichus's family is a high tomb of several stories, which is clearly identified by several archaeological markers. It is a moving moment to stand in the desert in front of the entrance to his tomb, looking at the statues above the threshold. There is the scene of a banquet, which is obviously related to the ritual celebrations of the Neoplatonicians. The wall plate below the statues gives some indications about the owner of this tomb. Here is an original translation of the text by a member of the Aurum Solis. It says: "Iamblichus of Mokeimos, son of Kaiakkaleios, son of Malichos built this eternal memorial gift, for himself and for his sons and for his grandsons, in the month of Xandikos of the year 314."[12]

I remember entering into his tomb, climbing up the stairs, and reading a few excerpts of his book *Mysteries of Egypt* as I raised the burning incense I brought to honor his memory. At a moment such as this, we can forge a link to, or increase the mystical link with someone. It was difficult to leave a place like that, and it was with regret and gratitude that I left that place under the burning sun, carrying these moments eternally in my heart. I can still hear his clear voice every time I open those of his books that have not been destroyed.

---

12. Macedonian calendar month.

*Figure 15: The Emperor Julian, who worked vigorously
to restore the greatness and values of Paganism.
(The statue is in the Museum of Cluny, Paris, France)*

During the period when Iamblichus was teaching, Christianity was rising rapidly, imposing its absolute and intolerant view. Unfortunately, and as is very often true in the history of humanity, it was not the moderate participants who shaped this new religion. It is obvious that the previous little Jewish sect was far from what Paul created. Even the teachings of the first apostles were very far in intent from the religious repression that was imposed by the first bishops all over the Mediterranean world. As always, uneducated people followed the doctrines that were the easiest to understand. No matter what the truth was, no matter what the facts were, followers acted as a herd to impose the law of the minority fundamentalists.

The sacred teachings were destroyed and the philosophers and initiates were hunted to death in some cases. This violence was everywhere. In Alexandria, the school was vandalized and the teachers were persecuted. The famous mathematician and Neoplatonician Hypatia was murdered with an absolute heinousness; her dismembered body was dragged all over the city by Christians. They destroyed the divine and sacred statues. They appropriated the temples or destroyed them. They forbade anyone in the city to even look at the destroyed statues.

A transformation was initiated in February 360 CE in Paris,[13] when Julianus (Julian) was declared Emperor of Rome. Julianus was the son of the Consul Julius Constantius (consul in 335) and half brother of Emperor Constantine I. He was raised as a Christian in Byzantium. After the execution of his family, he was banished. It was during this time that he learned philosophy and received the teaching of the second successor of Iamblichus, Aidesius, who was the founder of a school in Bergama. It was there that the Emperor Julian made his contact with Neoplatonism. Between 352 and 354 CE, he was initiated into the Theurgic practices and the philosophy of Iamblichus.

From his youth he had experienced the reality of the divinities. His Pagan roots were still alive, so he was initiated into the different Mysteries of this lineage and others such as Mithraism. After being acclaimed as the new Emperor he began an active effort to restore the greatness and values of Rome. In December 361 he promulgated an edict to return the temples to their traditional clergy. He imposed a law of tolerance and equality for every cult and divinity. He hired several philosophers to write books in order to explain the beauty and the higher good of this religion, and the tradition as it had been received from their ancestors. On June 26, 363 CE, he was killed during a battle against Persia. Rumors claimed that he died at the hands of Christians in his own army, but these rumors were never verified. What could have been an extraordinary opportunity for the whole world died at the tip of a spear on a battlefield!

For three centuries, persecutions would rage like a storm onto the last traditional believers. Naturally, this hatred was amplified against the Pagan clergy, and was at its most extreme against the intellectual elite, especially the philosophers who were initiated into the sacred doctrine and the secret Theurgic rituals.

The Emperor Justinian closed the philosophical school of Athens in 529 CE. The initiates were obliged to flee and find asylum in Persia

---

13. Archaeologists don't know the exact place where Julian was acclaimed by these troops, but it is likely to be close to a place called today Musée Cluny in Paris. A large statue of the Emperor still remains in these ancient Roman baths. You can see this statue in Figure 15.

for several years. After coming back to their homeland they held their meetings in secrecy in the ruins of the Temple of Demeter.

At first glance we might come to the conclusion that the sacred traditions and Theurgic lineage were eradicated and all the initiates were dead. However, we must remember what this tradition was founded on: a powerful teaching called Theurgy, and an intense understanding of the need for secrecy. Because they were the objects of persecutions, it reinforced the necessity for secrecy. When the Neoplatonicians came back from exile, they reopened the Academy. It remained open until almost the end of the sixth century. It is interesting to remember that until this time (600 CE) it was quite easy to find the masters and to secretly receive the Hermetic initiation I am talking about. Even during this very dangerous time, in a climate of tremendous persecution against their traditional philosophy and religion, the initiates were working to keep this sacred light alive. From the time of Pythagoras, secret signs were used to identify a brother or sister initiate of the same tradition. They had special items to prove their adherence.

Philae, the last temple in Egypt, was closed by the Emperor Justinian in the middle of the sixth century CE (551 CE) so that the beginning of the seventh century was the first time when the visible Pagan structure completely disappeared. One thousand years later, in the fifteenth century, Hermetism reappeared prior to what was called the "Renaissance." This reappearance would mean that the visible traditional structures appeared to be invisible for over nine centuries— only slightly less than the duration of the Platonic school in Athens.

It was the disappearance of science, medicine, etc., that was the worst disaster in the history of humanity. We lost centuries of progress. Meanwhile, initiates preserved their spiritual inheritance for the future generations we are currently living in now. It is essential to understand how we can be sure that this is the truth. Even if we have no access to information about what was happening during this dark period of persecution, it is possible to clearly identify a consistent lineage by recognizing several signs and manifestations that were always a part of this tradition. The signs help us to identify the presence of the tradition, even when the initiates had to hide in order to keep the lineage alive. Of course there is no exhaustive list of signs and manifestations, but we can start by looking at the Pythagorean and Neoplatonic philosophy as the first element. Theurgic and magick ritual practices are the second element. Loyalty to the pre-Christian religious beliefs is the third element. Don't forget that in a period of crisis, as it was from the sixth century until the end of the Inquisition, many initiates from this tradition had to hide their real beliefs, disguised as Christian scholars or theologians.

Keeping these elements in mind, it is possible to say that the Hermetic and Theurgic tradition was maintained in Byzantium, Greece, and Italy. First of all, I would like to highlight the names of Leon the Mathematician, and philosophers Michael Psellos and Michael Italikos. All of these men respectfully learned the *Chaldaean Oracles* and wrote extensively about these texts. Italikos was even named the "second Plato." It is indubitably the case that magick and even Theurgy were used by many scholars. (See the bibliography for more on this subject.) Of course, for now, it is not possible to show the ritual texts that were used by these great men, but there is absolutely no problem discussing the life and work of Georgius Gemistus Pletho.

In my book *The Divine Arcana of the Aurum Solis*, I wrote extensively about Pletho and his role as a master of the Hermetic tradition. If you read that book, you will be able to understand how the fundamentals of the Neoplatonic tradition and several hidden keys were given to the Italian Hermetic circles. Here I must emphasize the real existence of a secret brotherhood of initiates led by Pletho. Because many of the documents between the ninth century and the fourteenth century are lost or not yet translated, finding reliable information is really difficult. This lack of information can be circumvented, because there is more information about the organization and the goal of this secret society in the fourteenth century, fifteenth century, and thereafter. According to the French translators of Pletho's book *Laws*, C. Alexandre and François Massai, it is obvious that Pletho organized (or inherited) a secret society in Mistra (a city in the south of Greece). The letters and documents that survived help us understand the process and the goal of this brotherhood. It is clear that politically, Pletho was a nationalist who was eager to restore the greatness of his country—Greece. Even with this consideration, his actions and his goals were essentially focused on the spiritual and religious level. It was for this reason that he initiated famous religious people from Italy and not just from Greece. A real initiate does not care about borders and origins of birth, and so it was for him. The goals of this society were, as they were for the Emperor Julian, to rejuvenate the pre-Christian traditions, to re-establish the cult of the Immortal Divinities, to teach the works of Plato and the Neoplatonicians, and ultimately to marginalize Christianity.

As I explained previously, the desire to defend such goals was very dangerous in a time when the Inquisition was active. It was for this reason that some parts of the Order remained visible and other parts remained in secrecy. As in the Platonic Academy, the outer circle was the only place that deeper oral teachings were offered. Some students, not all, were then accepted into the inner circle, probably through initiations. Next, the rituals were revealed and the new brothers were able to receive the full teaching and the inner manual. This religious manual, *Laws,* is a presentation of all the elements needed to understand and practice Paganism as the early Neoplatonicians did. Philosophy, theology, creed, calendar, prayers, hymns, gestures, etc., were clearly explained. This book was publicly known after Pletho's death and the Patriarch Gennadius II was horrified by the text. As a good political Christian, he burned most of the text. Fortunately, in order to show that he was right to do so, he kept the contents and some parts of the text. For us, this provides a confirmation of the goals of that brotherhood. This material is still in use in the Ecclesia Ogdoadica (public religious branch of the Aurum Solis).

It was also necessary to be very prudent before revealing one's membership in the Order to anyone. In 1450, one of Pletho's students, Juvenal, was condemned for his Pagan religious beliefs and for being a member of the brotherhood. He had his tongue and right hand cut off before being thrown into the sea and drowned. Scholarios, the Patriarch of Constantinople, was a philosopher and theologian who denounced Juvenal and asked that he be condemned to death. He wrote: "His masters [he was talking about Pletho and the masters of the brotherhood] protected Hellenism with their words and writings, trying to resurrect the genealogies of Gods, clean the traditional texts [sic], develop a true liturgy, and many other things that had decayed and died. They do not dare to publicly attack orally or in their writings without any moderation the words of Christ, his dogmas, his works, and the ceremonies of our holy religion. Juvenal did just that." As Scholarios wrote: "The Pagan faith enlightens their souls to the point they can accept martyrdom." And Juvenal was not the only one to be persecuted. Yet this religious group was comprised of true siblings, in which all the initiates were loyal and active protectors of every member of the group. Scholarios explained that this secret group had members everywhere in the Italian-Greek world. Cardinal Bessarion, who was a member of the group, played an essential role in the protection of the other members. Several texts prove that he was a member of the inner circle.

In *The Divine Arcana of the Aurum Solis* I explained in detail why Pletho went to Italy and how his teachings initiated the rebirth of Hermetism. A new Academy in Florence was later placed under the direction of Marsilio Ficino. This Academy, including the group in Mistra, was created with an inner circle that performed sacred and Theurgic rituals, and an outer circle that was in charge of translations. The *Hermetica*, as well as the works from Plato, Iamblichus, and other Neoplatonicians, were translated and used there. The heritage was kept alive and used in an organized movement between the first visit of Pletho in 1438 and the visit of another initiate (Argyropoulos) in 1457.

Answering a letter I sent to the former Grand Master Melita Denning about the Florentine Academy and its relation to the initiatic process in Aurum Solis, she wrote (this letter is part of the Aurum Solis's archives): "Your experience [in the Aurum Solis] may have been of any circle of the Florentine type, and it certainly would be true of Careggi, to which such eminent visitors as Reuchlin or Erasmus probably never knew that their hosts were anything more than a particularly distinguished society for philosophic discussion.

"You are entirely correct in perceiving the presence of two distinct currents in our tradition. There is the Neoplatonician and the Pythagorean current, and the North African and Semitic, which we term Ogdoadic because it is distinguished by the high significance of the number eight. In the course of history these two currents have become considerably intermingled, so that we take the name Ogdoadic to denote our whole tradition, but in our history the meeting of the two initiatory currents can be traced, demonstrably, to Marsilio Ficino himself."

Ficino, protégé of Cosimo de Medici, was a devoted pupil and without a doubt the initiate of Chalcondylas and his associates, the fruit of his great studies under their guidance being his monumental *Theologia Platonica*. But then another influence entered into his life and work: that of the "Fideli d'Amore."

It is of tradition—and it is stated as a known fact in a book on Dante written by an eminent French Freemason and published in a numbered edition in the 1960s—that Dante was introduced into the Fideli d'Amore by his friend Guido Cavalcanti, another Florentine poet.

The history of the Fideli is curious. The Florentine family of Cavalcanti seems to have been particularly active among them. Coming from Dante's friend Guido Cavalcanti, we find in the fifteenth century Giovanni Cavalcanti, friend of Ficino and, undoubtedly, Ficino's sponsor into the Fideli d'Amore. Having completed his Theologia Platonica, he delayed its publication to make certain revisions; he also at that time wrote his commentary on Plato's book *The Banquet*. That book is dedicated to Giovanni Cavalcanti, and the words of the dedication, to one who knows of the connection of the Cavalcanti with the Fideli, is conclusive. It declares plainly Ficino's initiation into the Fideli d'Amore as a result of his introduction thereto by Cavalcanti.

It is good to know that the new Academy at Florence was not the only Academy that was managed by initiates eager to continue the divine work of the masters. In fact, we have focused intensively on Florence because the rebirth originated in Florence with the work of the Florentine Platonists, but other Academies in Florence, Naples, and

Rome were even closer to the Pagan project than the first Academy. Fewer writings were discovered, but it is well-known that Pope Paul II condemned the "humanistic" members of the Academia of Rome with the charge that they were working to revive Paganism and prepare a revolution. Regarding their goals, it is clear that they were an extension of the same group.

After this period, it is clear that the tradition continued to exist. I should mention the group called the "Fratelli Obscuri," which was active in Italy during the sixteenth and seventeenth centuries. What we know about this occult group shows that they were working with keys and materials that came from the Hermetic tradition. In a book called *The Life of Thomas Bodley*, which was actually written by Sir Thomas Bodley himself toward the end of his life, he mentions that he left England in 1576 to travel to France, Germany, and Italy to increase his knowledge and he was travelling for four years. So it is clear that he visited Italy and was initiated sometime between 1576 and 1580. It is very likely that Forli, Italy was the city where Thomas Bodley joined a "Society which, under the Veil of Mystery and the modest title of the Fratelli Obscuri, concealed the laudable object of propagating the Sciences and the love of Virtue. The Fratelli Obscuri had been established in imitation of an older Society, which had existed since before the fall of the Grecian Empire in the towns of Constantinople and Thessalonica. It was divided into three Grades . . . and had a system of writing which was known only to them. It also had a distinctive calendar." It is interesting to notice that this secret society adopted the plant moly (now known as Peganum harmala) as their emblem. Moly is a Magic plant that Homer mentioned in his book ten of *The Odyssey*. When Bodley came back to England, he opened a branch of this society with the authorization of the head of the Italian Order. When Antonio Pizzalleti came to London, he installed the new Society under the name of the "Tavern of the Muses." In *The Life of Thomas Bodley*, it says, "A few years later William Sedley and Thomas Smith established two new Taverns, one at Oxford and the other at Cambridge." Another tavern was opened at York and many more were also opened at the time John Selden was head of the Fratelli Obscuri in England.

I have already explained how the Inquisition was always directed against this Hermetic tradition. In Italy they were accused of heresy and many of them finished their lives in the prisons of the Inquisition. In England in 1669, King Charles II prohibited the secret societies. Consequently, the Fratelli Obscuri in England transformed their society into the Tobaccological Society and adopted the allegory of the tobacco plant instead the moly. As the Quatuor Coronati report[14] states, "The last head of these illustrious personages[15] died in the year 1753, and from that date all traces of the Tobaccological Society seem to have vanished until, some fifty years later it is met with as a practically new Society under the French name of the Priseurs."

There are many similarities between the Hermetic circles in Italy in the 1600s and the Pythagorean secret societies that were active in England and France. The Tobaccologist (named Priseurs or Nicotiates in France) were known as the "Children of Wisdom." Neoplatonicians were called "Friends of Wisdom" and philosophers. A special calendar was used by Pletho in his society. The Priseurs, such as the Fratelli Obscuri, also used a special calendar of twelve months, each comprised of thirty days. The names of the months originated in Egypt and Greece: Amonis, Apidis, Herculeo-Apollineum, Hermanubis, Momphta, Isidis, Omphta, Typhonis, Arueris, Sothiacum, Canobicum, and Ichthonicum.

To each month they added five days called "Days of Sais." They divided the month into five weeks of seven days each, associating each day with a traditional divinity, as Pletho did: Selene = Monday, Ares = Tuesday, Hermes = Wednesday, Zeus = Thursday, Aphrodite = Friday, Chronos = Saturday, and Helios = Sunday. They spoke clearly about their associations with members of the Pythagorean tradition.

---

14. The Quaturo Coronati was founded in 1884 in England and is the first Masonic Lodge of research. This Lodge still exists and publishes regular reports.

15. Sir Hans Sloane was in fact the last head of whom we have a record. That doesn't mean there was not a head after him.

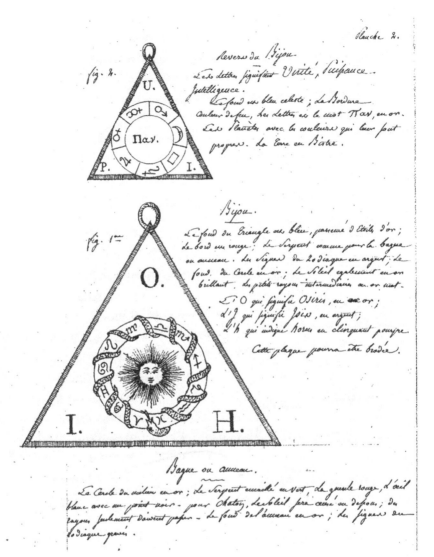

Figure 16: A page excerpt from the ritual of
the "Brothers of the Luminous Ring."

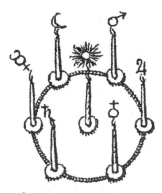

forme du Lustre.

Figure 17: A ritual chandelier used by the
"Brothers of the Luminous Ring," and the correspondences of the Lights.
(Excerpt from the Ritual Book.)

We might also mention several groups in France that were sometimes associated with Freemasonry, and which seem related to this tradition. Perhaps the most significant is the "Academy of the Sublime Masters of the Luminous Ring" (Académie des Sublimes Maîtres de l'Anneau Lumineux). The Hermetic elements in this occult society are numerous. A copy of the full constitutions and rituals from 1788 are currently held in the archives of the Ordo Aurum Solis. In the historical sections that discuss this Academy, we will find some surprising references. According to the founders of this society: "The name of 'Brothers of the Luminous Ring' is very old. It dates from the time of the Emperor Julian. Julian was one of the Christians of this time. He was condemned as an Apostate, because he didn't share their rage and their subhuman understanding of the Divine. . . . Christians oppressed him with defamations before and after his death, but they never totally tarnished his reputation, because even they said that Julian practiced all the virtues and gave them numerous blessings. It is he who gave the name of 'Brothers of the Luminous Ring' to our society, which have always kept from that day to this."

It is not surprising to find that the symbol of the sun is central to this society, associated with the seven planets and the twelve signs of the zodiac. Sacred names are associated with ancient Egypt and Greece.

You must also know that the groups just mentioned seemed to be focused on philosophy and the continuation of the Pythagorean and Neoplatonic tradition. They continued to use rituals, but they used them more symbolically than magically. We can compare that with Freemasonry, as it is today.

The other part of our heritage was very focused on Theurgic rituals. It retained this aspect, but remained very involved with the heritage from Iamblichus and Pletho. This line continued to be fully loyal to the Immortal Divinities and the Masters of the Golden Chain. The philosophy and rituals, as defined by Iamblichus, remained the central axis of all their work and mission. Perhaps the most obvious figure in this period was the Italian philosopher Tommaso Campanella, who practiced the Theurgic rituals to continue the tradition of Pletho and Ficino. It is important to know that, as a consequence of his beliefs, writings, and rituals, Campanella spent more than thirty years in prison, went to France, and remained there until his death. He died in 1639. It is impossible here to trace the lives of every historical figure of this time who travelled to Italy, France, and England. I wrote a book in French about the Christian Qabalah, and it is obvious that most of the famous figures of this time interested in the ancient traditions that originated in Egypt, Greece, and the Neoplatonic Academy learned this Hebrew Occult Science (Qabalah). They used these principles as tools. Some of them never confused a tool (such as the Hebrew or Christian Qabalah) with the religious and spiritual axis of their lineage. We can see this is true by the constant use of the Neoplatonic principles, the absence of Christian dogmatic restriction, and the individual rituals they practiced.

Even if the precise details of this time are not clearly known, it is clear that two currents survived as distinctly different secret groups.

According to the oral tradition of the Aurum Solis, an "Order of the Helmet" was established in England during the reign of Elizabeth I. This Order combined the Fideli d'Amore and Careggi successions. Francis Bacon, Edmund Spenser, Christopher Marlowe, and many other notables were among its initiates. Deeply involved with the beginnings of this Order was the "Italiante" movement of the early years of Elizabeth's reign. She herself had, during her sister's reign, been tutored by a Platonist scholar and had avidly studied the works of Castiglione, an intimate of the Medici. Under Elizabeth's personal patronage were Giacomo Aconcio, an initiate of the Ogdoadic Guild Mysteries, and Bernardino Ochino, a Sienese. Ochino, before traveling (by way of Geneva) to England, had narrowly escaped the trials of the Inquisition in Rome through the timely warning of another initiate, Cardinal Contarini.

The "Order of the Helmet" in its full development surrounded the Mysteries in England with a surge of new, intense feelings about the identity and power that characterized that age, and which survived well into the seventeenth century in its initiates.

A collation of Ogdoadic teachings and practices was begun as early as 1689, and the tradition was continued under the guise of antiquarianism from the early years of the eighteenth century. Certainly by 1689 the "Order of the Helmet" had ceased to function.

Figure 18: In the eighteenth century a "Societas Rotae Fulgentis," or "Society of the Burning Wheel," appeared as part of the Aurum Solis tradition.

As the history of the Order Aurum Solis indicates, a "Societas Rotae Fulgentis" (SRF) or "Society of the Blazing Wheel" appeared in the eighteenth century, bringing together the last adepts of the "Order of the Helmet."

Apart from initiation, SRF members were much concerned with their particular duty as they saw it to be: the preservation of the tradition as a whole, in as complete a condition as they were able to achieve for it.

This Society inherited important techniques based on those energies that are linked with the cycles of nature. It is absolutely true that the Baptistery of Florence synthesizes a certain number of symbolic elements that ultimately became part of the tradition of Aurum Solis. For example, their pavement reveals an interesting drawing that an Eastern person might describe as a mandala. On this figure it is possible to see a large wheel containing many concentric circles, with various colors, like a rose-colored stained-glass window. In the center there is a sun with twelve rays. Around this sun we read one of the key sentences of the Order: *En giro torte sol ciclos et rotor igne* (The Spiritual sun compels the Aeons to revolve around the periphery of a wheel, which it impels to turn with the force of fire!). Around the sun there are twelve drawings in the first concentric circle and in a second, outer concentric circle, we find the twelve signs of the zodiac. For the time being, we will not enter into an analysis of this Christian symbolism, but we may notice that the central place of the sun was a heresy at the time that this mosaic was assembled.

As you remember, the Academia Platonica directed by Marsilio Ficino reserved an honored place for the traditional forms of astrological Theurgy. The adepts of their time worked on the inner being with the techniques of planetary re-harmonization, utilizing such traditional elements as: correspondences, gestures, sounds, hymns, music, colors, etc.

This work on the inner being is the fundamental contribution of those techniques by which we may achieve harmonization with the universe; such techniques are at the heart of the Hermetic/Ogdoadic tradition. One of the fundamental contributions of the "Society of the Blazing Wheel" was the transmission and the deepening of this heritage of the Academia Platonica, both philosophic and Theurgic. The text of Plato's book *The Banquet* was explained by those initiates, including Marsilio Ficino himself; it remained an important basis of the work, reflection, and practice for the "Societas Rotae Fulgentis."

Yet, let us now be even more precise regarding the techniques transmitted by the SRF. The message that the Baptistery of Florence delivers to us is not only a part of our Outer Order. It is also a part of the Inner Order. As the history of thought (philosophy) reveals to us, the initiates of antiquity held many exchanges of information with the East. The theories of the "Bodies of Light" or "psychic bodies" were well-known at the same time, in both the Mediterranean world and in the East. Even the name of the Society of the Blazing Wheel, reveals that we do not speak only about the external representation of the universe, but also about the centers that animate our psychic being, those centers that the Eastern traditions called the chakras.

The SRF used techniques of animation, energization, and balance of the subtle parts of our energetic body. That was accomplished primarily through techniques of visualization, gesture, and breathing. If we were in an Eastern tradition we would be able to speak about visualization, meditation, Hatha yoga, and pranayama (or the yoga of breathing). You will be able to discover some explanations about these Eastern forms of meditation in some of the books of the Grand Masters of the Aurum Solis. Whether you are initiated into this Order or not, you will notice that (for example) the breathing techniques are elements that constitute a fundamental part of its rituals, and this is true from the beginning of the formation, and progressively throughout the student's advancement through the degrees. For example, we find a true teaching of Western pranayama in our own system. We are forced to admit that these aspects and teachings are seldom found in other Western initiatic orders.

The same thing may be said for the use of gesture in our rituals. For example, the sequences of positions that characterize the planets can easily be made to resemble certain parts of Hatha yoga, especially the famous "Sun Salutation." The meditations we use that are based on sounds and hymns are very close to mantras. All these elements were the center of the work and the transmission of the "Societas Rotae Fulgentis" and this transmission gives a characteristic power to the rituals of the Ordo Aurum Solis. All these techniques are still standard parts of regular training within the Aurum Solis.

Around the year 1860, the SRF was transferred from the West of England to London (specifically to the home of the Martin family, located at 1, St. Paul's Churchyard). From this time it began to explore in depth the practical aspects of its heritage, and was formally constituted as Aurum Solis in 1897. In my book *Secrets and Practices of the Freemasons*, I spoke in detail about the Rose-Cross lineage. Even if this tradition has several currents and influences (including the Hermetic, Christian, and magical aspects, etc.) the Aurum Solis has always remained independent from this line. It was the place where Theurgy, Neoplatonic faith, and teachings were preserved and taught.

Today, the surviving material of SRF remains within the keeping of the Grand Master's lineage of the Ordo Aurum Solis.

Hopefully, it is now easier to understand the importance of a lineage whose principle function is to do the necessary work by utilizing the magical principles of the Ogdoadic tradition. Three main principles define the validity and the effectiveness of this spiritual family, which is also called a "Theurgic lineage."

The first principle of the Ogdoadic tradition is that there is a direct link between each Grand Master and all the Grand Masters who preceded him or her. That link is part of the unbroken lineage that extends back to the time of the earliest Grand Master. It is through this link that each new Grand Master of the tradition is charged with his office. In a Theurgic Order such as this one, the office of the Grand Master is not the result of an election or the personal will of an assembly. The presiding Grand Master chooses his successor and transmits forever the occult office of the Order to him during a specific initiation. (It must be noted that, today, as in the first Pythagorean school, both men and women can be initiated and can become officers.) This is accomplished by connecting the new Grand Master to the unbroken Golden Chain of the past Grand Masters. This linking process makes the chosen Grand Master able to assume the full power of his office.

The special rites of the Grand Master give him the ability to maintain the egregores[16] of the tradition in a living, active, and dynamic state.

The second principle that establishes this legitimacy is the power to transmit the initiation, and the ability to connect the initiate to the egregore of the Order and the spirit of the masters of the Golden Chain. Those who are familiar with this kind of work recognize that an initiation must be coincident with an awakening of the consciousness of the initiate. This connection with the egregore facilitates that process and protects the aspirant in his work. This capacity, of being able to link an initiate to an egregore that protects and aids in the evolution of their consciousness, is a direct result of the active initiatic chain of the Order. The act of initiation causes these changes to occur in the aspirant. These changes make that person part of the unbroken chain, so that he or she is able to perform rites using a directly transmitted material basis. Initiation manifests these changes in the aspirant and links the aspirant to the Golden Chain.

The third principle, rooted in the Hermetic initiation, is that of the transmission of the "sacred objects" or, more exactly, the transmission of "consecrated objects." The tessera,[17] as a specific example of such a material basis, was made public by the Aurum Solis. A presentation of one of the models was offered in the public writings of Melita Denning and Osborne Phillips (husband and wife writing team who penned many books for Llewellyn). These tesserae constitute a direct occult link to the heart of the Order. As such the tessera forges another link for each new member to that unbroken occult chain, which ensures the constant aid and protection of the egregore to each member. This process and these teachings have their origin in the heritage that came from Iamblichus, Proclus, Apuleius, and Marsilio Ficino.

---

16. An egregore is an important notion and is extensively explained in the Glossary.

17. A tessera is a specific engraved stone consecrated during a ritual ceremony and given to the initiate with precise instructions about its goals and purposes. This very rare and ancient principle is still used in the Aurum Solis and is the manifestation of its Theurgic origin.

Exercise One—Harmonization with Thoth

This exercise can be performed in your own ritual room or in any quiet place. You will find information about how to set up your ritual space in the "Ritual of the Seven Gates" in Part 7. In the Ogdoadic tradition the altar is called a "bomos." Traditionally, the bomos is a wooden cube of 10.22" x 10.22" x 20.44". If you like you can paint this cube black or leave it in its natural state. For this exercise, you can use a white altar cloth made of linen or cotton.

Face east with the bomos directly in front of you. After a moment of silence, light a candle of natural wax (such as beeswax).

Raise this light three times prior to turning in each direction (east, south, west, and north). This action cleanses the place of working and increases the presence of the spiritual Light.

Walk to the west of the bomos and return the candle to its place on the top of the altar in the west.

Light the incense.[18] Walk to the eastern side of the room, and face east. Raise the censer four times to the east. Walk to the southern side of the room, visualizing a beautiful wall of vibrant golden light. Raise the censer to the south four times. Continue in the same way for the other directions until you return to the east. Walk to the western side of the bomos and return the censer to its place on top of the altar, in the west.

Sit down facing the altar (facing east) and meditate silently for a few minutes.

Visualize in front of you, to the east, a naos[19] in Egyptian style. The naos is in sculpted wood, covered with golden leaves. The two doors of the naos are open, and a statue of Thoth is just outside. Thoth has a human body and an ibis head. His hands are on top of his thighs, palms down.

---

18. Specific incenses can be found on the Aurum Solis website. You can also use Dragon's Blood in this instance.

19. The naos is a wooden engraved box often covered with gold leaves. This box contains the statue of the divinity. We also can find naos in stones.

In front of him are offerings, flowers, perfumes, and burning candles.
Contemplate Thoth, silently and respectfully.
Stand up; raise both hands in the direction of Thoth and say:

Let Thoth now be invoked!

Hail to you, Moon, Thoth!
     You, who makes a place for the Gods!
     You, who knows the secrets and inscribes them in the
sacred characters!
     You, who knows how to recognize the truth of discourse!
     You, who is the judge of each of us!
     You, the God of penetrating gaze, who stands on the
million year bark!
     You, the messenger of mankind, who knows each man by
his spoken word!
     You, who returns every evil action against its author!
     You, who satisfies Ra!

You, who advise the unique Lord and ensures that He knows
everything that happens!
     You, who calls the skies at sunrise and does not forget the
reports of past events!
     You, who protects the sun bark during the night and
accompanies the bark of the day, standing with your arms
extended at the prow of the ship!
     You, who seizes the ropes, when the bark of day and the
bark of night are at the fete of the crossing of the sky!
     We respectfully salute you!
     The Ennead in the bark of night adores you, O Thoth,
saying:
     "Hail to you, son and glory of Ra, you that Gods acclaim!
     Be honored, O Thoth!"

Stand, with your arms hanging naturally at your sides and remain silent for a little while.

Kneel in silence, so that you are seated on your feet. Place your hands on top of your thighs, palms up.

After few seconds of silence, say:

Thoth, noble Ibis, I call upon you!
O God who loves Knoum;
O writer of the Ennead;
Great God, who resides in the sacred city of Hermopolis, manifest yourself at this instant!
Hear my call!
Let your manifestation be powerful and let it make me great!
I ask that, by my pure desire, the chain of the Theurgic tradition be manifested at this instant!
O Thoth, I want to be a servant of your house.
May I speak of your valiant actions and tell with the multitude:
"Great are you, Thoth, and great are your actions!"

Remain silent for few minutes, while visualizing a shining golden light coming from Thoth, and illuminating all the levels of your being.

Stand up, raise both hands toward Thoth, and say:

May your power protect me during my Theurgic rites and in my daily life!
May I always render myself worthy of your protection!
So mote it be!

You may then extinguish the flame upon the bomos, return everything to a state of order, and write some notes about the ritual.

Note: The Magick Journal

Another basic tool that you should use regularly is your Magick Journal. Obtain a notebook to be used solely for this purpose; after each ritual, record your experiences, dreams, emotions, impressions, and so on. Any experiences that you believe are related to the rituals you are assigned to perform should be recorded there, along with your thoughts regarding the texts of this book.

Self-Test One

These questions are intended to help you to challenge your knowledge about the subjects you have been studying. You can use them before you read the materials or after. Try to answer the questions before checking the answers in the Appendix.

1. Who were the founders of the Western magical tradition?
2. Does a myth describe true events?
3. What is the Egyptian Ogdoad?
4. Who is Djehuti?
5. Are Thoth and Hermes the same figure?
6. What is the "Golden Chain of the Initiates"?
7. Which country was the birthplace of the tradition of High Magick (Theurgy)?
8. What ancient Masonic rituals are associated to the history of the Theurgic tradition?

The following questions are related to your own experience. It is good to use them as personal meditations.[20]

1. Can you provide some examples in your life of positive effects that stem from your knowledge of your familial lineage?

---

20. You can share your thoughts about these questions on the forums of the Aurum Solis website.

2. Find an Egyptian God and an Egyptian Goddess that attract you and meditate several times on their representations and their symbols.

3. Find a Greek (or Roman) God and Goddess that attract you and meditate several times on their representations and their symbols.

Part 2
The Pillars of the Theurgic Tradition

Constructing a Healthy and Safe Life as a High Magician and Theurgist

The two major pillars of the Theurgic tradition: The Theurgic tradition has two major pillars that support and delimit the healthy life of the student: philosophy and ritual.

The first pillar, philosophy, is not a sterile and useless intellectual discourse. Philosophy is a real spiritual exercise that helps you to develop three essential parts of your magical personality: 1) it helps you develop a healthy and rational mind; 2) it helps you discover how to enjoy your life here and now; 3) it helps you understand and prepare for the process of your death.

The latter of these two pillars, ritual, is different than magick. When you understand that Theurgy is a ritual work focused on raising your soul with the help of divinities, you can begin this path without any risks.

The Love of Wisdom

In the previous historical teaching we saw how the Greek philosophers from the Pythagorean and Platonic schools became the heirs to the Hermetic tradition. It would be too ambitious in this context to attempt a summary of the Greek philosophy, such as the one developed by these schools. To begin with, I must emphasize that, consistent with its etymology, the essence of this philosophical Greek movement is called "the Love of Wisdom." For some contemporary scholars, it is possible to really talk about philosophy only in reference to the period of Socrates or the pre-Socratic thinkers. According to those writers, this method of discourse was not in evidence before that time, and it certainly did not exist in ancient Egypt. This kind of conclusion is not acceptable as such. It might be acceptable if we reduce philosophy only to a theoretical discourse while hiding all its spiritual and esoteric goals. However, these philosophies are characterized by the idea of an inner desire to ascend from the physical world to the spiritual and divine plane.

As humans, it is believed we are incarnated into a realm of illusion and pain that is related to our physical nature. Inwardly we are not considered to be from this place. To use the Orphic declaration: "We are sons of the earth and the starry skies." This means that we live in this world, but our real existence is in the world above. As death is inevitable, we must be prepared for this moment. This is only possible if we train our spiritual body to go outside our physical body while acclimating ourselves to the higher levels of consciousness. This training is precise and is a secret that has been kept alive in the Theurgic tradition. It allows you to make this inner transformation and illumination without any help from a specific religion or priest. We have to work directly on ourselves. This is one of the reasons that Theurgists were considered to be real threats to the dogmatic religions. I will speak more extensively about this process in Part 6 of this book.

You must remember that, when we use Theurgy, this ascent is possible with the help of various Theurgic rituals. For a philosopher who is not a Theurgist, this ascent is made possible by the use of a special mental practice called "maieutics," meaning "the art of giving birth." The teacher uses this special method of rhetoric to deliver the ideas and knowledge that are already in the mind of the student. A part of his method is also used to help the students to ascend to the highest spiritual planes. According to Plato this is not a transmission of knowledge such as is provided in an old-fashioned school. This is a sacred work that allows the student to practice a real introspection and to begin climbing the spiritual path that leads them to the highest divine world. Plato wrote clearly about this process in several books, including *The Symposium*, *Phaedo*, and *Phaedrus*. Maieutics was a part of the oral teaching of Plato and this topic was taught in his school. These books remain the external and public part of this special and private teaching.

The discoveries made in modern times in Nag Hammadi (Egypt) motivate us to reconsider this Greek "invention" of maieutics. Jean-Pierre Mahé, a specialist in the Coptic language, explained how Thoth became the God of writing. Many books were credited to him. Most of them were writings about theology, astrology, magick, and the occult. Thoth is considered to be "the one who knows." He is supposed to be the creator of all philosophical teachings. As you will see, the Hermetic texts utilize a conversational form between Thoth and his initiates. These conversations are organized as didactic questions and answers. This method of writing is the same as the writing style in Platonic philosophy. Scholars frequently argue about the year these texts were written, but it is interesting and revealing to notice the relationship between the Hermetic method of writing, and the style of Platonic writings. According to the stories related by Maneton, the Egyptian historian, there was a family lineage of Hermes that passed the occult secrets of the tradition from father to son. According to this historian, the most ancient Thoth, who was the first Hermes, engraved his teaching on stone steles, which survived the deluge. After him came a second Hermes Trismegistus. His son Agathodaimon is supposed to have translated all the writings from his grandfather into Greek, in order to give them to his son Tat.

Clearly, even if Maneton is mixing mythology with stories, he is using an allegory to describe a priestly family who passes magick secrets from one member to the next, under the protection of the Temple of Hermopolis. In history, it is easy to see priests and wise men mastering the magical arts, who were then declared divine after their death. They became "symbolically" the God they embodied throughout their lives. We can read about a priest of the Temple of Thoth in Thebes who was named: "Grand God, master of the Truth, who protects the Temple and knows the two lands, writer of the truth for the Gods, bull of the divine cycle." It is clear that the real origin of philosophy, if we only consider its esoteric and initiatic parts, was the Hermetic tradition. The public manifestation of philosophy appeared later in Greece, in a more and more specific style of writing. It is plausible that this is why the first distinction between exoteric and esoteric was established by Pythagoras, a Greek who knew the Egyptian tradition very well.

We can now understand why the Platonic and Neoplatonic traditions are so important to someone who learns Theurgy. It is a kind of mental discipline that helps us to better understand the world. This is an inner training that enables us to develop a rational mind and a precise intellectual faculty of analysis. This training helps us to avoid all mystical delirium. Classical philosophy is something that can give a structure to our inner personality. It helps to avoid any religious dogmatism. It is interesting to remember the words from the German philosopher Nietzsche: "If you want peace of your mind, just believe. If you want the truth, then you must search for it." The wise use of human intellect, the development of a critical mind open to a large range of possibilities was named "Religio Mentis": "Religion of the mind." It was the Religio Mentis that was developed in the Hermetic writings.

As several scholars have shown, the *Corpus Hermeticum* seems to develop into two different kinds of gnosis. These two theories, which we might also call "points of view," could be considered as opposites. As a matter of fact, such initiates as the Platonic philosophers accepted the postulate of dualities: body vs. mind and visible vs. invisible. This is what is called "Classical Idealism or Platonic Idealism." This approach has been developed differently all throughout history. Some "spiritualists"[21] oppose the spiritual and physical worlds. They try to demonstrate that these aspects are two radically different modalities of existence, even if they both originate from God. This is the dualist form of spiritualism, which most closely approximates the Platonic philosophy. Other spiritualists believe in the reality of a spiritual world but refuse to accept the existence of a God.

For the ancient Greeks, the word "matter" didn't have the same meaning as it does today. For them it was only a substance that received a shape, such as wood, marble, bronze, etc. Matter always requires a shape in order to be manifested. For Plato, matter is indeterminate (Apeiron), a wet nurse (titene) from whom beings receive the elements that compose them, a place (Kora) where they live. With Aristotle, matter became that power that is about to manifest itself. What we have said doesn't mean that matter and shape are two distinct and separate essences. The soul, for example, is the matter of ideas, the power that manifests them. Consequently, spirit and matter are not in opposition.

If we presuppose that the goal of philosophy, which is the same as the goal of initiation, is to free the soul in order to rise above the world of illusions in which we are living, we might think it is logical to believe that our body is an obstacle. Consequently, an adept would have to liberate himself from his body in order to reach the divine spheres. If all the heads of this tradition agreed on this philosophical goal, then the way to reach the divine spheres would be quite different. We could reject our body as if it were an adversary. Contrarily, we could consider our body to be an ally that we must bring into balance, even while enjoying the pleasurable activities that enable us to perform the work. For example, if you are hungry, it would be very difficult for you to meditate, or to practice any kind of introspection. In the same way, if you eat to excess you will also be disturbed. It is better to find a good balance in your body. As we become more balanced, our body will

---

21. This word is related to the spiritual world and is different than the modern religion of Spiritualism.

become our assistant, helping us by becoming the solid basis on which we will be able to build our spiritual practice. This is what is called "optimistic gnosis." In the case of "pessimistic gnosis" we must assume that our body is useless and has to be strongly disciplined. Good examples of this approach are the anchorites and the stylites who stripped naked and climbed to the top of a column, starving themselves until they were unconscious. Without cleaning their bodies, they attempted to come into the presence of God in filthy, stinking rags. This was also true for those Christians who used self-flagellation to eradicate their desires and passions. Members of the modern Catholic organization called the "Opus Dei" are still obliged to regularly wear around their thigh an instrument called a "cilice," which is a chain mail band with pointed metal spikes fixed to it used to scratch the skin so that it bleeds. Hermetic philosophy is just the opposite!

Hermetism and Theurgic philosophy (explained by Iamblichus) presents the world as a place for experimentation, which is very useful for the development of our being. We are not the subject of any "fall" or some "original sin" followed by a banishment from the spiritual worlds. We are not condemned to suffer by a God who is supposed to be good, kind, and benevolent. Our human condition is not the result of a fall from grace, but from an incarnation, a descent of the soul, the descent of our psyche into a physical body. This descent was progressive, through several spheres that are associated with seven divinities. The Hermetic explanation for the descent of man is the foundation for the divine magick that we call Theurgy. The darkening of the Body of Light during our descent is the cause of the pain, the limitation of our consciousness, and the loss of memory of our past lives. It is essential to remember that it is not a malediction, but really a consequence of our descent into flesh. Even more positively, all our feelings, which come from our body, are a unique opportunity to feel pleasure and beauty. These sensations and feelings are a real source of joy for the optimistic gnostic.

From this perspective, Hermetism is really associated with Epicurism and to the Platonic search for beauty. In short, the Hermetic tradition is taken from Epicurism, whose goal is to live a well-balanced life while enjoying that life. Of course, excesses are not recommended, but enjoying life is a fundamental part of this process. From Platonism, the Hermetic tradition takes the idea that cultivating beauty in our life helps us ascend to the spiritual world from whence we came: the world of the Immortal Divinities.

Optimism and spirituality are united. In the Hermetic tradition, there is no denial that there is evil in the world. But evil is completely absent from the divine world. It is inconceivable for a Theurgist/Hermetist to believe that the supreme divine principle could have any evil parts. It is contradictory to suggest that a divine being commands or creates something violent or evil that results in pain and suffering for us. The more we progress and ascend on the spiritual path, the closer we get to the divine, which is necessarily composed entirely of all Beauty, Truth, Justice, and Good. As Epicurus wrote in his famous letter to Menoeceus: "Do not fear the Gods." We can easily see that this is true in all the texts that are considered sacred by Theurgists and Hermetists. God is not bad, violent, or wrathful. The supreme principle, sometimes called Nous Pater, doesn't ask for murder, sacrifice, or violence. You can now understand why the Hermetists were (and still are) horrified with biblical texts in which God is very often portrayed with these penchants.

Theurgy, the Divine Magick

Anyone who is interested in the Western tradition will soon hear about the word "magick." From the time of the Renaissance, and right up to modern times this word has been used by many authors, but the meaning of this word is not as obvious as we might imagine.

I already introduced the concept of Theurgy, but it is worthwhile to advance our understanding of this important part of the Western tradition. "Destiny of the Soul" in Part 6 will develop the relationship between Theurgy and destiny. You will remember that many books about Theurgy, and the *Chaldaean Oracles*, were destroyed or lost during the first few centuries of the Common Era. A few excerpts were miraculously preserved as quotations in various books, and scholars have given us a reliable translation of these texts. The main original writings about this divine practice are from Iamblichus, Porphyry, Plotinus, and Proclus. Of course, it is not an obligation to read all of these ancient and sometimes difficult books, even if they are fascinating. All of these honorable writers were real practitioners, but at the same time they were scholars, philosophers, and theologians. So their analyses are precise and sometimes too detailed and specialized. This is why it is not necessary at the beginning to learn all the details of a complex philosophy. The goal of this book is to explain the main principles and to help you to clearly understand what Theurgy is and what the unique characteristics of those principles are.

Neoplatonicians (Proclus, Plotinus, etc.) introduced a distinction between Theurgy and magic (or Goetia). The first was considered to be a "high form of magick." The latter was considered to be a "low form of magic." Modern authors and practitioners generally follow this distinction. I am not analyzing the etymology and evolution of these words in detail here, but there are still basic elements you have to keep in mind regarding these words. In the ancient Mediterranean world, the terms magic and Goetia were nearly equivalent. The origin of this custom may be found in the names given to the priests in Mesopotamia: "the Perfect, the Perfected One = Magi." Later on, in Neoplatonic philosophy, Goetia was progressively associated with the idea of sorcerers, who were frequently looked on as being evil and held in low regard. Even with this distinction, the meanings of the words magic and Goetia were not clearly defined until the Middle Ages. A book entitled *The Lesser Key of Solomon* was composed during the seventeenth century from different sources. In this book the distinction between bad and good daimons is explained.[22] When the word Goetia stands alone it is clearly associated with bad daimons. When Goetia is associated with the word Theurgy, it concerns generally good daimons. As a matter of fact, no matter what the evolution of the words "magic," "Goetia," "witchcraft," etc. may be, the word Theurgy has always been

22. Remember that during this century there was a difference between the word "daimons" (a Greek word related to "spiritual beings who work as messengers or intermediaries," which approximates the idea of the "Christian angels") and the word "demons" (a more recent word that only describes "bad invisible spirits").

associated with positive and divine work. Today we might remember that there is a kind of magic (Goetia) that is mostly focused on working with invisible spirits. There is also something called "High Magick" that is more clearly defined by the word "Theurgy," which is focused on magical rituals that are used to elevate the soul by creating contact between the person and the highest spirits and divinities.

Someone who works with the Goetic aspects of magic can be compared to someone who goes to the pharmacy and chooses the medications that seem appropriate to their symptoms at that moment. An untrained person would find this to be a dangerous practice. In order for this strategy to be useful, you must have a good description of the medicines, a good catalog of all medicines, and a good understanding of the side effects produced by each medicine, in addition to an understanding of the effect of combining various medicines and their interactions. By contrast, you could decide to see a doctor or a specialist who would evaluate your problems and your body as a whole. When he gives you a prescription, you have to take it for a while before you feel the results. These results are usually effective and they last. As you can see, everyone is able to buy medications for minor diseases on his own (doing magic and Goetia), but for major diseases, the assistance of a specialist and a real treatment (Theurgy) is certainly safer.

Both magic and Theurgy agree on and accept the existence of a spiritual world that is invisible to our physical senses. Both also accept the existence of a spiritual and invisible body that is intimately linked to our physical body. Our double nature, body and soul, is easy to understand and is the source of what a Magus or a Theurgist does.

Even if modern Wiccans do not frequently use the word Theurgy, their use of the power of magic, their moral statements, and the relationships that Wiccans create with their divinities place them very close to Theurgy. It is clear that most of the time they are not on the path of "low magic." This is equivalently true for modern druidic groups.

According to the Hermetic and Platonic philosophy, the material world that surrounds us is an iconic representation of spiritual principles. Today these principles are called archetypes and are a reality in the spiritual world. Thus, everything we see around us is the shadowy reflection of these divine principles, sometimes called "Ideas." Consequently, everything that we see in the world is linked to a spiritual archetype. The occult law of correspondences states that a reflection corresponds to its ideal reality. There is a link between these two elements. Knowing these correspondences is essential as the key to accessing these invisible powers. What I have called symbols can be material artifacts, plants, stones, etc., or anything that acts as a true link for accessing the divine ideal to which it is linked. For example the light emanating from a candle is the symbolic representation of the Divine Light; a pentagram is the representation of the four elements balanced by the upper presence of the Aether,[23] Spirit, etc. Using such symbols in a ritual and being aware of this connection really does connect us to the corresponding invisible power. Of course the use of one symbol doesn't make a ritual. To do that and to be able to increase the power, we need to associate several symbols with our ritual, and then activate them in a precise sequence. For example, we can think about the engine of our car. If we consider just one part, a piston for example, we would agree that it is related to the power of the engine, but in order for the engine to work, we cannot just activate one part. All the parts must work together in a precise way. That is how a ritual works. This is also why the study of symbols and correspondences are so essential. This is also the point where magic and Theurgy radically differ.

The magus (Goetian) uses his knowledge to perform rituals in order to obtain material results without any intention of raising his soul to the divine. The magus works with the chthonic daimons in order to obtain what he wants. He uses the less spiritual invisible levels of his body, closest to the material world, and his own abilities to impose his will on the daimons. This is a utilization of tools for the purpose of tricking the daimons into a relationship in which the magus has power over them. As a result, the magus is always involved in a power struggle, and he has a constant need to be protected from the powerful, invisible daimons. Of course he cannot be sure that he will always be the most powerful

---

23. This Greek word is sometimes spelled "Ether." (Greek: ΑΙΘP)

force in this contest, even if he has very impressive Theurgic capabilities. Such a magician is able to perform divination, spells, talismanic magic, etc. This kind of magician can also invoke inferior divinities that are close to our world, but always with the same material goals in mind.

By contrast, the Theurgist relies on his relationship with the divinities for his spiritual work. This is radically different from what a magician does, whose work can be seen as a horizontal action focused on simply getting what he wants. Thus, the Theurgist is focused on a higher and purer form of magick, which is called Theurgy. The essential Theurgy is the liberation of his soul and the ascent to the Divine by the use of precise ceremonies. This is a vertical ascent and relationship between one person and the God(s). The Theurgist is someone who uses piety, devotion, and ritual together and in conjunction.

Aurum Solis has a moral requirement that must be met before any person is initiated, because the Theurgist must be a moral person before he performs any ritual work. The relationship he wants to develop with the Immortal Divinities is rooted in respect and devotion, instead of relying on the pretense that he can impose his own will on another being. The relationship he establishes with the divinities results in a relationship of sympathy, attraction, and love. It is because the Theurgist loves the divine and Immortal Divinities that he is able to contact them in a very balanced and safe way.

When we perform a Theurgic ritual guided by a true love, mistakes can be forgiven and minimized. When (in our personal life) we call our lover to apologize because we have made a mistake, or we forgot something, etc., we will immediately be forgiven. This kind of relationship and ritual practice is safe and the Theurgist's life will be better in several ways as a result of this practice. His physical and psychological balance will be improved. His influence will be felt by others. What ancient Greeks called the "kairos" will be strengthened. Kairos is this strange faculty that some of us have that allows us to be at the right place at the right moment. This is a truly remarkable consequence of a deep Theurgic work. All these gains are a consequence of our relationship with and love for the divine, and not only because of our use of Theurgy.

Because he is aware of these essential elements, the Theurgist will use a progressive method for his spiritual ascent. It will involve both devotional practices and ceremonial rituals. Hymns and prayers are used in his daily life. This is the best way to establish and maintain an intense and intimate relationship with the divinities that have been chosen by the Theurgist. The ritual ceremonies involve the use of specific symbols to invoke the epiphany of the divinities. The precise steps of this initiation include using statues composed of the appropriate medium in order to call the God into the statue by the use of specific inner preparations, gestures, invocations, repetitive sounds, and holy words, perfumes, specific musical instruments, secret artifacts, etc.

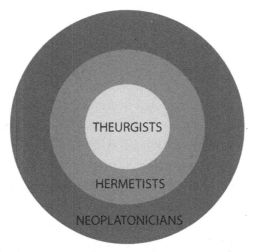

Figure 19: The three groups: Theurgists, Hermetists, and Neoplatonicians.

You must remember that Theurgy is a real tradition, which was totally associated from the beginning with the Hermetic and Ogdoadic tradition. The relationship between these schools is not often clear. The principle you have to remember is simple. There are three groups: 1) Neoplatonicians 2) Hermetists 3) Theurgists. A Hermetist is necessarily a Neoplatonician, but the reverse is not necessarily true. A Theurgist is necessarily a Hermetist, but the reverse is not necessarily true. Consequently, a Theurgist is at one and the same time a Hermetist and a Neoplatonician.

It is for this reason you see people who are interested in the Hermetic tradition, but not involved in Theurgy.

I must now underscore various facts you have to know about this classification.

- These three groups have a specific share in Platonic Theology, but each group developed a specific aspect of this philosophy, which is more focused on its specifics.
- These three groups worship the Immortal Divinities in the same way. The religious aspect is a primary constituent of the belief system of every Neoplatonician.
- Rituals may have been performed by each group, but they are at the heart of Theurgy.

The divine and sacred work of Theurgy can be learned and performed safely with an initiation and in the presence of a master who knows the process and has, himself, accomplished this spiritual journey. This information is precisely revealed in certain ancient fragments from the original text of the *Chaldean Oracles*. There, we read certain very specific terms, such as "myste," "initiates," and "initiations." This is the way that the Order Aurum Solis still works today, fully integrated in a direct line with the Masters of the Golden Chain.

Ultimately the initiate will be able to turn his soul toward the divine and progressively ascend to his origin following what is called "the sacred way of the return" by the use of the sacred Mysteries, which are directly transmitted.

Exercise Two—Remembrance [24]

The technique of anamnesis is an important example of how to use this system. I encourage you to begin this practice right now.

This exercise is very ancient and has several purposes. It was taught by Pythagoras. In the Pythagorean aphorisms called the "Golden Verses," it says: "Do not allow sweet sleep to take you before you have reviewed

---

24. *Remembrance* in Greek is "anamnesis."

every action of the day." Plato also taught this exercise as a way to train memory, so we can remember our entire life and even past lives. This training will help you to preserve the memory of what you learned in this life when you pass away, which is a very essential key to spiritual progress.

When you get into bed, before you go to sleep, lay down on your back, with your arms relaxed on both sides of your body. Relax and breathe regularly.

After few minutes of relaxation, declaim mentally the hymn to the Greek Goddess Mnemozyne:

> Mnemozyne, you who knew Zeus and gave birth to the Holy and Sacred Muses of pure voices, I invoke you!
>
> Hearken, I ask that you remove any unwanted lapse of memory; give me a steady and united Mind and Soul, and improve my ability to reason.
>
> Mnemozyne; you are the attentive and careful Goddess who brings to remembrance my heart's thoughts. Help me retain them without failing, recalling them swiftly to a clear mind whenever necessary.
>
> O blissful Goddess, I am your initiate. Awaken in me the memory of the Sacred Mysteries, and take away forgetfulness forever.

Review the events of your day in memory. Always start with the most recent events and then gradually run through them in reverse until you arrive at the beginning of your day.

As you consider each event of the day, take the measure of this event by fixing your attention on it (focusing on the time and place when it occurred) and proceed to assess your attitude and yourself at the time under examination.

Decide in your heart and conscience if the attitude you have been examining was good or bad in accordance with your principles. If you have acted contrary to the principles of good, regard it as your imperative duty to rectify your attitude as much as possible the very next day.

Having reviewed the activities of the day, take a few minutes to consider your projects for the day to come. Allow yourself to release everything related to the previous day, and all of the concerns that weigh on you. Devote the very last thoughts of the day to whatever gives you a true inner peace and joy. The last thought of the day must always help you tend toward a greater state of inner harmony, a better sense of inner congruence. It seems like a very simple thing to accomplish, but, over time, it will begin to be of tremendous importance to you.

Self-Test Two

These questions are intended to help you challenge your knowledge about the subjects you have been studying. You can use them before you read the materials or after. Try to answer the questions before checking the answers in the appendix.

1. What is the meaning of the word "philosophy"?
2. Why is philosophy important in our lives?
3. Are Neoplatonism and Hermetism optimistic or pessimistic philosophies?
4. Do the Theurgists believe in "original sin"?
5. What is "High Magick"?
6. Is Goetic magic dangerous?
7. What is the goal of Theurgy?
8. Is a Neoplatonician necessarily a Theurgist?

The following questions are related to your own experience. It is good to use them as personal meditations.[25]

1. Did you learn philosophy in school? If so, what was the most important thing you remember from your lessons?
2. Can you really enjoy something without being aware of it?
3. What do you think "bad magic" would be?

---

25. You can share your thoughts about these questions on the forums of the Aurum Solis website.

4. For you, what is the best moral principle when performing magical rituals?

Figure 20: Thoth revealed the sacred books,
later entitled the Hermetica.

Part 3
The Sacred World

Discovering the Presence of the Divinities in the World and Understanding Why Monotheistic Religions Separated the Divine from Our World

A disconnected world: We are living today in a world that has become disconnected from the sacred and the divine. Monotheistic religions have severed the direct relationship that existed in the Pagan world between believers and their Gods. The monotheist chiefs used their dogmas as weapons to gain supremacy over Pagans and their world.

A Pagan world full of divinities: In the pre-monotheistic world, Gods and Goddesses were present everywhere. Worshippers and Theurgists used many ways to reach the Gods. The existence of a divine principle above this spiritual ladder (which is impossible to define) was accepted, but without rejecting the notion of sacredness in the world.

This part is intended to clearly explain how this spontaneous and original relationship to the divine was distorted in order to take it from you.

Discovery of the Sacred World

For more than a century Western people have been living with a moral and religious foundation that they are quite unconscious of. In a way, our thoughts, reactions, and feelings have been shaped by the Judeo-Christian values. As I previously explained in this book, religions that existed before the spread of Christianity were declared false when Christianity arose, and were condemned as the divagation of fools. At times, Paganism was also considered to be a predecessor, or an earlier stage of the monotheistic religion. In this way, Christianity came to be considered as the final and perfect culmination of the religious mind. This idea was also accepted by most of the Western esoteric schools.

If we study about the true essence of a human being, we will discover an inner nature that is really different than the one described by Christianity or modern science. Human beings appear to have a dual aspect: rationality and magick. As a result of understanding this, we may start becoming aware that the world around us is not limited to what we can see. Evidence of this intuition of the existence of the invisible world can be found in the records of archaeological digs in various prehistoric caves. Artifacts such as gifts and food associated with funerals are gifts to the dead, which demonstrate an awareness of life beyond death and consequently the invisible world.

The education we have received shaped what we see in the world around us and could limit our understanding of the world. Being unaware of our beliefs and of their origin is a real limitation of what we can perceive. The new Christian religion also taught a specific representation of the world, which then became a new mental limitation. Despite all these attempts, the primitive and spontaneous magical part of our inner being is still there. It is a real blessing to recognize this original pattern, which is helping us to break down these artificial limits and to recover from this long period of darkness.

It is interesting to discuss religion, angels, and divinities. It is exciting to follow the psychoanalytic, psychological, and philosophical theories. It enhances us to learn new esoteric teachings. It is possible to believe that several conceptualizations of all these theories are correct, but none of them succeed in fully explaining our original religious essence. On this point there has been no evolution. We are no more advanced than our earliest ancestors when they sat at the entrance to their cave, anxiously afraid as they watched the Gods of the storm. This ancestor still exists inside us and coexists with our rational, modern consciousness. It is necessary to understand this in order to incorporate this reality into our lives.

On one side there is something we might call the "understanding of the earth," which may be thought of as the feeling of the most primitive and authentic parts of our being. As I said about the optimistic gnosis, what is essential for everyone is happiness here and now. No matter what theory we propose, or how we talk about the goals of life, the goal is always the same for everyone: to achieve peace and happiness in this world.

On the other hand, as I just explained, every human being feels the existence of the invisible world. Yet this dimension cannot be demonstrated and is only perceptible as the result of an inner certitude. No matter what time we look at in history, Gods, God, angels, and demons are related to an irrational faith. Despite this irrationality, everyone must accept this as a real and essential part of our being, which is rooted in experience.

In our modern consciousness, this spiritual world appears to be both simple and complex at the same time. We might say that the Universe is a realization of a unique God upon whom our existence and future is dependent. It is also possible to understand the unique God as an inaccessible principle connected to us by a hierarchy of divinities and angels. It is also possible to see the world full of divinities just as the Pagans did.

No matter what the beliefs are, it is logical to challenge them in order to make progress in the direction of being able to see reality as it is. It is true that for now there is no way to prove the existence of these spiritual planes. We might ask ourselves whether the monotheistic explanation of the universe and the world is the best way to reach happiness in this life. Is it an obstacle, or does it help us achieve real progress?

When I taught philosophy several years ago, I sometimes had to explain the Western religious background to the students. I remember a Christian student saying that Egyptian and Greek Gods were just mental creations that never existed. When I asked him why, his answer was surprising: "Because there is just one God!" he said.

My reply was a simple question: "If you are a believer, what differences can you see between the one God you are talking about, and Zeus, for example?" The conversation continued:

—Zeus doesn't exist . . .

—How can you be so sure? What proof do you have?

—I know that, because it is written in the Bible.

—This book was revealed by God speaking directly to someone. Am I correct?

—Yes, you are.

—So without considering the statements of this book, which are, of course, subjective, it seems that if you accept the existence of a divine being, you have to agree on the fact that other cultures can also believe, but they may believe in a different divinity.

—No, I cannot.

Over many years of teaching, I saw the same way of thinking many times. It is this exact image of the monotheistic theology that brings people into a contradictory rhetoric. Mental limitations were artificially created and even human logic has a very hard time breaking the bars of this jail.

By contrast, the first time I read books written by polytheists or animists, I read that divinities can be seen as different ladders put all around a house. They are all useful to climb on the roof. You may prefer one over the other, but the only way to claim that there is only one real and unique ladder is to break all the other ladders. For me, this was a clear confirmation of what I was feeling deeply. You can be a materialist and reject all the divinities, but to say that you believe in one God and that the others don't exist is just absurd.

It is not my intention to say that this is the only and definitive truth, but I will remember all my life the look of someone who realized that the monotheistic limits are artificial. Suddenly the horizon gets much wider and so does the way we see the world and other people. This is what I call a real "conversion."

As a matter of fact, and from a general point of view, it has never been possible for humanity to believe in just one God. Even in Judaism, Christianity, or Islam, hierarchies of spiritual beings were added to create a kind of link between the higher levels and the bottom level where we live. They did not call the beings that populated their hierarchies Gods and Goddesses, but they are so close in meaning, that a real theological evaluation would be necessary to explain the difference. For the believers it was quite the same. A real power was associated with these invisible powers.

Of course the unique God continues to be the original reference, but it was considered so perfect that any contact with human problems or mundane life was unworthy of him. This is why angels replaced the traditional divinities, to fill the gap. But even angels sometimes seem too far from people. This is why Christian religions created the saints. This is not the place to explain in detail how these countless saints were often invented and organized. It is enough to see that the popular faith and religion has always needed invisible creatures that are closer to the human level in order to help and reassure us.

This feeling and relationship is the same as the polytheistic tradition I am talking about. This is something natural and spontaneous. It is a demonstration that an essential part of human nature cannot be destroyed or replaced. If there is a reality, even if it is invisible, we will see its manifestation and finally its return. It is impossible to twist the reality and install a contradictory philosophical system. The Immortal Divinities will always return to us because they never leave us. They were just sidelined by the political religious powers of the day. For this reason, we can unveil this spiritual path to the divine again today by showing how our ancestors conceived the sacred, which is really present in us and in the world around us.

Gods and Angels

To our ancestors, the divine and the sacred worlds were present all around them in this world. If we consider the Hindu religion in India, it is a modern example of this pre-Christian world.

A kind of cosmic energy constitutes the hidden structure of the visible world. This principle of order is a power that organizes chaos into a very well-structured cosmos. We can call this principle "Physical Laws," but science has shown these laws are not limited to the visible world. Fractals and quantum physics are good examples of such hidden structures. Greeks named this universal principle, "the Nous" and Freemasons call it "The Grand Architect of the Universe." Undoubtedly, this is a universal principle. To know whether or not this principle is an "intelligence" or a "Supreme God," is a philosophical question beyond our intellectual abilities. Meanwhile, it is easy to see that the world expresses order, not chaos. These principles of balance and order are also the basis of our existence. Nonetheless, that doesn't mean we have to obey and follow orders from this power. Of course we may feel appreciative and respectful, but there is nothing obligating us to a blind worship of this principle, leading to intolerance.

For Pagans, the cosmos is inhabited by numerous divinities with whom it is possible to communicate through ritual and worship. This is what Theurgy is about. It is difficult to say with precision exactly what the divinities were from the perspective of the first humans. Undoubtedly they were as close and present as the rain and wind.

It might be tantalizing to organize or rank the various divinities in order to establish a relationship with them. This is what occultists have done in the past. Other traditions organized these divine powers into two distinct categories, male and female. Indeed it is possible to conceptualize the universe as being fundamentally based on a duality that constitutes the two aspects that balance it. Even if all these classifications can help us in our understanding of the divinities, this is not exactly the way that was used by the initiates of the past. There were two other methods traditionally used by Theurgists in their work, and are still used today.

The first method is to use the astrological associations between the stars and the divinities. We will find examples of this kind of use later in this book, in the ritual practices that are devoted to the seven planetary divinities.

The second way is to think about the life of the divinities, as it is related in legends and myths. Symbols, correspondences, and certain abilities are more easily understood and provide a clear coherence that will be useful in rituals. Reading these stories will give us a good foundation, which we will use later to build our own inner world.

It is possible to advance our understanding of the divine world even further. The following explanations are not new. Authors such as Celsus and Plato talked about them. The point here is to figure out whether the Gods and Goddesses with whom we are creating a link during our rituals are outer or inner realities of ourselves. In short, you might ask: are the divinities a reality outside the consciousness that worships them?

To answer this question, we must first understand that it is really difficult to put an absolute limit on the extent of our consciousness and what it can perceive. If you touch your head it is very easy to realize your personal physical limitations, and consequently the nature of your brain. These limitations do not apply to your ability to think. Your thoughts are not limited to your cranium. They are far more extensive in scope. This question is, of course, different if we are discussing our thoughts and our soul. In that case, the divine powers must be considered to be external to our being and internalized as archetypal principles. Some pantheistic schools claim that we are a God, but I would add that we are, at the same time, a Goddess, and even a multitude of Gods and Goddesses. A part of us is divine, but this may be revealed in multiple facets. After centuries of brainwashing it might be difficult to believe in our own divinity and to understand what it is. For this reason, it is useful to be helped by an outer divinity, which has a close relationship with who you are. You will see later that there are several possibilities when it comes to finding out which divinity best suits you, and who you essentially are in this life. This is very useful at the beginning of magical work.

What is called the "One," or the "Good," remains quite unapproachable, but between this higher plane and us exist several divine beings ready to help us. Our relationship with these divinities will help us to make our being and life sacred, enabling us to be more aware of the presence of the divine and sacred in us and in the world.

It is time now to formulate a very important conclusion, which might be understood to be heretical from the perspective of the common way of understanding religion in the Neoplatonic tradition: we are free to choose the divinity we feel is the most appropriate for us.

According to the Theurgic tradition we were associated with a specific divinity (or a group of divinities) prior to our incarnation. Knowing this divinity will allow us to reconnect with him or her. Consequently, they will help us in our rituals and you will be able to ascend to the higher planes. Another aspect to this is the good influence the divinity will immediately have in our daily life. We can ask for its help with very effective results.

This idea of choosing a divinity is now present and even central in numerous spiritual groups such as Wicca, Druidism, Neo-Paganism, etc. There are several ways to choose this divinity and of course these methods are complementary. For example, from a very young age, I felt a strong relationship to the divine power of the storms. When I was a child, I would frequently run away from my parents when a storm was approaching in order to be at the center of it. Later on, I developed this relationship on another level: the magical level. I became aware that the emotion of love gives us the key to directly access the divinity. The name of this divinity can be different depending on where we live, our cultural background, or our initiatic tradition. This is a relationship we build all throughout our life. Theurgy can give us other opportunities to choose. We can find specific divinities that are related to the astrological positions of the stars at the moment of our birth. These Gods and Goddesses are directly related to us and we will obtain a great advantage to know them and build a loving relationship with them.

The Theurgic way of performing rituals has always been done this way: we create a loving relationship with the divinities, which is rooted in precise, simple, and beautiful rituals. This is the way I felt approaching storms when I was young: a pure pleasure, admiration, respect, and a powerful magick.

Most people are accustomed to the idea of a unique God, who must be the only object of worship. Consequently, two attitudes are possible: we must accept this idea as adequately describing our feelings, or we must reject this idea, just as the materialists and atheists have done. With regard to this last possibility, our rejection also eliminates any possibility of considering the notion of sacredness in the world, or a religious nature that is proper to every human being. As we can see, there are other alternative and traditional options.

A second conclusion must also be considered, which follows logically from the first: we can choose more than one divinity. We can even change from one divinity to another.

The choice of divinities is sometimes the result of a family lineage, but it is also possible to add one or more divinities that seem appropriate to us. We must also realize that these choices are not the result of a game. We have to remember the purpose of such choices, as well as why we are worshipping a divinity. As I explained before, this relationship with an outer divinity will help us to inflame the divine part in us. As we are not all identical, everyone has a different sensitivity, therefore we must choose a divinity that has a close relationship with who were are. For example, an artist who is always focused on beauty would choose Diana or Apollo; a politician would choose Zeus; a soldier Ares; a young lover Aphrodite, etc.

Another way to choose, which is complementary to the first, consists of creating a relationship to the divinity that can help us to increase missing abilities and balancing excesses and deficiencies. For example, someone who is irascible and nervous would choose a peaceful divinity; by contrast, a person with a lack of energy could compensate for that by worshipping a dynamic divinity such as Dionysus.

The Hermetic and Theurgic traditions have developed this very coherent system to help the initiate to progressively illuminate the different levels of their psyche.

To conclude, I would like to underscore the fact that divinities have historically gone through periodic cycles of awakening and being asleep. This was the case with the Egyptian and Greco-Roman divinities who went through a sleep cycle several centuries ago. Many people have assumed that the Gods and Goddesses disappeared, and somehow that proved they never existed. However, strong relationships were maintained with the Gods and Goddesses by initiates and masters of the Theurgic tradition, working under the veil. Today there are many signs that show the Gods and Goddesses are progressively awakening and beginning to manifest their presence. It even seems that some of these divinities have changed their place of residence. The reactivation of the relationship with the saints and the angels was clearly a transitional step that was conducive to the rebirth of these traditions.

Humanism and Spirituality

It is usually admitted that the birth and development of atheism, which is sometimes called the "death of God" is a logical consequence of modern scientific discoveries. The modern age seems to drive us to live in a world that is strictly dominated by rationality. For example, the development of the theory of evolution seems to be the end of human beings believing themselves to be the creation of God. In brief, it seems we were divine creations who suddenly share a common ancestry with monkeys. The consequence of this shift was a rejection of all moral and spiritual religious principles. As you may know, today it is not that simple. The research of anthropologists in recent years clearly shows that the sacred has been closely associated with human beings throughout history. The mistake was to confuse religion and spirituality. This is why it is essential to be reminded that religion and spirituality are two different and independent manifestations of the sacred. This mistake was the cause of many social and political problems that ended in fratricidal wars. The religious political power in the West, which has been monotheistic from the time of Constantine, defined several dogmas and froze the sacred into a unique manifestation, which they called "revealed religion." The consequence was a negation of our demiurgic potential as human beings and a dismissal of our ability to perfect ourselves. This temptation to become a monopoly is very old. We find it in all clergies who held both political and spiritual power. In our age, we have rediscovered the notion of freedom of religion and the free expression of the divine and sacred. As a matter of fact, everyone is capable of manifesting sacredness in an original way. We are all capable of freely expressing our beliefs and of worshipping what we believe without fear. Being able to maintain this attitude implies the necessity of accepting others as they are.

Hermetists have taught us from the beginning that we can always learn something from the examples set by the people around us. It is always interesting to learn how others practice their religion, what their beliefs and rituals are, etc. When curiosity is present, intolerance cannot exist. When we have this tolerant attitude, we will always be surprised to see dogmatic groups claiming they can decide they possess the unique way to meet God and that "their" truth must be considered to be "the only" truth. In the modern world, contacts with different cultures are increasing. Although it is quite easy to be curious about another country or their culture, the subject of religion is somehow different. This is something very intimate to each person, and as such, it is necessary to give it respectful consideration. When we look at the dispositions with regard to this matter, we have seen the manifestation of two main behaviors: 1) the totalitarian hegemony of fundamentalism; 2) the total freedom of religion in the US protected by the Constitution.

It is clear that the second solution is the only one that can guarantee social peace and respect for others. Under the Constitution, spirituality is respected as the individual's right to have a relationship with whatever divinity, God, Goddess, or any absolute power the individual chooses. When everyone is only concerned with an ascent to the divine, all religions will be more and more positive, allowing more human inner development. There is nothing to fear if there is no central chief to whom we must submit. The cosmos is all around us and we have the freedom to choose the expression of worship that most suits us. Fundamentalists are the perfect opposite of the spiritual human nature. Trying to force someone, or even entire populations, to the orders of a God or a Goddess is the root of violence and tyranny.

Every human being must be free at any time to worship the divinity he wants, as long as he doesn't try to force his beliefs on the public and political sphere, or try to impose his beliefs on others by using intimidation and fear. Increasing this respect for others will eliminate the religious hatred that must be considered to be what it is: a hatred of our fellow human beings.

People have a duty to act on their own, considering that being a human is not definitive. Everyone must determine for themselves what they believe. Humanity is fragile. It is easy to return to violent and primitive actions. For example, it is astonishing to witness the crimes that are perpetrated in the name of religion by believers who tell us that their God is a God of peace and love. Many people are trying to impose their religious views on others about social issues such as abortion, contraception, marriage, etc. Mixing politics and religion has always been very dangerous. By contrast, Hermetism teaches that all parts of a human being are sacred: soul, mind, and body. Through its evolution, humanity has developed an extraordinary ability: the ability to reason. This means that if everyone uses reason to control their passions, it will be possible to establish rational laws and principles, assuring a balanced and peaceful society. I am not saying that this process will be easy, but this is the solution that has always been used by the initiates of this tradition. They succeeded in balancing reason and spirituality by evolving the form of social tolerance that the Emperor Julian tried to implement. The core of this system is awareness and individual responsibility with regard to nature and other people.

It is always tempting to ask for precise rules when we undertake an esoteric or spiritual path. Philosophers and initiates of the past wrote extensively on these subjects, and I would have to say that these subjects are complicated. Paradoxically, it is not necessary to learn extensively about philosophy in order to understand what the Golden Rule teaches us:

"Do not do to your neighbor, what you would take ill from him."
—PITTACUS (SIXTH CENTURY BCE)

"Avoid doing what you would blame others for doing."
—THALES (SIXTH CENTURY BCE)

"What you do not want to happen to you,
do not do it yourself either."
—SEXTUS THE PYTHAGOREAN (FIRST CENTURY BCE)

"Do not do to others what would anger you
if done to you by others."
—ISOCRATES (FOURTH CENTURY BCE)

"What thou avoidest suffering thyself, seek not to impose on others."
—EPICTETUS (FIRST CENTURY CE)

As you can see, these sentences express the same moral principle we can summarize as follows: "In every action, harm no one. For all the rest, you are free to do as you wish."

If we agree with these sentiments, then it will be easy to decide whether or not we want to undertake the initiatic way of Hermetism and Theurgy. The moral commandment is to urge you to be responsible for yourself. After we have met this prerequisite, we will be ready to receive the teachings and training needed to ascend to the divine with the use of symbols and rituals.

Exercise Three—The Solar Blessing of Your Day

This exercise is intended to re-activate a deep communication between you, your own inner divinity, and the invisible powers that surround you. You may associate this exercise with any other daily practice you have. It will give you a first insight into the Egyptian part of the Ogdoadic tradition.

Morning

When you wake up, stand up, face east, and say:

In your rising, I salute you, Khepera!

Heru-Khuti Khepera, you are the creator of your own manifestation!

When you are in the bark of the morning, the winds rejoice your heart.

At the limits of day, your beauty is before me, O living Lord, and my soul proclaims that you are my Lord forever.

In your rising, I worship you, Khepera!

Visualize the sky as it gets lighter, starting from the horizon, as if the sun were nearing dawn. See the bark of Amon-Ra emerge. Construct this image precisely, carefully composing the shapes and colors.

The bark is made of emerald. The God Amon-Ra is seated on a pedestal of lapis lazuli. He appears in his hieracomorphic form; that is to say, he appears in a human form with the head of a sparrow hawk. In his hand he holds an ankh made of lapis lazuli. His head is surmounted by a scarlet sun resembling a garnet. Before him, at the front of the bark, is the solar disc, shining like topaz.

Imagine you are standing inside this disk of yellow sun, which is shining on the bark, and you are standing directly in front of the God. While maintaining this visualization, recite the following:

Master of Life, may your power enter into me.

May your contemplation uplift me each day, bringing me closer to my divine nature.

May my eyes behold your beauty and my ears delight in your song.

I am the Word of Truth!

I am a master of the Magical Universe!

I am as a God!

Maintain your visualization of the shining yellow sphere and imagine its rays emanating from you, spreading in streams toward all the creatures of the material earth and your own material body.

Noon Adoration

Visualize the same bark at its zenith overhead. Lift up your hands toward the radiant sun while reciting the following adoration:

On this resplendent day, I salute you, Amon-Ra.
Heru-Khuti Ra, you are the master of the Gods!
When you are in your bark above the skies, your spreading golden light rejoices my heart.
At the zenith of the day, your beauty is without parallel, O living Lord, and my soul proclaims that you are my lord forever.
On this resplendent day, I worship you, Amon-Ra.

Imagine you are standing inside this disk of yellow sun, which is shining on the bark, and you are standing directly in front the God. While maintaining this visualization, recite the following:

Master of Life, may your power enter into me.
May your contemplation uplift me each day, bringing me closer to my divine nature.
May my eyes behold your beauty and my ears delight in your song.
I am the Word of Truth!
I am a master of the Magical Universe!
I am as a God!

Maintain your visualization of the shining yellow sphere and imagine its rays emanating from you, spreading in streams toward all the creatures of the material earth and your own material body.

Sunset Adoration

Stand in the position opposite to that of your morning adoration, and visualize the bark facing in this direction (thus you see it behind you).

Its prow is starting to exit through a door of lapis lazuli strewn with golden stars.

Lift your hands in this direction, while reciting the following adoration:

Beautiful in your setting, I salute you Temu!
    Temu-Heru-Khuti, your rays are splendid to my eyes.
    When your bark approaches the evening, the wandering
stars glorify you and the sentinel stars praise you.
    At the limits of day, your beauty is before me, O living
Lord, and my soul proclaims that you are my Lord forever.
    Beautiful in your setting, I worship you Temu!

Imagine you are standing inside this disk of yellow sun, which is shining on the bark, and you are standing directly in front of the God. While maintaining this visualization, recite the following:

Master of Life, may your power enter into me.
    May your contemplation uplift me each day, bringing me
closer to my divine nature.
    May my eyes behold your beauty and my ears delight in
your song.
    I am the Word of Truth!
    I am a master of the Magical Universe!
    I am as a God!

Maintain your visualization of the shining yellow sphere and imagine its rays emanating from you, spreading in streams toward all the creatures of the material earth and your own material body.

Midnight Adoration
(Note: You may also perform this adoration just before you go to bed instead of at midnight.)

Visualize the bark at its lowest point, within the womb of deep night. No light illuminates the scene, except for that of the stars.

Keep your arms alongside your body, while reciting the following adoration:

I salute you during your hiding.
   Your rays have withdrawn from the world.
   As your bark proceeds silently through the deep night, the wandering stars glorify you and the sentinel stars praise you.
   In the deepest night, your beauty is hidden, O living Lord, and my soul proclaims that you are my Lord forever.
   In your hiding I worship you O Immortal God!

Imagine you are standing inside this disk of yellow sun, which is shining on the bark, and you are standing directly in front of the God. While maintaining this visualization, recite the following:

Master of Life, may your power enter into me.
   May your contemplation uplift me each day, bringing me closer to my divine nature.
   May my eyes behold your beauty and my ears delight in your song.
   I am the Word of Truth!
   I am a master of the Magical Universe!
   I am as a God!

Maintain your visualization of the shining yellow sphere and imagine its rays emanating from you, spreading in streams toward all the creatures of the material earth and your own material body.

Self-Test Three

These questions are intended to help you challenge your knowledge about the subjects you have been studying. You can use them before you read the materials or after. Try to answer the questions before checking the answers in the appendix.

1. Can you be a completely rational person?

2. Is God unique?

3. Can you choose your own divinity?

4. Are the divinities immortal?

5. What are the two methods used by Theurgists to "work" with the divinities?

6. What is the difference between religion and spirituality?

7. What important virtue can enable us to resist against intolerance?

8. What moral principle can be useful in most aspects of your life?

The following questions are related to your own experience. It is good to use them as personal meditations.[26]

1. What are my rational tendencies?

2. What are my irrational tendencies?

3. What God(s) and Goddess(es) would I choose, and why?

4. Am I sometimes intolerant? If yes, on which subject and why?

---

26. You can share your thoughts about these questions on the forums of the Aurum Solis website.

Part 4
The Sacred Books

Recognizing a True Sacred Book
and Understanding Its Role

The revelations: From the beginning of humanity, Gods and Goddesses have spoken with people who were trained to receive their messages. This was the birth of what is known today as "sacred books."

Sacred books are not equivalent: Paganism, including Theurgy, has teachings that offer the student fundamental information about the philosophical and ritual processes. However, you must learn why all sacred books are not equivalent, and why some of them are even dangerous. To do that, you must first learn how to recognize the validity of divine revelations.

This chapter will also provide you with an original translation of the first book of the *Corpus Hermeticum*.

The Divine Revelation

Most of the spiritual groups and traditions use sacred texts as a reference. This was also the case in antiquity, and in the tradition I am describing here. Long before the first manifestation of the monotheistic religions, which are currently called "religions of the book" (Judaism, Christianity, and Islam), Thoth, and other such divinities, gave their teachings to mankind. Thoth asked initiates to write this knowledge down and to conceal it from the eyes of the uninitiated.[27] In the Hermetic text called "The Ogdoad and the Ennead," discovered at Nag Hammadi, Thoth says that this revelation was protected in such a way that it will remain indestructible, so that it is always accessible for future initiates: "O my child, write this book for the Temple of Diospolis (Hermopolis—the Temple of Thoth).... You must engrave it in hieroglyphs and remember the name of the Ogdoad, which reveals the Ennead. For that, you will use turquoise steles and you will put them into the sanctuary under the protection of the 'eight wardens' and the 'nine of the sun'". [28]

You may ask yourself how the revelation of this God is manifested. It is well-known that in the monotheistic religions, God reveals his word and laws through prophets, who act as their intermediaries. Some men are chosen by God, who uses various criteria, but the process itself is the same for all religions. God manifests itself to the prophet inwardly or outwardly, or may even use both internal and external revelations in combination. Words, sentences, and texts are given and the prophet just writes these down like a scribe. There is no analysis of this process in the Bible, because the foundation of this tradition is not reason, but faith. God reveals himself when he wishes and his word is definitive.

---

27. This also occurred when the Christian Bible first appeared. The text was only accessible to priests and was restricted to them. Thus, believers were just authorized to use a compilation made of excerpts that were carefully chosen by the priests. It was centuries later that the Bible became available for everyone to read.

28. Due to its esoteric nature, the text doesn't clearly explain the meaning of these names. Nevertheless it is clear they are related to the group of divinities described in the myth of the creation previously discussed in this book.

In the Theurgic tradition, some explanations about this process are provided in various texts such as *On the Mysteries* by Iamblichus. This master explains that there two main forms of divination: public and private. He explains that the divination he is talking about is performed by the prophet or oracle "who stands on the characters," and the method used is the "adduction of the light," meaning the act of receiving the divine inspiration through the descent of spiritual light. This is represented by the descent of the divine light, the sun, which during the Theurgic ritual enlightens the "Ethereal and luminous vehicle which is linked to the soul" (*On the Mysteries*, 3:14). Once this step of connection with the light has been achieved, the Gods use our ability to imagine by imprinting in our imagination the images, ideas, and messages they want to give us. As Iamblichus explains, this phenomenon can occur in two ways: 1) the Gods use the channel of light and enter into us; 2) the Gods manifest themselves from the outside and inscribe the information upon our soul. This is the moment when our spirit is able to receive messages from the God or Goddess. Iamblichus clearly explains that this is not our human imagination creating these messages on its own, but that we receive the impulse from the Gods. Of course it is necessary that the augurer or the Theurgist has received the proper training in order to practice this kind of divination without adding any personal elements, repressed desires, or phantasms. I will say more about this when I describe the criteria which allow us to recognize a real sacred text.

According to Iamblichus, in Theurgy, all the techniques of divination are actually just one technique: "illumination by the Light," no matter the place or the tools used for this illumination. This is how the first sacred books of the Hermetic and Theurgic traditions were received. Thoth gave his message and asked that it be engraved with the most sacred magical characters. Unfortunately, nobody found these steles of stone, yet the tradition was perpetuated. We still have several fragments from the first book that are used in the Theurgic tradition: the *Chaldaean Oracles* and most of the *Corpus Hermeticum*.

The authors or sources of foundational texts are often difficult to find. In the case of the Theurgic tradition we are lucky to have some information we can use to better understand the historic sources.

First, two famous figures revealed a doctrine that was supposed to have come from the Chaldeans or Theurgists; these adepts were referred to as the Julians: Julian the Chaldaean and his son Julian the Theurgist. Together, they unveiled a sacred book called the *Chaldaean Oracles*. According to the scholar Polymnia Athanassiadi it was in Apamea, Syria, that this famous book was written. This was also the place where Iamblichus taught.

With the help of his father, Julian the Theurgist was supposed to receive a book using prophetic divination. His work was entitled *Logia di èpon*. This book was the exact transcription of the message received from the God(s), without any commentary. When the book was fully received, it was considered "closed" as an accomplished revelation.

This book presents and elaborates a spiritual doctrine and a ritual process that enables the initiate to re-ascend to the divine. Unfortunately, it was largely destroyed and the remaining parts are only quotations that may be found in several other books. There were several attempts to reconstruct the book from these fragments, but they were only marginally successful. I should also highlight two things about these oracles: first, the text is not easy to read; secondly, the text is foundational. Therefore, I suggest you read it from time to time. It is undeniable that Neoplatonicians were familiar with this text. It quickly came to be considered a sacred text by everyone who was dedicated to learning Theurgic rituals.

The *Chaldean Oracles* is the real heart of Theurgy and it is the main reason why chiefs of the new monotheistic religion have done their best to destroy the book. Fortunately, Iamblichus, the second founder of Theurgy after the Julians, created a clear and definitive "Theurgic Philosophy," which is a union of Neoplatonism, Hermetism, and Theurgy itself. I will speak precisely about that in Part 6 of this book.

The Hermetists that came later provided commentary on the *Chaldean Oracles*, but the text itself has never been modified. It is terribly sad that this work was lost or destroyed. Today, even if we have only fragments of the original, their study is considered to be fundamental for the magical tradition I am describing in this book.

Later, between the seventh and eleventh centuries, a set of texts were assembled that are considered to be sacred by the Neoplatonicians and Hermetists. It is called the *Corpus Hermeticum*, or the *Hermetica*, and it was composed in Egypt. This book is comprised of several treatises. As the French scholar Françoise Bonardel wrote: "The Nous-God, called Poimandres, revealed this divine wisdom to Hermes Trismegistus; it was given to chosen disciples and constitutes the foundational teaching of what became the Hermetic tradition." Other books were added such as: "Asclepius" (also entitled the "perfect discourse") and various "fragments from Stobaeus." (Stobaeus was a compiler of various Greek texts.) Magical papyri, Greek alchemical texts, and other short Hermetic texts that were found in Egypt have been added to this corpus by the Aurum Solis. Historically, they were not part of the original corpus, but it is clear, according to the scholars who studied and wrote about them, that they are from the same source. The *Hermetica* is markedly different from the *Chaldaean Oracles*, because these Hermetic texts present both direct revelations from God and philosophical discourses. Even if this set of texts seems closer to the "Platonic dialogues" than the *Chaldaean Oracles*, it is undoubtedly a fundamental corpus on which the tradition was built and developed. The *Hermetica* was considered to be, and was used as a sacred book. Today the Ecclesia Ogdoadica uses it in the same way. It might be possible to add other short texts, which were preserved by Arabian alchemists and philosophers and revealed during the Middle Ages. This is also the case for the texts entitled *The Seven Chapters Attributed to Hermes* and the famous "Emerald Tablet," presented by Albert the Great (1193–1280).

To conclude this subject, it is important to say a few words about the divine nature of the sacred books. I explained before that in some cases, the reception of information given during the divine revelation could be mixed with human errors and psychological proclivities. Based on this concern, it is legitimate to look for objective standards that enable us to discriminate what is divine and what is human in the revelation. As I said, God and the Gods in the Theurgic tradition are all good and righteous. They manifest their presence through what we call Beauty and Truth. Every injunction that expresses violence, cruelty, or murder is radically opposed to the divine essence. Any text encouraging such behaviors cannot be considered to be sacred by Hermetists. It is for this reason that the Hermetic and Theurgic sacred texts have never encouraged violent actions, even in symbolic terms.

This is not the case in the Bible. Several of the texts that were supposedly revealed by God are far from meeting the Hermetic definition of sacredness. As an example, I have provided an excerpt from Exodus: "Then Moses stood in the gate of the camp, and said: 'Whoever is on the Lord's side, let him come unto me.' And all the sons of Levi gathered themselves together unto him. And he said unto them: 'Thus saith the Lord, the God of Israel: "Put ye every man his sword upon his thigh, and go to and fro from gate to gate throughout the camp, and slay every man his brother, and every man his companion, and every man his neighbour."' And the sons of Levi did according to the word of Moses; and there fell of the people on that day about three thousand men.

"And Moses said: 'Consecrate yourselves this day to the Lord, for every man hath been against his son and against his brother; that He may also bestow upon you a blessing this day'" (Bible, Exodus 32:26–29).

No matter what your beliefs are, it is easy to understand that such recommendations cannot blindly be accepted if you are a Neoplatonician. Even more than that, it is simply more logical to remain very cautious with regard to such injunctions.

The Texts

Corpus Hermeticum—The Creation

The *Corpus Hermeticum* contains a very interesting creation story. You are certain to appreciate the style of these sacred texts. The following text is the original transcription used in the Aurum Solis and the Ecclesia Ogdoadica.

Book one: Hermes Trismegistus—Poimandres

One day, as I was gazing into the depth of my mind and reflecting upon the nature of beings, I felt a torpor overcoming or pressing down on my body. It was as if I was sinking into a deep sleep after being tired by a heavy meal, or by exhaustion. Most strangely, my spirit progressively rose from my body, soaring above me in the gentle Aether. At this moment, I saw a gigantic being of incredible size. It came to me, swallowing the immensity of space.

Its voice echoed in my mind as it said: "What are you seeking? What do you want to know?"

I replied, without hesitation: "But you, who are you?"

"I am Poimandres," he said, "the Nous, the absolute Sovereign of all. I am with you at all times, and I know what you are looking for, although you are unable to name it."

"Oh, I seek to know the beings of the world, and the nature of God. My Soul's deepest desire is to understand the Universe!"

"Your desire is rightful. Keep it to yourself and I shall teach you the mysteries of all things."

Uttering these words, he then changed his appearance. His being became an intense and lively Light bathing me in rapture and joy, yet unknown to me I could not perceive the limits of this all-encompassing Light. Each and every instant in his presence further opened my heart. Loving without any reserve, my Soul was wholeheartedly united to the Light I perceived and felt in blissful harmony.

It was at this moment that I perceived a sinuous movement far below. A tenebrous and terrifying undulation crept where I had been standing earlier. It moved forward, in ominous silence, approaching as a dark snake coiled in spirals. Obscurity then slowly faded as the air grew heavy with humidity. Clouds of steam rose toward me as gigantic winding arms, whistling with the rhythms of their upward movements. The world, which had been silent, came alive. Inarticulate cries seemed to gush out from the fire filling the air.

The Light then grew in intensity, and a vibrant Breath spurted out of it. I felt my eardrums vibrate as this inaudible sound rushed below and mixed itself with the strange nature in formation. As it touched the humid obscurity, a magnificent and shining fire rushed upward to where I was standing. The resounding flames rose up, whirling, carried by the winds and the circling air. This intense and marvelous dance was a true celestial enchantment. Below, water and earth were intimately mixed, one to the other. In unison, their respective movements could not be distinguished.

Then rang anew the voice of Poimandres: "Do you understand that which you now see?"

"No," I said.

"The Light you contemplate is mine; it is the Light of the Nous; I who existed well before obscurity was manifested, before humidity revealed itself through it. As for the Breath, this luminous word resounding in the silence, it is he who rushes out of my heart; the son of God."

"I do not understand this language . . ."

"Bring closer to your own self what I have just revealed to you. The Verb, or Logos, is sound and Light, and the faculty of seeing and hearing. God the Father is your Nous. These two natures should never be separated. Your life depends on their union."

"Thank you, O Poimandres."

I felt his attention focusing on me, an intense force rose in the air around me. He then said: "Fix your gaze at the centre of the Light. May the understanding to which you aspire grow in you."

This tension grew in intensity and my whole being trembled. It seemed as if this part of me, which he had named Nous, harmonized itself with the center of the Light I was contemplating. I then saw a Light made of multiple Powers, extending so as to form a limitless world. This powerful fire in extension was maintained by an even greater Power which kept it, giving it structure and stability.

Lost in the contemplation of these Luminous Powers, I heard his resounding voice again: "You saw the archetypal form, the first principle, which existed before the beginning of that which is without end."

"But," I inquired, "where do the elements of nature come from?"

"The Will of God, which, contemplating the Beauty of this archetypal and ideal world, shaped every soul according to its own nature.

"Now, listen to the story of what happened at this very moment:

"The Nous God, which is both male and female, life and light, used the Word to give birth to the second Nous Demiurge. This new Nous, the God of Fire, Breath, shaped seven Governors (seven planets) into existence, organizing them into circular paths around the material world. From the Power of these Governors, destiny was born.

"At this precise moment, the Word of God freed itself from the Elements of the pure nature it had just formed and organized, and united itself to the second Nous Demiurge, because both were of the same essence. The Elements that were of an inferior nature, left on their own recognizance by the Logos, became physical matter.

"While the Elements were becoming matter, the Nous Demiurge united with the Word that was enveloping the seven circles of power and imparted unto them a divine circular movement, which has no beginning and no end. When these rotations began to impart rhythm to the cosmos, the Nous extracted the Elements from the animals that were unable to reason, because the Word was no longer inside them. He formed flying animals from the Air, from water he formed all the animals that live under the water. Earth and water were separated and for the first time, terrestrial animals, reptiles, wild and domestic animals appeared.

"Then the Nous, the power of life, the light of the world, gave birth to a Man like himself. This Man was so beautiful that the Nous fell in love with his image; he fell in love with his created image, and therefore, he gave it everything he had.

"When the Man looked at what the Demiurge had organized in the Nous father, he wanted to make a creation of his own, after obtaining the Father's agreement. Therefore, he entered into the sphere of the Demiurge, in order to use his power. Seeing this new creation for the first time, the Governors fell in love with him, and each of them gave to this new creation a specific part of their own power. Knowing their essence of the Governors, because he now had part of each of their natures, the created being wanted to go through each of these circles in order to know the power of him which has authority over the Fire. It was at this point that he had power over all mortal beings and all the animals that were unable to reason, looked down through the cosmos, broke their shells, and revealed the marvelous appearance of God to the entire natural world. Nature had already seen the Man's reflection in the water, but when she saw this endless beauty, the power of the Governors united to the shape of the Father God, she suddenly realized the power of her love for him. The Man also saw his reflection in the water. Instantaneously, he fell in love with her and wanted to join her in order to stay with her. As soon as he desired this, it immediately happened. He penetrated the shape without thought, and Nature received her beloved into herself. Nature embraced him and they united themselves with a burning love.

"It is for this reason that Man is the only living being on earth who has a dual nature; he is at one and the same time mortal, having a mortal body, and immortal, because he has an immortal spiritual aspect. In fact, even though he is immortal and has power over everything around him, he suffers the same plight as all mortal beings, because he is subject to the workings of destiny. Even if his being originates from above the seven divine spheres, as his power indicates, he has become a slave to destiny. He received this duality from his Father. Just as his Father, he is, at the same time, both male and female; but he is different than his Father because there is a part of him that is subject to the natural world."

After these last words had been pronounced, I said: "O my Nous, I love this conversation."

Poimandres said with a low voice:

"What I have to say is a mystery that has been hidden until this moment. When Nature united herself in love to the created Man, she produced an extraordinary miracle. He whom she embraced was composed of the nature of the seven Governors (the planets), mixed with the Elements Fire and Air. As a result of their union, she gave birth to seven different men; each kind of man has a special relationship with one of the seven celestial Governors. Everyone, both male and female, stood up and looked up at the heavens."

I interrupted his speech, saying: "O Poimandres, I burn to hear you. Don't speak about other things; continue to explain what you began to unveil!"

"Be silent! I have not even finished explaining the first point."

"I will remain silent," I answered him—fearing that he might stop offering the revelations he was giving to me.

He resumed his story: "That is how the first seven human beings were generated. Earth is the feminine Element, Water is the genitor, and Fire brought maturity to the mixture. Air, which is also called 'the Aether,' is the vehicle of the vital breath, which was mixed with Nature. It was at this moment that the body was formed into the shape of the Man. The immaterial part (life and light) respectively gave birth to the soul and the intellect. Thus were all the beings of the sensible world created, until all the various species had appeared.

"Hear now what you desire to know. When the first part of this creation had been accomplished and we were at the beginning of a new cycle, God's will cut the link which united all things. All the animals, and all the humans, were instantly separated into two parts: male and female.

"After this, the sacred word of God resounded: 'You who were created, grow and become a multitude. May the one who has the greatest intellect know that he is immortal and that death is the result of desire. May he step forward and be cognizant of all beings.'

"At the moment when he stopped speaking, providence created a union between the beings who were under the influence of fate and the structure of the spheres, after which all beings grew in number, each one according to its species. Thus, everyone took the first steps on the path. Some were united with their soul, their beloved, which was among those progressing towards the ultimate Good, while others remained attached to their physical body, full of desire, staid in darkness, suffering the torment of the death in their flesh."

I asked again of Poimandres: "What could this terrible error have been, that was committed by those who refused immortality and remained in ignorance?"

"It seems to me that you have not really thought about what you just heard! Didn't I ask to you to be attentive?"

"I am doing the best I can to be attentive; I will do my best to remember what you have unveiled for me and I give thanks to you for all things."

"So if you have been listening attentively, please explain to me why those who are already dead, deserve to die again."

"The source of the individual body is the darkness from which the humid Nature came. It is from this nature that our envelope was created in the sensible world. It is here that death finds its origin."

"This is correct, but then how can you explain God's word, which says that: 'He who recognizes his inner essence, progresses toward God?'"

"The Light and the Life of which the father is composed gave birth to that which constitutes our essence: the soul and the intellect."

"This is as you say, and it is certainly from God the Father that humans are born. So if you learn how to know yourself as a being made of life and light, then you will come back to life," said Poimandres.

Full of bafflement and confusion, I said: "O my Nous, tell me how I can become alive! God said, 'May the one who has the intellect know himself,' yet it seems to me that all humans have the intellect."

"Don't think like that! I, the Nous, I am with those who are holy, good, pure, merciful, and pious. For those pious ones, I help them know everything. When they raise their souls to the Father with the help of love, benedictions, and the required hymns, they create an essential link to me. They begin to understand the influence of the senses on their bodies prior to their death. I, the Nous, will not allow their physical body to disturb them, because, as the Warden of the Gates, I will close the entrance to all negative thoughts that arise from their imaginations.

"As for the senseless, evil, vicious, envious, avaricious, murderous, and impious, I am not on the side of those wicked ones. Therefore, I yield my place to a vengeful demon. It is he who pierces humans with his goad of fire, torturing them through their senses, giving them the punishment they deserve. These are the humans who are always full of desire, always driven by unsatisfied appetites. Nothing succeeds in satisfying them; therefore their torture increases, while the flame devours and burns them."

"Thank you for explaining that to me. Please explain to me how the soul ascends."

Poimandres answered: "First the material body dissolves, deteriorates, and then the physical body progressively disappears. The self is abandoned to its personal daimon.[29] The corporeal senses return to their origins and are again part of the astral energies. Meanwhile, that part of the human that is full of wants and desires returns to nature. The deceased person progressively ascends through each celestial sphere. As he passes through the first sphere, he abandons his capacity to grow and decline. At the second sphere, he sheds all malice, at the third he gets rid of the illusion of desire, at the fourth he sheds the pretentious need to command others, at the fifth he gets rid of his impious audacity and pretentious temerity, at the sixth he gets rid of those illicit appetites, which give him wealth, and at the seventh the lie that traps him in death is eradicated.

"Purified from everything that was placed into him during his descent through each sphere; retaining only his own power, he enters into the eighth circle, the circle of the Ogdoadic essence. Numerous beings are there, shining, luminous, and always singing hymns to the Father. He comes among us and they are delighted by his presence. He unites his voice to them and begins to feel this divine ecstasy. Just as those who surround him, his song rises as an offering of his whole being to the Divine. Above the eighth circle, a soft and Ethereal voice reveals the presence of the celestial powers. All ascend toward the Father, surrendering to these Powers, becoming similar to them, in order ultimately to enter into God. Hear what I have to say: the goal of the wise being is blessed, because he intends to become God."

A silence follows his last words. I do not dare to move, speak, or even think.

---

29. There is a distinction between daimon and demon. To learn more, go to the Glossary.

Poimandres speaks loudly to me. "What are you waiting for? Why are you still with me? As you have now inherited what you desired to know, go and become the guide of those who are praiseworthy! With your help, and the help of God, humans will be saved."

As his voice begins to fade into the innermost parts of my being, Poimandres rejoins the Powers who surround him and he disappears from my consciousness. I addressed thanksgivings and benedictions to the Father. Now, invested with this power, having been taught about the essence of the Whole, and the supreme vision, I left these divine beings. I began to proclaim to humans the beauty of respect, love, and knowledge, saying, "O people, sons of the earth, you who are abandoned to drunkenness, sleep, and the ignorance of God, be sober and temperate, cease to be drunk, for you are cursed by the sleep of your reason."

As soon as they heard my words, they joined me. Speaking to them, I said: "Sons of the earth, why are you still dying, when you have the power to become immortal? Change your behavior, abandoning the erroneous path you are currently on and relinquishing the ignorance you have associated yourself with. Liberate yourself from the tenebrous light and take part in immortality, eradicating the dissolution of your flesh forever."

Some of those who were on the path of death made fun of me and moved away. The others kneeled and asked for me to teach them. I raised them and became the guide of humankind, teaching them science and the ways which allow them to become immortal. I placed wise words in them and they were drenched with ambrosial water. When the night fell and the light of the sun began to disappear, I told them to thank God. After the hymns were sung, everyone went to sleep.

For myself, I engraved these moments that I had been wishing for, for such a long time, on my heart. I closed my eyes and an extreme joy filled my whole being. My soul was slowly reaching the serenity I was searching for. From my closed eyes went forth a true vision, while from the silence the unchanging good began to resonate.

I had just received from the Word, Poimandres, the full authority and I was full of the divine breath of the Truth. With all my soul and all my powers, I offered to the Father God this hymn:

Holy is God, Father of all things,

Holy is God, for by his Will, everything is accomplished by his powers,

Holy is God, who wants us to know him and who belongs to those who know him,

Holy art Thou, you are the Word who brought everything that exists into existence,

Holy art Thou, for all Nature represents you,

Holy art Thou, whom Nature hath not formed,

Holy art Thou, for you are more powerful than any power,

Holy art Thou, you who are greater than everything,

Holy art Thou, you who are above all praise. Receive the pure sacrifice of these words offered by a pure soul. You the inexpressible, the unspeakable, you that only the silence can describe, my heart is open to you. Protect me from falling, which might separate me from the knowledge which my essence deserves. Grant me these requests and fill me with power. Only then can I enlighten all those who are in ignorance, those who are my brethren, your sons. Yes, I believe and I witness that I am going toward the life and the light. Blessed be our Father, and may the power you have given me help me to assist you in this work of sanctification.

The "Emerald Tablet" of Hermes

Here is the text of the famous "Emerald Tablet," attributed to Hermes the Thrice-Greatest. The first source of this text can be found in an Arabic book entitled the *Kitab Sirr al-Asrar,* which is supposed to be a letter from Aristotle to Alexander the Great.

Several websites will provide you with numerous translations of this text. Here is the translation by Newton:

This true without lying, certain most true.

That which is below is like that which is above that which is above is like that which is below to do the miracles of only one thing.

And as all things have arisen from one by the mediation of one: so all things have their birth from this one thing by adaptation.

The sun is its father, the moon its mother,

the wind hath carried it in its belly, the earth its nurse.

The father of all perfection in the whole world is here.

Its force or power is entire if it be converted into earth.

Separate thou the earth from the fire, the subtle from the gross, sweetly with great industry.

It ascends from the earth to the heaven, again it descends to the earth and receives the force of things superior and inferior.

By this means ye shall have the glory of the whole world thereby all obscurity shall fly from you.

Its force is above all force. For it vanquishes every subtle thing and penetrates every solid thing.

So was the world created.

From this are and do come admirable adaptations whereof the means (or process) is here in this.

Hence I am called Hermes Trismegistus, having the three parts of the philosophy of the whole world.

That which I have said of the operation of the Sun is accomplished and ended.

Exercise Four—The Oracle

This simple exercise associates two different aspects of the Theurgic and Pagan traditions: connection with a divinity and divination. This is useful to develop your inner abilities, and of course to obtain spiritual insights on whatever situation you want to work on. Usually this ritual is performed by a woman, but a man can use it with great beneficence.

Arrange your temple as you did in the first exercise of this book when you worked with the God Thoth. The bomos must be located in the western part of your room.

On the top of the bomos, place the representation of Apollo [30] (center), a cup of spring water (to the left), and few laurel branches (to the right).

Stand up directly in front of the bomos, facing west, and extend your hands over the cup of water, palms down, saying:

May this water, which issues from Okeanos, purify me.

Moisten the tips of your fingers in the cup and use them to purify your face. Wipe your face with a white towel.

Place a chair at the eastern side of the bomos, facing east. This chair should be approximately four feet from the bomos.

Light the incense and place the censor on the floor approximately at two feet in front of the chair (east of it).

Come back to the bomos; pick up the laurel branches, raising them toward the representation of Apollo and say:

O divine Apollo, deign to consecrate these laurel branches that their action will assist me in receiving your messages.

Place the laurels in contact with the representation of Apollo for a few seconds, and sit down on the chair facing east.

Raise the laurel branches into the smoke of the incense and pronounce the following invocation:

O Apollo, you who reside in the secret heaven of the fourth sphere, grant me your blessing and your aid in my enterprise.

Remain in silence for few seconds, then continue saying:

O Apollo, sovereign of the long days, omniscient arbitrator of planetary powers, you who give the wisdom of prophecy, the

---

30. You can use the Major Arcanum of Apollo from the Aurum Solis Tarot if you have it. This Tarot is explained in my previous book the *Divine Arcana of the Aurum Solis*. You can find more information about it on the Aurum Solis website.

ecstasy of music, the rapture of poetry, and the suddenness of the mystical search belong to you!

You are the one who discerns the truth from the shadows of illusion and fate!

In the bosom of the dawn and in the incomparable splendor of the star of day, you offer the sacred image of your magical being, so may your power arouse glory in us and raise us toward the accomplishment of our quest!

Glory to you!

Close your eyes, and, while extending the laurel branches, say:

May the vibration of the sun be manifested in this place and may Apollo descend progressively into me.

Today, I . . . *say your name* . . . invoke you, divine Apollo. I would like to know . . . *explain your question clearly* . . .

Add incense if necessary. Close your eyes again and begin to shake the laurel branches, visualizing Apollo coming from the west (the direction of the bomos) and entering into you.

Continue to shake the laurel branches throughout this entire process, repeating the divine name:

Apollo.

Let the presence of Apollo be manifested in you, as you listen to His message.

When this is done, mentally thank Apollo for His presence and shake the laurel branches more rapidly for one or two minutes until you feel that the divine presence has returned to its representation.

Stand up. Place the censer and the branches on the bomos and declaim the following while facing west:

Hear our voices, O blessed Apollo, you the Powerful, the Brilliant.

Dispensator of riches, you who came from the black soil of Egypt, I invoke you as of old with the cry of "Ié."

You, Titan who bears the bow and the golden lyre, Holy art thou!

You who slew Python, light-bearer, Holy art thou!

Brilliant young man full of glory, you whose head is crowned with golden hair, Holy art thou!

You who conducts the Muses and the Choirs, Holy art thou!

You who shoots your arrows above the infinite spaces, Holy art thou!

You, the Oracle whom one questions and prays to at Delphi as at Didyma, Holy art thou!

You, Lord of Delos, who sees all things and bears the intelligence of the mortals that we are, Holy art thou!

Pure are your omens and luminous your responses!

You who contemplates from high in the infinite ether the earth and all this that you find, hear with a benevolent heart my words that ascend toward you.

The beginning and the end of all things belong to you and there is not a place, infinite or near, dark as well as luminous, that is not found under your regard.

The harmonizing notes of your golden lyre equilibrate the cosmos and the destiny of men. Each sound, each ray of light, brings the manifestation of your divine harmony. The seasons succeed one another and the meadows in springtime are covered with flowers whilst resounding with your melody.

O Resplendent God of light and of power, I address you as of old did those who prayed to you.

Apollo, Lord Resplendent, you whose voice reaches me, carried by the wind, you whose seal-mark is the entire cosmos, manifest yourself to me in this instant, so that all the initiates here assembled may pray to you.

Divine APOLLO, may you return to your kingdom in peace, with my profound gratitude!

You may then extinguish the flame upon the bomos, return everything to a state of order, and write your notes about the ritual.

Self-Test Four

*These questions are intended to help you challenge your knowledge
about the subjects you have been studying. You can use them before you
read the materials or after. Try to answer the questions before checking
the answers in the appendix.*

1. What are the "religions of the book"?
2. Are there any books that are considered to be sacred in the
   Theurgic tradition? If so, what are they?
3. Who is the author of the *Chaldaean Oracles*?
4. Are the sacred books of the Theurgic tradition still available?
5. What criterion do we use to determine whether or not a book is
   sacred?
6. In the first book of the *Corpus Hermeticum*, does the Nous-God
   have a specific gender?
7. What does this first book of the *Corpus Hermeticum* teach us
   regarding our human nature?
8. What famous sentence is often quoted from the "Emerald
   Tablet" of Hermes?

*The following questions are related to your own experience. It is
good to use them as personal meditations.* [31]

1. What book do you consider to be sacred and why?
2. What things do you dislike seeing in a sacred book?
3. What constitutes a divine revelation in your opinion?
4. Did you ever receive an inner message that has been significant
   in your life?

---

31. You can share your thoughts about these questions on the Aurum Solis website.

Part 5
The Divine Cosmos

Understanding the Macrocosm

Life is enjoyable: Once we have become aware of the roots of this Theurgic tradition—know that our body and our physical life should be enjoyable, understand how the rituals must be used, and feel the divine presence all around us—we are ready to unveil the cosmic order.

Structure of the cosmos: The first step that is unveiled in this part is the simple structure of the cosmos. This is the first structure you have to use in your Theurgic journey. There are no complicated or unrealistic notions here. The pre-Christian Theurgists always used those elements that are well-known to everyone who practices Theurgy: four elements, seven divine spheres, the Aether, and twelve divine powers.

The Occult Structure of the Cosmos

The Theurgic tradition teaches that systems such as the Qabalah, Eno-chian magic, the Tarot, etc. are representations, structures, or maps of an invisible reality. They do not represent the truth per se. It is for this reason that Theurgists who have been initiated into this tradition used and still use such systems only as magical tools. They never forget that the theological doctrine associated with such systems did not origi-nate with them. Powerful energies exist in the cosmos. Theurgists be-lieve it is possible to draw on and utilize these powers with the use of signs and sacred words. It might be surprising to hear some Hebrew Qabalists saying that the modern and Magical Qabalah are not a true expression of their tradition. Some even state that a modern magical use of Qabalah has no substance and that it is an empty body. As a matter of fact, this is totally true. Magicians, Theurgists, and Esoteri-cists use Qabalah for their own purposes. So it is essential to remember that when we use Qabalah as Hermetists and Theurgists, that doesn't mean we have any obligation to accept the principles of this system as the absolute and definitive truth. The Neoplatonic School has never manifested a desire to be part of the Hebrew or Christian theological doctrine. A Theurgist neither rejects nor accepts these parts of the Western tradition. As long as believers do not try to convert anyone and they remain tolerant, all is well.

The Qabalistic philosophy is not the same as the Neoplatonic sys-tem, but it is always possible to take what is good, interesting, and helpful from these traditions without being obliged to blindly accept their dogmas. It is interesting to know that a spiritual tradition such as Qabalah can generate dogmatism and "fossilization of the mind" in its believers. When I wrote a book about the French tradition called "Martinism," [32] I began to realize the harmful effects of a dogmatic Qabalah. I met several sincere initiates who were in real pain, perform-ing daily rituals rooted in the "Psalms," which were excerpted from the Bible. Their whole vision of the world was based on pain, reconcilia-

---

32. A spiritual and initiatic school originating with the French mystic, Louis Claude de Saint-Martin.

tion with their divine father, and the fight between good and evil. They were taking a dangerous religious philosophy as absolute truth and this acceptance had deep consequences for their whole lives. Their feelings during their rituals were always of cold, invisible presences. The power was there, but there were also so many problems in their lives.

Many times I have seen the auras of such practitioners and their auric colors were always darkened by these invisible beings, which were building a real screen between their soul and the upper light. Of course, there is a "relatively safe" way to use the Qabalistic tools in a luminous way. This is what we were taught in the Aurum Solis in the books published in the past. The main principle for using the Qabalistic tools in a luminous way is to be aware of the egregores involved. There is a way to use a knife without hurting ourselves, and there is also a way to use these tools without creating an invisible barrier around us. In this case, the positive effect on our aura will be tremendous!

It is now time to explain the way Hermetists understood the cosmos.

Astrology has been well-known for thousands of years. This ancient science, often despised in modern times, still remains a primary reference tool all around the world. There are many controversies about using it as a tool for prediction, but the ancient Western societies didn't use astrology in only one way. As we can see today in India, astrology is used to choose the right moment to be married, to begin a new work, to be elected as an official, etc. Some of these uses remain active in the initiatic world, but eventually they were condemned and eradicated by the monotheistic religions. Modern science generally rejects the affirmation that planets can have a physical effect on us. Of course, it is obvious that the nearest celestial bodies have an influence on earth and consequently on us. The Moon and the Sun are good examples of powerful effects we can feel and see all around us. Despite the fact that a physical influence of Mars or Saturn on our physical body has not yet been detected or proven by scientists, that does not mean that such energy doesn't exist. By using mythology, symbolism, and Theurgy as a basis, modern psychologists have elaborated different theories that associate the deep structures of our unconscious to universal archetypes. In order to understand this interesting theory, let us visualize these relationships.

From the modern perspective we are composed of two main parts: a conscious and an unconscious mind. We can compare our unconscious to an inner world full of memories, symbols, powers, desires, etc. The ancient representation of the ocean from which we all originated and filled with things we cannot see offers us an interesting image of the mind and its layers. I love cooking and, as you will see, the process used in cooking can help us understand these difficult notions. It is always interesting to visualize the preparation of a pancake as a means of understanding our unconscious. Imagine we want to make pancakes, but instead of progressively adding the water to the flour, we accidentally add the water too fast without stirring these ingredients properly. The preparation will not be homogeneous and lumps will appear. The dough can be compared to our unconscious and these lumps to what we might call "archetypes"; so we see that lumps are not always bad. One aspect of this representation must be considered. When we cook we need to use a sound receptacle that has no holes in it, but this is not the case for our inner being. Instead, we may think of our unconscious as open to, and in a constant contact with the universal unconscious. It also contains universal archetypes, as well as the universal principles of everything we can see or imagine around us. The archetypes inside us are the images of other similar and universal archetypes. This similarity provides a kind of relationship between them, and underlines the existence of a real link. We are also in contact with the unconsciousness of other people but indirectly, by the use of certain universal principles.

Once you understand this organization, you will easily understand how astrology can be associated with this notion of archetypes. If everything visible in the cosmos possesses an invisible counterpart that is connected to a specific power, we can easily understand that Mars (for example) is the visible aspect of a particular archetype. It is not necessary to look for the potential existence of this kind of martial energy on the visible level. Since all the cosmic and inner archetypes are connected, any possible planetary influences may have an echo that can directly affect our unconscious. This martial character emerges as a wave or a tide from the deepest level of our inner self. Sometime in the future, science may discover a physical influence, but we do not have to wait for that discovery to understand and utilize this system right now.

Do not forget that even if I explain astrology by using this model of inner communication, that doesn't mean we should eliminate the divine powers and divinities that are present in Theurgic work. A Theurgist never uses these concepts as a passive form of understanding. They are always utilized and understood to be part of a rich system we can use in our rituals to enable us to ascend to the Divine. You must understand that astrology can be used to obtain very useful and effective results in our being and daily life. This knowledge and understanding has been kept alive by the Hermetic tradition from ancient to modern times.

The use of the astrological magick as developed during the Renaissance by Marsilio Ficino was rooted in the tradition of "signatures." This concept uses a set of invisible relationships between different elements of the cosmos. Let us take solar power as an example. Someone eager to increase his energy, self-confidence, health, etc., would naturally use the power of the sun. In order to do that, we must attract and hold this power in our aura. Different elements around us can be used for exactly that purpose. Ancient initiates drew many charts that will enable us to attract and hold any kind of energy. In this example, we might choose something that has the color gold, such as yellow plants, specific resins, oils, perfumes, liquors, sounds, days, etc. All these elements are related to the sun and will be organized in a coherent sequence of ritual practices. This Theurgic way of using astrology and signatures comes from the famous affirmation of the "Emerald Tablet" attributed to Hermes: "True, without falsehood, certain, most certain. What is above is like what is below, and what is below is like that which is above. To make the miracle of the one thing."[33]

---

33. It seems this text was written during the sixth century. The translation provided here comes from a twelfth century Latin version.

At the time of the Florentine Academia Platonica headed by Marsilio Ficino, the members used this law of universal relations to organize powerful symbols in their rituals, enabling them to ascend to the Divine. It was a real continuation of the Theurgic tradition defined by Iamblichus. They tried to balance and harmonize their lives by using these principles and ritual practices, and they often succeeded. Happiness is really possible in this life when we harmonize our inner being with the upper levels of consciousness we can reach using rituals and worship. As I explained previously, there is a real communication between our inner cosmos and the cosmos that surround us. The balance between these inner stars and powers will give us health, success, serenity, and peace. Of course it is easy to see that this happiness of the soul and the health of the body are not always fully manifested. A loss of balance, anxiety, and sorrows are more often present in our life than the more desired states. These states of our inner being (and their regulation) are related to the order of the whole cosmos. Therefore, astrology becomes a way by which we can come to understand the powers that comprise our personality. Theurgy, which was also called "Celestial Magick," allows us to take action instead of remaining passive so that we can recreate the harmony we have lost during this current life or in our previous existences.

The Cosmological Basis of Theurgy

The fundamental concept of these ancient traditions is a representation of the cosmos, which has been the foundation of the Western world. From its beginnings in Sumer and Egypt, astrology was structured according to a system of four elements, seven planets, the Aether (sometimes fifth element), and the zodiac.

As I already stated, these archetypal powers are simultaneously inside and outside of us. It is worth noting that most of the time the astrology we know doesn't offer us any keys as to how to be active instead of passive. After presenting our cosmological situation, no solution is proposed. When I began to work in the Theurgic tradition, I was immediately disappointed with this lack of information describing how to manage the conclusions of astrologers. I felt as if I had gone to a doctor who gave me a diagnosis, without offering me any prescription. I realized later that Theurgy is the prescription and I clearly understood that there was room for action.

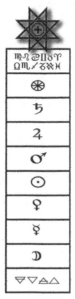

Figure 21: From its beginnings in Sumer and Egypt,
this system was structured according to a system of four elements,
seven planets, the Aether (sometimes fifth element),
and the zodiac crowned by the Mysterious Ogdoad.

If we want to be able to do something, we must take action and consider the Theurgic options that will enable us to really work with these powers. We have to create a contact inwardly and outwardly with them in order for the divine powers to hear us. Of course we can learn about the theoretical and symbolic concepts of the planets. Without this connection, we may be able to understand and perhaps feel the martian, venusian, or saturnian character, but this is not enough to enable us to take action. The goal of the Hermetist is more ambitious. One of the goals is to feel the essence of the divine power inwardly and to create a strong and effective link to it. This connection will be established progressively, step by step. In this way we will discover the characteristics of these specific energies, these divinities, and we will be able to work more effectively on ourselves. For the founders of this tradition, this set of elements, planets, and astrological signs is the manifestation of an order we can immediately see if we raise our eyes to the heavens. When we consider the physical level, we adopt a geocentric point of view. We are looking at the visible level for the purpose of developing a cosmological and mythic consideration of the cosmos.

We are really at the center of the cosmos. Our consciousness is the foundation and the positional reference point from which we see the world that surrounds us. The place where we are standing in this world defines the way we see, feel, and understand the cosmos. If we work to understand that in the same way the Theurgists always did, we will discover that we are at the center of the six primary directions of space (East-West-North-South-Zenith-Nadir). It seems obvious to everyone that what is material and visible is under our feet, and what is invisible and aerial is above us. The planets and the stars are logically associated with a higher state of being. This observation also explains that planets are perceived in sequential order from our reference point here on earth according to their motion. These full cycles (orbits with respect to the stars) are well-known by ancient astronomers, and you will find their values in the following table. We see the planets moving as if they were in front of a fixed starry sky, which was originally, symbolically conceived of as an eighth sphere, a sphere of fixed stars that resides above the seven planets and the Aether.

Planet	Sidereal Cycle
Moon	29.5 days
Mercury	88 days
Venus	224.7 days
Sun	365.25 days
Mars	687.1 days
Jupiter	12 years
Saturn	29.5 years

Figure 22: The planets and their sidereal cycles.

To understand what is above this eighth sphere is a complex problem. The answers of the Hermetists varied, depending on who was writing the article. Some of the Hermetists talked about the Nous and Nous Pater. For Christian Qabalists such as Dante, this sky was crowned with a celestial rose composed of nine angelic choirs surrounding God itself. What you might want to consider is that what is beyond this celestial veil is yet another reality. I agree with the Theurgists, that this matter can only be decided by those who have really risen through the seven skies. An explanation of the essential nature of these spheres is easier to obtain, because they were clearly associated with the divinities everyone is familiar with: Moon-Selene, Mercury-Hermes, Venus-Aphrodite, Sun-Helios, Mars-Ares, Jupiter-Zeus, and Saturn-Kronos. Of course, in this list I am using the names from the Greek and Roman worlds, but we can easily find Sumerian or Egyptian divinities that have the same characteristics. Hermetists have always been eclectic in their work and approach. This mental attitude defines their consistent approach toward all other religions and philosophies. They maintained a strong commitment to ensure a deep moral tolerance and respect for the beliefs of others.

The Four Elements

Throughout the sixth and fifth centuries BCE, Greek philosophers began to investigate the structure of matter and the nature of life forms. Pythagoras believed that the world was the result of an admixture or combination of the four original elements: Earth ($\triangledown$—solid state), Fire ($\triangle$—imponderable substance), Air ($\triangle$—gaseous state), Water ($\triangledown$—liquid state). The Aether was associated sometimes as a fifth element, sometimes as a principle of animation, which is placed between the planets and the starry sky.

The importance of the Pythagorean Tetractys is well-known. The quaternary structure organized into four lines using a total of ten dots is one of the central sacred symbols used by the initiates of Pythagoras school. It is interesting to note that the oath was pronounced in front of this representation, as the initiate said: "I swear by whomever revealed to your soul the Tetractys (meaning the representation of the number ten, using four series of dots to represent the numbers 1–4), which has in it the source and the root of the eternal nature." A text from Philolaus the Pythagorean reveals this organization into four elements very clearly: "There are five bodies in the sphere: Fire, Water, Earth, Air, and the circle of the sphere, which constitutes the fifth." It is well-known that the pentagram or pentalpha was a sign of recognition secretly used by Pythagoreans. It is easy to combine these symbolic representations to understand how the pentagram used in the Theurgic rituals came to be associated with the five principles I just mentioned. I will speak more precisely about this topic later in this book.

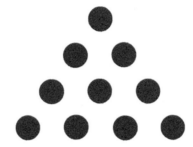

Figure 23: The quaternary structure known as the Divine Tetractys.

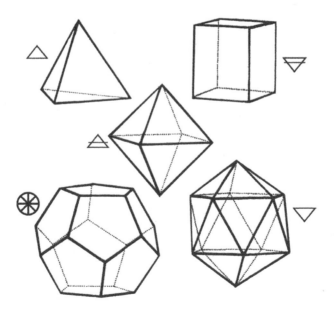

Figure 24: The five Platonic solids.

Greek philosopher Empedocles agreed with this theory, saying that all animals' bodies are the result of a mixture of these four elements.

Figure 25: A copy of a Gallo-Roman artifact representing one of the Platonic solids.

We can find geometrical representations as early as the Neolithic period. Plato used this ancient idea and associated geometric volumes with the four elements. Earth was associated with the cube (*Timaeus*, 55d), Air with the octahedron, Water with the icosahedron, and Fire with the tetrahedron. Plato linked the dodecahedron with the All, the universe (*Phaedo*, 110b; *Timaeus*, 55c), because for him it was the representation of volume that most closely approximated the sphere. In another part of the *Timaeus*, Plato presents four levels in nature: the Gods and the celestial order (Fire), winged animals (Air), terrestrial animals (Earth), aquatic animals (Water). Aristotle added a fifth element, Aether, which was considered to be that part of the air that is purest. He claimed that the skies were composed of this element, but he did not associate this element with the fifth solid of Plato.

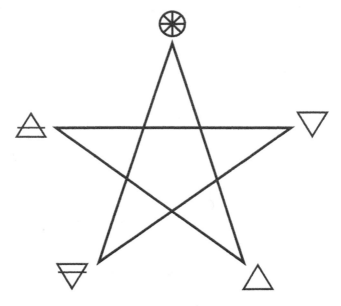

Figure 26: The pentagram, the elements, and the Aether.

In the *Corpus Hermeticum* we will find a very interesting text[34] that is related to the five elements and alchemy:

Isis said to his son Horus:

All things in this world are shaped by words and actions; the source of everything is in the ideal world, which emanates to us, through the principles of order and measure, all of manifest reality. Everything in existence came from above, and everything in existence will rise to go down once again.

From this movement, the holiest nature places in the living being the following clear sign: the breath we take in from above, we take in from the air, then we send it back to what is above, and draw another breath in again. To accomplish this, we have a pair of bellows: when we have closed our mouths, which we used to receive the breath of air, then we are no longer in this domain. We have returned to what is

---

34. *Corpus Hermeticum* XIII-17 and a fragment from Stobaeus XXVI–13.

above us. We have other abilities that derive from a specific dosage of these elements in a corporeal mixture.

Each human body is comprised of these four elements, from which a condensation is exhaled which surrounds the soul, and then spreads throughout the body, yielding something specific for that person. This is the way psychic and corporeal modifications occur.

If there is overmuch of the element of fire in the structure of the body, then the soul, which is naturally hot, and which became even more ferociously hot as a result of the increase of heat it received, is manifested in the living being by them developing an enthusiastic nature with a strong and ardent body.

If there is overmuch of the element of air, the living being becomes lightweight and more unbalanced in his body and soul.

If there is overmuch of the element of water, then the soul of the living being vacillates, and is always ready to increase and enlarge its presence into the surrounding area. Water has the capacity for uniting with other elements; therefore these living beings will tend to develop relationships with others. When water spreads out all around in large quantity, it dissolves everything, absorbing all these things into itself and becoming what it absorbed. Due to the water they contain, it is quite impossible for the body to keep its inner agglomeration. Consequently, when disease appears, it dissolves and loses its inner principle of cohesion.

If there is overmuch of earth, then the soul of the living being becomes rigid, because, as the organs of perception thicken, the pores are not large enough for it to get out so it stays inside the body, isolated by itself, hindered by the weight and the density of the mass of the body. The body is firm but inert and heavy. It moves unwillingly under the impulse of the will.

Eventually, if all the elements in the body are well-balanced, then the living being has enough heat for action, light for movement, a temperate condition in the joints, and adequate firmness in their cohesiveness.

May the whole nature of the world hear now, because these are the words of the one who has mixed fire, air, water, earth with order and moderation and who stands at the heart of the power of the breath and Aether.

"Powers that are within me, sing in concert with my Will!

"Blessed Gnosis, by thee illumined, with your assistance I can celebrate the Light of the Divine, and rejoice in Joy of Mind.

"Ye, all Powers, sing the hymn with me!"

The following quaternary division was developed extensively by Agrippa in his book about Celestial Magick. Occultists have often used the following correspondences:

- The four letters of the name of the Hebrews' God, called the Tetragrammaton: Yod, He, Vav, He.
- The four humors of human beings: blood, phlegm, red bile, and melancholy.
- The four parts of the year.
- The four quarters of the moon.
- The four winds (name in Greek/name in Latin): Eurus/Vulturnus (East wind), Zephyrus/Favonius (West wind), Notus/Auster (South wind), Boreas/Aquilo (North wind).
- The four rivers of heaven.
- The four terms of mathematics: dot, line, surface, and volume.
- The four terms of nature: substance, quality, quantity, and movement.
- The four terms of physics: the power of germination, natural growth, the ability to change shape, and specialization.

- The four terms of metaphysics: being, essence, potentiality, and action.
- The four moral virtues of philosophers: wisdom, equity, bravery, and temperance.
- Etc.

The occultists in the nineteenth century, such as Eliphas Levi, explained the four elements in the following way: "the subtle and the thick, the fast and the slow solvent, hot and cold things; in occult physics constitute the two positive and negative principles of the quaternary. Air and earth are the male principles; fire and water are the female principles, because the philosophical cross of the pentacles is an original hieroglyph of the lingam of the gymnosophists.

"These four simple forms are associated with the four following philosophical ideas: spirit, matter, movement, and rest."

To summarize what I have just explained, all the traditional representations (Hermetic, astrological, alchemical, etc.) indicate that the symbol of this hierarchy is the pentagram: the set of the four traditional elements (Earth, Water, Air, and Fire) plus the Aether, which is above them.

In the ancient mythological texts several divinities were associated with the elements. The Ogdoadic tradition of the Aurum Solis, following the classical symbolism of the Renaissance, associated the elements with the figures of Ouranos, Gaia, Pontus, Eros, and Aether. You will find more about these divine powers in my book *The Divine Arcana of the Aurum Solis Tarot* (Llewellyn Publications).

The following table presents the main correspondences you should use in your rituals.

Elements	Earth	Water	Air	Fire	Aether (Universe for Plato)
Symbols					
Platonic solids	Cube	Icosahedron	Octahedron	Tetrahedron	Dodecahedron
Description of the Platonic solids	It is composed of 6 sides, which are squares. It has 8 points and 12 edges. It has 3 edges joined at each point.	It is composed of 20 sides, which are equilateral triangles. It has 12 points and 30 edges. It has 5 edges joined at each point.	It is composed of 8 sides, which are equilateral triangles. It has 6 points and 12 edges. It has 4 edges joined at each point.	It is composed of 4 sides, which are equilateral triangles. It has 4 points and 6 edges. It has 3 edges joined at each point.	It is composed of 12 sides, which are regular pentagons. It has 20 points and 30 edges. It has 3 edges joined at each point.
Divinities	Gaia	Pontus	Ouranos	Eros	Aether
Greek letters	Gamma	Delta	Rho	Pi	Theta
Hebrew letters	*No Hebrew Letter**	Mem	Aleph	Shin	*No Hebrew Letter*

* The Hebrew alphabet has only twenty-two letters. This is different than the Greek alphabet with twenty-four letters. Consequently, in Hebrew Qabalah there is no letter for the elements Earth and Aether. To learn more about this surprising lack of these elements in the Hebrew Qabalah, you can read my article "Did You Miss Something? Qabalah Versus Hermeticism" on the Llewellyn website at: http://www.llewellyn.com/journal/article/2230

The Seven Divine Spheres

It is always essential in the Hermetic and Pagan tradition to maintain a relationship with the cosmos, while never forgetting our body. Astrology was built up according to this principle. Following this logic, we can easily reenact what the ancient priests and initiates of Chaldea and Egypt did when they constructed astrology. They went out, considered the four axes and the eight directions, and then looked up to contemplate the divine realm of Gods and Goddesses. From our perspective on earth, we can easily see that there are a few celestial bodies (planets[35]) moving with respect to the stars, which are called fixed. We can categorize these special stars, just as the ancients did. It is difficult to know precisely if they considered these celestial lights to be real planets or divinities. We have to remember that, for the ancients, the cosmos was full of Gods, and celestial phenomena were never separated from these divine presences. We will find seven such stars; if we try to order them according to their brightness and relative velocity we will find what is called the Chaldaean sequence. This is a scale you will be able to use in your Theurgic rituals to undertake the way of the return to the divine. The table below shows these correspondences.

Planets	Divinities	Greek Letters	Hebrew Letters
Saturn	Kronos	Omega	Resh
Jupiter	Zeus	Upsilon	Tav
Mars	Ares	Omicron	Gimel
Sun	Helios	Iota	Dalet
Venus	Aphrodite	Eta	Kaf
Mercury	Hermes	Epsilon	Pe
Moon	Selene	Alpha	Beth

Among those divinities associated with the planets, some of them have been closely associated with the Theurgic tradition. Of course

---

35. The word "planet" comes from the Greek root "Plan" (πλαν) that means "to wander." The word "planetos" (πλανητός) means "wondering" versus "fixed stars."

this is also true for Hermes as well as Hekate, one of the Goddesses of the Moon. Plato associates Aphrodite with the desire of the initiate. For this reason, I will now highlight some of the main aspects of the divinities lives and symbols.

The Twelve Divine Powers
The Divinities and the Calendar

The idea of a group of twelve divine powers is very old and goes back to the earliest period of Western mythology. It is not my intention to change this book into a book about astrology; rather, I wish to give you some insight into this traditional representation of the cosmos.

The Greek astronomer Cleostratus of Tenedos (ca. 520 BCE to 432 BCE) is believed to be the first person to organize the signs of the zodiac into the sequence we recognize today. I am always amazed to see that such symbolic representations have been in use from ancient to modern times. The only explanation I can think of for this phenomenon is that these perfectly symbolic numbers and structures resonate deeply with the human unconscious. Mythologists used the symbolic number twelve on several occasions and you can easily do a search and find that there are twelve Olympic divinities in the Greek pantheon. This pantheon was represented in various ancient monuments and artifacts. The traditional list can be found in the following table, along with their Roman names.

DIVINITIES	
GREEK NAMES	**ROMAN NAMES**
Zeus	Jupiter
Hera	Juno
Poseidon	Neptune
Demeter	Ceres
Dionysus	Bacchus
Apollo	Apollo
Artemis	Diana
Hermes	Mercury

Athena	Minerva
Ares	Mars
Aphrodite	Venus
Hephaestus	Vulcan

The Roman calendar was established during the first century and is clearly inspired by the Olympians.

ROMAN CALENDAR		
MONTHS IN LATIN	MONTHS IN ENGLISH	DIVINITIES
Ianuarius	January	Juno
Februarius	February	Neptune
Martius	March	Minerva
Aprilis	April	Venus
Maius	May	Apollo
Iunius	June	Mercury
Iulius	July	Jupiter
Augustus	August	Ceres
Septembris	September	Vulcan
Octobris	October	Mars
Novembris	November	Diana
Decembris	December	Vesta

As we can see, there is a correspondence between the months of the year and specific divinities. It is important to say immediately that all the authors of the past have not always used the same attributions. It is good to keep that in mind. Different monuments and even manuscripts were preserved. These allowed us to reconstruct the calendar provided above. There is no reference to the astrological signs. As matter of fact, at this time these divinities were very much associated with the month, rather than the zodiacal signs. Remember that the Hermetic tradition was born in Egypt. It is likely that this country received the influence of Mesopotamia regarding this religious subject and used it to develop its own system. The first real zodiacal reference is found in a Ptolemaic temple in Denderah (first century BCE).

The Roman astrologer Manilius, in his astrological text "Astronomica," which was written between 30 BCE and 37 CE, highlights the relationship between the signs and the divinities. There are some differences between these attributions and what are called the "Rustic Calendars."[36] It is important to consider the explanation given by Manilius. Instead of being a simple civil calendar that is associated with the twelve months of the year, the result of his work graphs the religious, symbolic, and magical relationships among these twelve signs.

ACCORDING TO THE ASTROLOGER MANILIUS		
MONTHS IN ENGLISH	SIGNS	DIVINITIES
March	Aries	Minerva
April	Taurus	Venus
May	Gemini	Apollo
June	Cancer	Mercury
July	Leo	Jupiter
August	Virgo	Ceres
September	Libra	Vulcan
October	Scorpio	Mars
November	Sagittarius	Diana
December	Capricorn	Vesta
January	Aquarius	Juno
February	Pisces	Neptune

These correspondences are strengthened by the finding of various artifacts, and I discussed of some of these in *The Divine Arcana of the Aurum Solis*. Maybe the most obvious and well-preserved of these artifacts can be seen in the Louvre Museum in France. This artifact is the top of an altar found in Gabii, and was sculpted during the first century CE. Surprisingly, this artifact, which is so important to the history of

---

36. Calendars from the time of the reform of Julius Caesar (first century).

astrology and Theurgy, is currently seated on the ledge of a blind corner, and it is very difficult to find[37]. These artifacts are important as a witness to, and an archaeological confirmation of these astrological writings.

In my work about the Aurum Solis Tarot I also underlined the relationship between the letters of the Greek and Hebrew alphabet, and the astrological signs. Obviously the astrologers and Theurgists of the Ogdoadic tradition used this precise and clear system from its inception right up to modern times. This venerable pattern provides us with a precious guideline that is congruent with the Neoplatonic and Hermetic philosophies. It was also true during the Renaissance and the so-called rebirth of Hermetic magick.

I use the Greek names of the divinities in the table on the next page and offer their associations for your information with the Alchemical steps of the Great Work.

Classic Astrological Attributions of the Signs

It has been well-known for centuries that parts of our body and different aspects of our character are associated with the astrological signs. Here are the main attributions that are generally accepted by modern astrologers. These associations will be useful in some of your ritual exercises.

Figure 27: Astrological signs on one of the traditional representations of a zodiacal chart.

---

37. You can go to the Aurum Solis website (www.aurumsolis.info) to see the map of the museum and its locus, as well as a list of other artifacts that hold an interest for those who want to understand more about the Theurgic tradition.

Signs	Aries	Taurus	Gemini	Cancer	Leo	Virgo
Divinities	Athena	Aphrodite	Apollo	Hermes	Zeus	Demeter
Alchemical steps of the Great Work	Calcination (putrefaction, black matter)	Freezing (clotting)	Fixing (firing of the purified matter)	Dissolution (reduction of matter to its primitive form)	Digestion (preparation for distillation)	Distillation (circulation of the matter called "Rebis")
Greek letters	Beta	Zeta	Kappa	Lambda	Mu	Nu
Hebrew letters	He	Vav	Zayin	Het	Tet	Yod
Signs	Libra	Scorpio	Sagittarius	Capricorn	Aquarius	Pisces
Divinities	Hephaestus	Ares	Artemis	Hestia	Hera	Poseidon
Alchemical steps of the Great Work	Sublimation (purification of matter)	Separation (dissolution of matter by the use of its solvent)	Burning (preparation for multiplication)	Fermentation (separation of sulphur and salt)	Multiplication (repetition of all the steps, resulting in glorified matter)	Projection (transmutation)
Greek letters	Xi	Sigma	Tau	Phi	Khi	Psi
Hebrew Letters	Lamed	Nun.	Samekh	Ayin	Tsadi	Qof

Aries

Nature: Cardinal, male, angry, passionate, irritable, energetic, and vital.

Bodily structure: In the physical body, Aries governs the skull and facial bones.

Other organs: Aries governs the brain and cervical nerve centers. It governs the head, face, nose, ears, eyes, and mouth (in astrologically detailed anatomy, different parts of the head are governed by different planets).

Taurus

Nature: Fixed, female, stubborn, tends to gluttony, healthy but easily depressed by disease.

Bodily structure: In the physical body, Taurus governs the cervical vertebrae, the occipital region, and tendons and muscles of the neck.

Other organs: Taurus governs the cerebellum, pharynx and esophagus, carotid artery, jugular vein, salivary glands, larynx, vocal cords, and trachea. It governs the lower jaw, chin, neck, and throat. This sign has a close relationship with the generative organs.

Gemini

Nature: Mutable, male, irritable.

Bodily structure: In the physical body, Gemini governs the clavicles, scapulae, humerus, and arm bones in general (although a more detailed subdivision assigns the elbows to Cancer, the forearms to Leo, and the hands and fingers to Virgo).

Other organs: Gemini governs the organs of respiration, the lower part of the trachea, bronchi, bronchioles, the thorax, and upper lung. (In general, the whole lung is under the dominion of Gemini, but in a more detailed classification, pleura, and lower lobes of the lungs are associated with Cancer.) Gemini governs the shoulders, chest, and arms.

Cancer

Nature: Cardinal, female, cold, wet, sensitive, receptive, passive, strong but apparently weak.

Bodily structure: In the physical body, Cancer governs the chest, ribs, and sternum.

Other organs: Cancer regulates the mammary glands, body fluids in general, blood serum, stomach, bladder, and the matrix; it governs the chest and epigastric region.

Leo

Nature: Fixed, male, hot, electric, dry, active, constructive, and vital.

Bodily structure: In the physical body, Leo governs the spine, especially the thoracic vertebrae.

Other organs: Leo governs the heart and circulation in the arteries and liver (this organ is more governed by Jupiter than the sun, but its zodiacal sign is Leo). Bile is under the dominion of Leo and Scorpio; it governs the back and the heart region.

Virgo

Nature: Mutable, female, cold, dry, melancholy, irritable, exuberant.

Bodily structure: In the physical body, Virgo rules the lower thoracic vertebrae, but more accurately the large muscle conformation that forms the peritoneum, or the cavity that contains the intestinal organs.

Other organs: Virgo's domain includes the intestine, pylorus, duodenum, jejunum, colon, mesenteric section, spleen, large intestine, the abdominal area, and stomach.

Libra

Nature: Cardinal, male, hot, humid, without much resistance, lethargic.

Bodily structure: In the physical body, Libra governs the lumbar vertebrae.

Other organs: Libra governs the kidneys, especially the upper and the cortical and medullary surfaces, including the work of distillation and filtration of urine but not its elimination. The renal papilla and the renal plexus are also under the dominion of Libra; the ovaries and testes are partly under this sign, in the sense of the accumulation of vital force but not its distribution.

Libra governs the lumbar region, groin, lower trunk, back around the lumbar spine, buttocks, and the area around the anus.

Scorpio

Nature: Fixed, female, hot-cold, irregular, passionate, ardent. This is the sign of life and death.

Bodily structure: In the physical body, Scorpio governs the pelvic bones.

Other organs: Scorpio governs the lower part of kidneys, eliminating urine from the kidneys and the bladder, urethra, ureter, elimination of fecal matter, rectum, anus, and the genitourinary system of both men and women. Strong influence on the glandular system; Scorpio governs the iliac and inguinal regions.

Sagittarius

Nature: Mutable, male, hot, dry, angry, fast, adventurous, honest, undisciplined but willing to listen to good advice; having a healing power because of a strong will and optimism.

Bodily structure: In the physical body, Sagittarius governs the sacrum, coccyx, and pelvis, the hip bones and the hip joints, including the muscles of locomotion and the muscular system in general.

Other organs: Sagittarius governs the iliac arteries and veins, and the sciatic nerve; it has an influence on the nervous system in general and the liver, due to the influence of Jupiter. Sagittarius governs the hips and thighs.

Capricorn

Nature: Cardinal, female, cold, anxious, and enduring.

Bodily structure: In the physical body, Capricorn directly regulates the legs and knees. The bones of the body are governed by this sign, as well as the joints, but joint movement belongs to Saturn.

Other organs: Capricorn does not have a large scope of governance, except for the bones and periosteum; it governs the entire system of the skin, hair, and teeth.

Aquarius

Nature: Fixed, male, hot, humid, strong, rational, active with good vitality.

Bodily structure: In the physical body, Aquarius governs the leg bones, especially the tibia and fibula, and talus bones of the ankles.

Other organs: Aquarius particularly governs blood and the circulatory system, as well as breathing, because it is related to the oxygenation of blood; this sign governs the calves, legs, and ankles.

Pisces

Nature: Mutable, female, cold, wet, lymphatic, helpful, sensitive, compassionate, generous, dependent, with low spiritual vitality.

Bodily structure: In the physical body, Pisces governs the feet, and directly affects these bones: the tarsus, metatarsus, and phalanges.

Other organs: Pisces particularly governs the lymphatic system, the glandular system, and the synovial fluids; their influence on health is very strong, but is almost always badly aspected.

Pisces governs the feet and toes. The influence of this sign is externally visible throughout the tissues.

Exercise Five—The Celestial Ladder

In the previous part of the book I described the simple structure of the cosmos we use in the Theurgic system. It is interesting and important to use the divine powers to connect your inner centers of energy to each level of energy of this Celestial Ladder.

In the Theurgic Qabalistic system, the Aurum Solis calls this exercise the "Rousing of the Citadels," which works with the six archetypal centers of energy. As I already explained, this logic is also true in the Qabalistic representation of the universe.

Here you will experiment with another level of consciousness that has been defined by the Ogdoadic tradition. In order to do that, you will use the connection between your inner energetic centers and the celestial bodies that have been well-known for centuries to theurgists, alchemists, and astrologers.

You can use this powerful training daily.

In order to invoke the divine powers and to welcome them into your inner being, into your aura, stand up, visualize above your head the Glorious Star, which you can see an image of in the section about the Celestial Ladder.

Hold this glorious symbol in your mind, raise your arms up to the sky, palms up, and declaim:

En Giro Torte Sol Ciclos Et Rotor Igne[38]

Lower your arms, allowing them to hang naturally at your sides.

Inhale and visualize a golden light coming from the center of the star and descending in a sphere just above the top of your head.

Exhale.

Inhale while you intensify the golden light in the sphere and then exhale as you vibrate the divine name:

Ὁ Κρόνος— Ho Krónos (Kronos)

Keep your lungs empty a few seconds without thinking about anything.

Perform this cycle two more times. Inhale, and vibrate the name once more so that you have completed three vibrations of the divine name.

---

38. "I am the Sun, I am the wheel moved by the fire which makes the spheres turn."

Inhale and visualize the golden light descending down through the center of the spinal column from this upper sphere to a second sphere, which is situated at the level of the forehead.

Proceed as you did for the first center with the vibration of the divine name:

Ὁ Ζεύς—Ho Zeús (Zeus)

Continue this process with the remaining five spheres, visualizing the golden light descending from one to the next until you have vibrated each divine name three times.

Throat: Ὁ Arhz—Ho Arēs (Ares)

Heart: Ὁ Ἥλιος—Ho Ἕlios (Helios)

Belly button: Ἡ Ἀφροδίτη—Hē Aphrodítē (Aphrodite)

Genitals (more precisely three inches above the genitals): Ὁ Ἑρμῆς—
　　Ho Hermês (Hermes)

Coccyx: Ἡ Σελήνη—Hē Selḗnē (Selene)

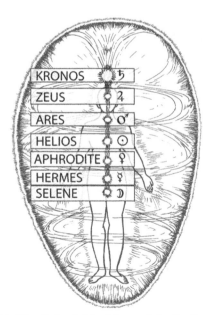

Figure 28: The Celestial Ladder and the Bodies of Light.

Inhale and hold the air in your lungs for few seconds. Visualize the golden light in your spinal column and in each sphere.

Exhale and breathe naturally.

Cross your arms on your chest, left over right, with your palms touching your body.

As you hold these spheres in your mind, visualize a ribbon of white light coming from your coccyx and rising in a spiral movement, turning counterclockwise. This ribbon is turning around you as a bandage is wound around a mummy. The ribbon continues to rise until it reaches the sphere located at the level of your forehead.

Proceed in the same way with a second ribbon of the same color, rising in a spiral but moving clockwise.

You must continue envisioning these cycles of ribbons rising until they reach the level of your forehead.

Visualize the golden light shining throughout your entire aura.

After few seconds of visualization, open your arms in front of you, palms up, and declaim:

May the power of the Glorious Star purify my being!
    May the powers of the Earth and the Starry Sky raise my
soul toward the Divine Ogdoad!
    So mote it be!

Lower your arms, allowing them to hang naturally at your sides.

Self-Test Five

These questions are intended to help you challenge your knowledge about the subjects you have been studying. You can use them before you read the materials or after. Try to answer the questions before checking the answers in the appendix.

1. Qabalah cannot express the only and absolute Truth. Why?
2. What is the relationship between "astrology" and "archetypes"?

3. What is one thing you can do to enjoy your life more?

4. What is the traditional representation of the cosmos that we also find in astrology?

5. What are the four elements? What relationship do they have to your body?

6. What Hebrew and Greek letters correspond to the elements?

7. What are the seven planets? Can you draw their symbols from memory?

8. What do you notice about the nature of each astrological sign?

The following questions are related to your own experience. It is good to use them as personal meditations. [39]

1. Do you think a complicated explanation (about anything) is more likely true? If so, why?

2. Find four aspects of your personal nature that you associate with each element and explain how they are associated.

3. With which planetary divinity do you feel the strongest relationship? Why?

4. Do you think that your astrological sign fits you? Why?

---

39. You can share your thoughts about these questions on the forums of the Aurum Solis website.

Part 6

The Divine Being

Understanding the Microcosm
and Revealing Your Destiny

The microcosm: In the Western tradition there is a well-known concept: the macrocosm (the cosmos) and the microcosm (us). The previous chapter unveiled the traditional structure of the macrocosm. The present part unveils the microcosm. You must learn how you are constituted in order to understand how your occult structure works, and what its purpose is.

The temple blueprint: The Theurgic tradition uses the representation of a traditional Greek temple to highlight the five principles of human beings: Body, Body of Light, Soul, Spirit, and the Divine.

From this point you will be able to understand the purpose of Theurgy and safely begin your Theurgic Great Work.

The Occult Structure of Human Beings

Everyone is interested in knowing more about the occult structure of human beings. It has been a subject of investigation for centuries and new theories continue to flourish. Most of the time, modern books that present the Western tradition use the Hebrew Qabalah as an outline for all cosmic or human structure. This is interesting and understandable. Since the structuring of this new system in France during the twelfth and thirteenth centuries, Qabalah was first used by Jewish people for the occult interpretation of their sacred books. Qabalah also influenced Hebrew rituals and eventually Christians became interested in this new system and used it to understand their own texts.

The Hebrew Qabalah has been progressively recycled and adapted to meet the needs of Christians and modern esotericists who are interested in the Western heritage. A collateral effect of this progressive recycling was that people began to forget the original system. These people became victims of this erosion of memory in the group mind, nearly exhibiting symptoms that rival amnesia. The original and traditional Western explanation of the occult structure of the soul was eventually forgotten completely. Fortunately, during this modern period, books were not burned and scholars continued to work. It is also fortunate that there were a few Theurgic schools, such as the Ogdoadic tradition of the Aurum Solis, that continued to teach both systems to their initiates.

When I am giving a lecture, I often use the example of tinted glasses to explain the effects of different systems. If we wear a pair of glasses tinted in a deep-blue color, all the world around us will be seen tinted with this color. It is the same if we wear a pair of Qabalistic glasses. No matter what the real nature of the world around us is, our perception of the world will be tinted by the glasses we wear. If you are like me and you have to wear glasses all day long, then you will come to understand another consequence of this interesting phenomenon. After a few weeks, we begin to forget that we are using glasses. The situation is the same here. Someone who is wearing the Qabalistic glasses will forget they have them on, and everything will become surprisingly Qabalistic. It is even more depressing to see initiates who understand they are wearing glasses, but who continue to wear them because they are incapable of questioning their own assumptions. Glasses are reassuring. We can see that when people understand nothing of the way an initiatic tradition works, they tend to reassure themselves by living in a golden age from the past. An initiatic Order with a real and enduring lineage is something different. It stays alive and is not frozen in an imaginary past. Of course we could certainly say the same for every belief system, including Buddhism, Hinduism, Freemasonry, etc. but the point is to learn how to see things as they are. For now, I do not consider the solution to be the removal of the glasses. It would be the same as trying to change our vision itself, or to remove our brain from our physical body without dying. Consequently, the best would be to use a different kind of glasses, which are appropriate to what we are doing at that moment.

Let us consider this solution. This is the best choice to avoid the most mistakes and to see things as they really are. But this is not a natural solution and it is not easy to do. If we want to be able to utilize this solution, we need to have a good intellectual background so that we can understand the different systems without adding our own projections and representations. This approach is like analyzing a sample of DNA and trying to avoid any contamination. It is very difficult to be aware of all the factors that might contribute to contamination, because it is difficult to be an expert in all the related fields. To be precise, if we want to avoid a Qabalistic contamination of our understanding, we have to know and understand Qabalah, but we must also be able to think about the problem from a critical point of view, without using Qabalah. This is a real challenge, because if we want to understand the whole Western tradition, we must understand Qabalah. The same thing is true for those who are not Christians, but who find an understanding of Christianity useful.

If we want to learn and practice the Hermetic tradition we have to learn and understand Hermetism as it is, not as our inappropriately tinted glasses might cause us to perceive it. We have to be aware of this possible contamination of our perception, of our understanding. It is the only solution if we want to see things as they really are.

Of course you could say "who cares?" or "are all these measurements really necessary?"

This book is about the Western tradition, and more precisely about the Hermetic and Theurgic traditions. As you now understand, Theurgy is the name of the ritualistic system that is used by the initiates of this lineage. The main concern for them, and for me as I write this book, is to offer you the opportunity to create a good balance in your inner and daily life. Theurgy is a specific system. The ceremonies and rituals we use to achieve advancement are organized and rooted in a specific and logical structure. Therefore, I do not recommend mixing different systems. For example, I would not recommend trying to apply a Qabalistic philosophy or theology to Hermetism. These two systems provide very different ways of using our senses to perceive the world. If you want to hike with the goal of reaching the summit of a mountain, the gear you need will be different than what is necessary for walking in the desert. Everything is not equivalent and interchangeable.

So, here is the exciting challenge that faces everyone who is interested in the Western tradition and eager to unveil the Hermetic heritage. Close your eyes, forget what was created during the Middle Ages and then repeated as an absolute truth. Imagine you are coming back to a time when monotheistic religions were just insignificant groups worshipping the God of their tribe, just as everyone else did. Now, open your eyes and you will see that there are still initiates of the Mysteries who invest in the study of philosophical teachings, and freely worship the Immortal Divinities they choose. Those who are interested in the occult dimensions join groups, can receive initiations, and practice magick and Theurgy. Wonderful systems are taught today to sincere adepts and nobody is trying to convert them into sinners.

If we want to understand the essence of Hermetism and Theurgy in order to be able to use its clear and living system, this is the way we must see things. Once we see things in this new way, the representation of the cosmos is simple. This is also why the explanation I have given you of our occult structure is quite different than the one commonly used as a tool, even though the old system is certainly true within its own context.

Naming the occult structure you will be working with is just as important as having a map when you are travelling. This is an essential tool of the work and a way to understand the teachings of the masters of the tradition, who taught from the earliest periods of civilization in the Western world.

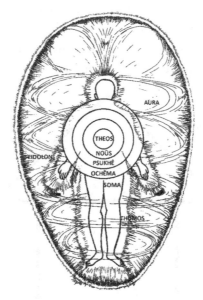

Figure 29: The occult structure of a human being according to the Theurgic tradition.

According to the Theurgic tradition, our real essence as a human being is our soul, and our body is its necessary organ. It is commonly taught that we are the result of the union of this soul and this body. In fact, this is not really true, because if we believe as the Theurgists do that we are really a soul, then our body is not what we are. Our body is something external, which is different from us. Have you ever stopped in front of a mirror, looking at your body as if you were looking at some-one else? Can you compare the differences in your body when you were very young, a teenager, and at your current age? All these bodies were "you," but, at the same time, you can feel deeply that they are not you. They are just mutable envelopes our soul needs in order to be incarnated, and in order to be able to experience this world. Of course this immaterial and immortal soul is not united with our body alone, without any intermediaries. Its essence is so subtle that it would be impossible for the soul to really be locked within the boundaries of our physical body. If you visualize the action of boiling water poured on snow, you will be able to imagine what I am referring to. If the soul (the hot water) were to be poured into the body (the snow), the body would melt in an instant. Consequently, there are steps used by the soul to form various bodies during its incarnation, and these different bodies have different rates of vibration.

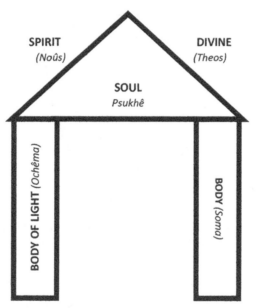

SPIRIT
(Noûs)

DIVINE
(Theos)

SOUL
Psukhê

BODY OF LIGHT (Ochêma)

BODY (Soma)

Figure 30: The occult structure of a human being in accordance with the five principles of the temenos.

The different parts of which we are composed can be symbolized in various ways. These different parts can be symbolized as the entrance to a Greek temple (called a temenos) with its two pillars and the triangular superstructure. They could also be envisioned as a pentagram crowned by the Aether, or the traditional representation of our body itself. In accordance with the structure of the elements I previously described, it is easy to remember that, in Hermetism and Theurgy, there are five parts used to describe our physical constitution. These different parts are:

Figure 31: The structure of the temenos and the Greek temple.

1ˢᵗ **Part:** The Body (called *Soma*—σῶμα)

2ⁿᵈ **Part:** The Bodies of Light (called *Hepithumia*— ἐπιθυμία | *Ochema*—ὄχημα)

3ʳᵈ **Part:** The Soul (called *Psuche*—ψυχή)

4ᵗʰ **Part:** The Spirit or Intellect (called *Nous*—νοῦς)

5ᵗʰ **Part:** The Divine aspect (called *Theos*—θεός)

The Body—Soma

It is impossible to be alive without a physical Body (*Soma*—σῶμα) and our Soul cannot do anything without it. Our Body is the material part of what we are. Its structure and shape is organized according to the principles provided by the Nous. It is important to briefly remind you of the status of the Body in the Theurgic tradition. The Body is not viewed as a curse or something we have to eliminate and forget.

Our Body is a kind of crystallization around our soul. You can compare it to the crystallization of salt around something when water evaporates. This physical Body is different than the essence of our being, but, at the same time, depends on it. The goal is to transcend this physical limitation.

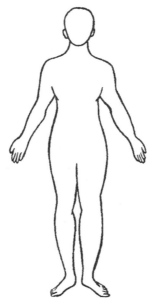

Figure 32: The Body—Soma.

The Bodies of Light

Today the idea of a "Body of Light" is familiar to most people. Since the beginning of the popularization of Western esotericism, questions about the aura have spread everywhere. It is true that its exact nature, origin, and function are difficult to define. This Body, called the ochema, is the vehicle of the Soul, the invisible and luminous body of the Soul, which is made of Aetheric material. The Soul is the part of the inner occult structure that gives movement to the Body of Light. Once it is perfected, it could be compared to a starry vehicle. You can easily understand in this context why this Body is sometimes called an "astral body." It allows the Soul to descend into the Body without being under the dominion of the flesh. The ochema is sometimes called the pneuma (breath).

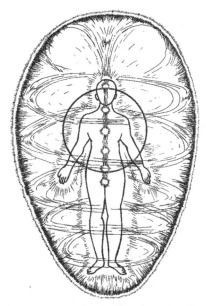

Figure 33: The Bodies of Light "surrounding" the Body.

Our Soul has previously used this vehicle to be embodied. This Body is indivisible, eternal, not subject to the influence of passions, and could be considered to be immortal. It is an intermediary between the Soul and the Body.

When you think about a luminous vehicle surrounding your physical body, something people refer to as an aura today, it is generally seen as an invisible and subtle envelope of the Body. Such is not the case here. I must make a clear distinction among three words that are often used in modern esotericism: etheric body, aura, and astral body.

The "etheric body," to use the common name that was chosen by the Theosophical Society, is a body of energy, a vital body, which is an emanation of our physical body. As you can see, the origin of the etheric body must be found in the physical body. In Platonic theology we would call this "etheric body" the "Thumos (θυμός)." [40]

---

40. Also spelled "Thymos."

The "aura" is also an invisible body, which surrounds us on a more subtle level than the etheric body. It reflects our inner life, passions, desires, urges, etc. The Theurgic tradition is using the same word: "Aura (αὔρα)."

To understand what I just called astral body, we have to consider two aspects that are very close to one another.

The first one is the ochema itself. As I just mentioned, the ochema is not derived from the physical body. In his book *Phaedrus*, Plato used the image of a chariot to describe the ochema, with the driver representing the Soul.

This vehicle is very subtle. You also have to consider another aspect, which is a sort of a reflection of this luminous Body. This reflection is not a pure illusion or fantasy. It is a manifestation of the ochema, called an "eidôlon" in Platonic Theurgy. It is also bonded to the physical and emotional bodies (*Soma* and *Thumos*), and as such, is always drawn toward their terrestrial inclinations.

Perhaps you have heard about what is sometimes called astral travel? In the Ogdoadic tradition, the exteriorization of the Body of Light is considered differently, depending upon the level we are experimenting with, or working with. Things are different depending on whether we are working with the eidôlon or with the ochema. There are various goals for working with each of these as well. The eidôlon is used in the first steps of the work, because it is the most accessible. The rituals using these levels are closer to magic than Theurgy. The second body, the ochema, is used for higher purposes and is the vehicle that is used to follow the path of return, and to ascend to the divine planes. In this case, when this Body of Light moves out of our Body, the driver does not come from below, but from above. These differences have a definite effect on the practical aspects of the ritual, such as the way you would exteriorize the invisible substance, and the part of the Body you would exteriorize this invisible substance from. As you can imagine, it is crucial to train with people who know all these aspects of the occult work before attempting this kind of ritual.

According to Iamblichus, because this vehicle is made from Aether and is not a mixture of other elements, it can be considered to be immortal. When we die, this vehicle will not disappear; but it will have a destiny that is independent of our Soul.

The Soul—Psuche

To give you an explanation that is as simple as possible, I would say that the Soul (*Psuche*—ψυχή) is "you." This is the spiritual and individual part of us, which is the origin of our individual creativity and awareness. All throughout our life, our body changes. Obviously we do not look the same today as we did when we were four years old. Nevertheless, we feel inside of ourselves that we are always the same person and we are certain that we are always us. Something in us maintains a cohesive identity throughout our life. It is the Soul that unifies our memories in a coherent way and organizes them into an inner self. This Soul came from above and it contains the memory of our previous lives. When we have completed our current life, our Soul will travel again to the outer world before coming back in another body. Hopefully, if we are lucky or well-trained, we will come back with a good part of our memory intact.

Our Soul is immortal. It is independent from the material world, but is also able to receive new elements, which are the result of our experiences in this world. The Soul may also be considered to be an intermediary between the upper levels of our being and our body. Consequently, a detailed analysis of the Soul could lead us to think that there are several parts of the Soul, or even different Souls in one person. Even if such a consideration is possible, we must think about and remember that the Soul has to be thought of as a whole. This is how a Theurgist must work ritually to improve the quality of the vehicle of his Soul (ochema) and will use Theurgic rituals to increase his proximity to his Soul. The Theurgist takes good care of his Soul. I am not just talking about a moral aspect, but a real Theurgic operation, which is intended to prepare the person for their departure from this life when the time comes. An initiate cannot improvise at the last minute. When our Soul leaves our Body, we must be prepared. As Plato said, "To philosophize is to learn how to die." This is completely true and the Neoplatonic tradition perpetuates this assertion. Iamblichus carries this idea even further. For Plato, when philosophy is considered only as an intellectual exercise, it is not enough to reach this desirable goal. Theurgic rituals are needed, and they are closely associated with philosophy. Taking care of our Soul is the first step in the Ogdoadic initiation.

The Spirit—Nous

The word Spirit (*Nous*—voῦς) is often used as a synonym for intelligence, awareness, and intellect. Everyone today knows the current meaning of intellect. It is for this reason that I must give you some precise information about the way this word was used in the past, and how it must be understood from the Hermetic perspective.

When we are thinking about something, we are using our intellect. Our thoughts are a result of a function of our brain called the intellect. We use our intellect in science, philosophy, and many aspects of our daily life when we want to decide between two courses of action. Plato called the mental process of making such a decision "discursive reason." The Nous is not the part of us that does discursive reasoning. The Nous is the ability to reason itself, the intellect, but not the active process of deciding. To say this in another way, the Nous is the engine of our car (our intellect) but not the motion of this engine (discursive reason). This is the reason that the Nous is considered to be the divine intellect. An interesting text entitled *Definitions from Hermes Trismegistus to Asclepius* offers more precise information about the essence of the Nous. In the fifth part of this document, Hermes explains that reasonable speech is the servant of the Nous. Reasonable speech comes from inner silence. This kind of speech is truly different than someone who just talks and plays with words without any contact with a real and inner understanding. We could say that the Nous is the divine inspiration that gives life to our speech and illuminates our understanding from the within.

Since I am explaining the Theurgic point of view, I must highlight something I believe you will find important and perhaps surprising. For the Hermetic tradition and for Theurgists, it is possible to make an inner distinction within the Soul. It is said that every human being

has a Body (Soma) and a Soul (Psuche) but not every Soul has an intellect (Nous). There is a divine part of the Nous and another one (less
divine) that belongs to the Soul. In the *Corpus Hermeticum*, Hermes
explained that God invited everyone to be plunged into a mysterious
cup in order to know why they were born. In fact, this immersion is
the way to manifest the desire to undergo the mysterious "way of return" to the divine world. As the text states, only some people answer
and will become, through this transmutation, the "initiates of the
Nous." The others who don't feel this spiritual desire, this inner call,
have the function of reason (Logos), but not the Nous. They are mortals while the others who are plunged in the large vase are immortals.
These mortals are almost non-humans who are totally subject to their
passions and desires. They are quite incapable of anything higher than
what an animal can do.

As you can see, the Nous is a fundamental articulation of the spiritual life. We might say that there are two categories of people around
us. Some live with a Soul that is without the Nous (meaning without
this divine part of the Nous) and another group lives with a Soul that
has the Nous. When I was a philosophy teacher it was really easy to see
who was able to question himself, and who had no clue what it means to
think about something beyond the material world. For many people
there is no spark, whether we are talking about the Soul, destiny, or God.
Their whole life is not an action, but a reaction. They copulate, work,
have children, and die. They can think, but not in a way that allows
them to develop a critical and personal mind. We should not despise
these people, but as a matter of fact they really are different. Theurgists
called them a "herd of men who are subject to fate." On the other
hand, you are reading this book and you are, of course, trying to understand something beyond the material realm. This is the first step
toward, and the manifestation of a true initiatic desire. You can decide
to take action; to be plunged in the large cup of initiation in order to
begin walking the path. Once you make this decision, the second part
of the Nous will be made manifest to you.

In the *Corpus Hermeticum* it says: "Agathodaimon said that the
Soul is in your Body, the Nous in your Soul, the Word in your Nous,

and God is the father of all that." Later the same text states: "The most subtle part of the Soul is the Nous, and for the Nous this is God."

The Divine—Theos

Before I discuss this point any further, it is necessary to keep in mind that I am explaining the structure of our inner being. In Greek "Theos" (θεός) means God, but Theos has nothing to do with the notion of a unique God. The upper part of the Nous is so high and subtle that we could come to believe, just as the initiates did, that it is the real presence of the Divine, of God inside us. This is different than the Supreme Divine Principle, which is present in everything. This is also different than the hierarchies of Gods and Goddesses we will learn about in our advanced Theurgic work. This is really a divine presence we can imagine as a light that is hidden at the top of our inner self and showing us the way. In the Platonic allegory of the cave, Plato used the image of a fire, burning at the top of a cliff in a dark cave. This is an image of our progress as we wander in the darkness of our desires—the passions that arise in our body. We felt the call and the desire was manifested in us. We stood up and began to walk, listening to the silent word (the Logos) emanating from our intellect (Nous) through our Soul (Psuche). We felt this divine presence. As we turned our eyes inward, we were guided by the luminous presence of the Divine in us (Theos), which is the reflection of the outer sun, the real manifestation of the One.

It is now time to consider the "spiritual destiny" I have mentioned several times in the previous explanations.

The Destiny of the Soul

Birth and Incarnation

You now understand the structure of cosmology as derived from the observation of the cosmos and the inner structure of human beings. It is from these codifications that the masters of this tradition developed a simple duality: matter-spirit and body-soul. Thus, we have a Body we can feel with our senses, but at the same time, we can think, remember, and imagine. All these actions are completely non-physical.

If a materialist argues that everything is a result of activities of the brain, the fact is that these mental processes are still non-physical. Consequently, it is logical to conclude, as I did in the previous chapter, that we have a Body and a Soul. Even though the Body deteriorates when we die, that doesn't mean the Soul will deteriorate. On the contrary, our Soul will be free to reach the world it belongs to.

Imagine a child playing with a balloon flying above him. This might be the representation of our Soul attached to our Body. If the child releases the string, the balloon will rise to the sky. This is a good way of understanding how the Soul rises after death. It is not necessary here to use other Qabalistic or Enochian systems to understand this. There is simply an above and a below, just as there is a visible and an invisible. I am always surprised to see how complicated the questions of attendees to a meeting can be before I explain the occult world to them in this way. After a few minutes of explanation everything becomes clear and understandable. Of course the considerations of the details of any system can be extremely complex. Nevertheless, complexity and dogmatism are never a guarantee that we have found the truth. As the philosopher Descartes explained, it is better to go from the simplest to the most complicated, but never the reverse. I understand that using complicated systems gives the teacher more power over their students. This is not the best way to teach a real initiatic system. On the contrary, simplicity is very often a good indication of a tradition that has been truly understood and lived. It is clear that you will have to learn more about all these aspects, but just as a child learns their letters before they can read a book, knowing principles and beginning ritual exercises are the necessary first steps.

To be more precise now regarding the Theurgic teachings of Body and Soul, it is useful to know that Iamblichus, following the theology of the *Chaldaean Oracles*, outlines three principal levels or worlds. In this Chaldaean representation of the world, these three levels are called: the Empyrean (the highest level), the Ethereal (the median level), and the Hylic (the lowest level). Iamblichus uses the words: Noetic (the intelligible, highest level), the Noeric (the intermediate world), and the Visible (the lowest level).

Our spiritual Soul descended from the celestial world to enter into matter in order to be embodied in a physical Body. As I explained in the previous chapter, all Souls are not equal, because of their actions in previous lives. Consequently, the descent itself will be different in some aspects, depending on the state of the Soul. It is important to remind you that there is not merely one explanation of this process. Here I am explaining the way of Iamblichus and the main Theurgists of his school of thought.

There are two scenarios to consider regarding the path followed by our Soul prior to its descent. The first scenario has to do with the first time our Soul began to exist. This is the point long before we had our first incarnation in the long chain of evolutions, up to where we are today. The second scenario has to do with the time previous to this present incarnation, in the period between two lives.

As you might expect, these two situations are different. You must understand that these points are complex and that they bring up several theological and philosophical consequences. (You can check the Bibliography if you want to learn more about these specific subjects.)

There are five main steps:

1. The Souls are separated from the hypercosmic Souls. [41]

2. The Soul is linked to its vehicle.

3. The next step is the moment that occurs when the Soul is associated with a celestial God, and placed under its care as well as the care of the celestial hierarchy that follow this God. This specific link creates a difference between the Souls.

4. According to Plato, this is the moment when the Soul receives its destiny. At this primordial moment, a specific divinity [42] is allotted to the Soul.

---

41. This is the first differentiation of the Soul from the cosmos and its distribution among the stars.

42. The Greek word used by Iamblichus to name this specific divinity is *oikodespotes*. This divine power can be understood as the "Master of the House." Traditionally in Theurgy, this is the divinity that governs the sign of our ascendant, if this planet is well aspected.

Even if all Souls are initially made equal, some differences may occur due to the fact that they each have different specific divinities.

5. Lastly, the descent of the Soul into its vehicle occurs and a personal daimon is associated with the Soul. You must remember that this descent of the Soul varies, depending on whether we are considering the original descent, or the one that occurs between lives.

Let's talk now about the original descent. This is both a theological and a philosophical problem. Thus the answer has never been simple. Indeed the answers from Plato, Plotinus, and others are a little different than those from Iamblichus. For Iamblichus (as the founder of Theurgy he remains our primary reference), the Soul is governed by natural law. There is no evil origin, no malediction, and no sin at the origin of this descent. Moreover, please notice that the term used is "descent" and not "fall." The meanings of these two phrases are very different; consider, "going downstairs" versus "falling downstairs." It would be even worse if I say that someone pushed you down the stairs. In the Theurgic tradition, there is no such reference. The biblical story creates a paradox in which a loving God decides to curse us by pushing us out of heaven. That is certainly a strange manifestation from a benevolent divinity. In Platonic theology, as understood by Theurgists, the Soul will "fall" during its first descent, just as we fall if we jump from a window. This is not a curse, nor a manifestation of evil, but merely a consequence of the natural law that is attributed to the divinities. Thus, the moral consequences of this kind of "falling" are totally different. The descent of the souls is a kind of completion of the universe. In some cases, pure Souls come into the visible world to manifest the presence of the Gods. They will help the visible Gods manifest in this world by performing rituals and drawing worshippers to the Gods.

When the Soul descends, it will cross through the different planetary veils. It will first encounter the veil of the fixed stars, which is the eighth veil; next it will descend through Saturn (governed by Kronos),

Jupiter (governed by Zeus), and so on. Each of them will bring to the Soul "symbolic clothing" made up of influences from each sphere. Each Soul has its own characteristics. As a matter of fact, the more deeply the Soul descends, the more this envelope creates a thick barrier that can block the inner light. Consequently, the divine higher essence will be difficult to perceive and express. In order for you to visualize this part of the process, just imagine a candle as the representation of the Soul. Imagine now that we put this candle into a dark-grey glass, then inside another glass that is white, then inside another that is red, and so on. After placing so many colored barriers around the light, it would be very difficult to even see the light of the candle inside at all. This is symbolically the situation of the embodied Soul. Plato explained that our Soul could be seen as a statue that has fallen into the sea; shells and corals have progressively covered it. Indeed the density and nature of these invisible influences differ with each person. These differences are a consequence of our past lives and the way we decided to descend into the visible world.

The second case (the descent of the Soul between lives) is based on the same natural law, which is symbolized by the law of gravity. In this case, the path of descent could exhibit several important differences. First of all, the Souls are no longer pure. They have lived, experienced matter, and become changed by that experience.

As we now know what the different parts of the Soul are, we can easily understand that some parts remain pure and divine, while other parts have become contaminated by contact with matter during previous incarnations. Because of these past incarnations, the Psuche has been darkened and we have lost the memory of our origin. This loss is not a radical, complete loss, and it is different for everyone. In fact we are trying to recover our original abilities, plus the experience offered by the lives themselves.

There are three main categories of Souls:

- In the first case, we see a Soul that lived a previous life full of animalistic urges, being prone to violence, anger, etc. Its return will be uncontrolled and unwitting. These Souls follow the natural law of descent as all Souls do. Consequently they are not allowed to choose the life they will live. Because of the influence of their previous lives, they would spontaneously choose the most attractive destiny; consequently their choice is not really free. This process will continue until part of their memory is reactivated, giving birth to a desire to change this otherwise inevitable destiny.

- In the second category, the Soul descends to train and improve its character. Remember that the metempsychosis in the Western tradition is quite different than what is generally taught in the Eastern religions.[43] In the Western tradition, souls can progress and are able to retain their progress from one life to the next. The work, the learning, the experiences we have today will not be lost when we die. We will bring these improvements with us if we consciously choose to do so. Surprisingly, this does not occur automatically. We must be trained before we can do that.

Both of these categories of Souls are subject to fate. Souls are different because their specific divinities are different and all the links they have to other spiritual creatures make a unique web of influences and relationships. This process is very close to the process used to construct a natal chart. In a properly constructed natal chart, you can see the unique signature of your natal sky, which shows the precise influences acting upon you. Nevertheless, you can choose whether to follow the best parts of this influence or the worst parts of it. For example a solar influence will direct you to perform solar work, but you can use it for good or evil and you will suffer the consequences of your choices.

- In the third category, the Souls are pure and have a luminous descent in which they keep the memory of their origins and

---

43. There are exceptions, such as in Hinduism (at least in Shivaism) and the concept of "sanchita karma." Some of these schools believe that this karmic part comes from past lives. There are younger and older Souls in an evolutionary view, since, at the end, all will be connected to their "One." According to modern scholars, this theory of reincarnation was defined in the Mediterranean world and eventually spread to the Eastern cultures.

goals intact. This quality allows them to maintain a strong and pure link to the different hierarchies of spiritual beings. Therefore, the fact that they are embodied doesn't imply a darkening of their Soul.

The Path of Return

As you read this book today, I am confident that you already have had this kind of inner experience, which has enabled you to feel the spiritual part of you. I know that this inner experience is usually difficult to understand. Philosophers are trained for a long time in order to theorize about such inner feelings, without eradicating them. You don't need this specific intellectual training to begin. As Plato said, this inner feeling is an essential step. It is a manifestation of a pure desire to remember our real nature and our spiritual origin. It is essential to catch hold of this desire and to nurture it as we would nurture a little flame in order to start a fire. We have to be careful and use our instincts and reason in a balanced way. At each step of this spiritual journey, always remember that practice is the cornerstone.

The first question you should pose to yourself is: why it is necessary to undertake this process of ascending to the divine? That is a good question. In fact, if we are in this world to have experiences and enjoy what it can provide us with, we could say that there is no need to work all our life to elevate our soul. It could even be considered the opposite of what seems needful. This is true, but it is still the wrong way of thinking about this issue if we consider the whole panorama. Someday you and I will die. We will leave our Body. When this time comes, we will be forced to deal with various situations.

If we do not take care of our Soul, we will leave our Body in an unconscious state. Consequently, our choices will be reduced and our memory will be quite totally darkened during the process of the descent.

If we take care of our Soul now, we will elevate our level of consciousness and we will leave our Body in a more conscious state. Consequently, we will have more choices and we will keep parts of our memory from this current life in our next life.

If we take care of our Soul and practice Theurgic rituals (or their equivalent) in a traditional way (not improvised) our destiny will be totally different. As Iamblichus taught, contemplation and meditation are not enough to obtain real results here and now. Theurgic rituals are required, and these rituals must be from a traditional and moral lineage. As we perform these rituals, our Soul will be trained to do two things right now: to find a good balance in an enjoyable life, and to elevate our Soul with the help of Theurgy. Both aspects will be associated with a clear mind that is well-organized with the help of science, philosophy, and theology. Thus, when we die, we will be able to cross over to the other side in full awareness.

On the other side, we will see the Noetic world without any veils. As the philosopher Pascal said about God, working for our Soul is like a wager: if there is something after death, our work will have been essential. If there is nothing after death, we have lost nothing. This is even more true because I am talking about a Hermetic and Theurgic school. This is not a religious system in which you have to despise your body and all the pleasures of the material life. You do not have to become a hermit. You just have to achieve a balance in your life between your Body and your Soul.

It might be helpful to learn how to do that, because no divinity is going to come and rescue us. In fact, as I have previously explained, the "saviors" are the pure souls of the initiates who come back to teach and train us.

From the Theurgic perspective, there are three main steps on this path of return. As in most of the trainings you may have studied, each of these steps includes other subcategories, but it is not necessary to teach these explicitly here. They are not required to understand the whole process.

The first step is to purify our vehicle in order to remove the material elements that darken our perception of the cosmos. If we want to understand the reason for doing so, there is a simple visualization that will help us. Imagine a diver at the bottom of the sea who is wearing a diving belt. If he wants to return to the surface, the easiest way is to progressively remove the weights he is wearing. If we compare these weights to our body, the removal process is the process of purification. The Body is useful as a weight, but if we want to ascend to the divine, the best way is to be trained to learn how to momentarily abandon the Body.

The second step is the re-ascent itself and the liberation of our fate. As you can easily imagine, this is a special moment. An old and sacred mystery is hidden in this teaching. In the first part of the book, I extensively described the status of Thoth as the founder of this Hermetic tradition. It is easy to understand the relationship between this "God of the Eight" and the Ogdoadic tradition. But it is paramount to understand why the initiatic Order that has charge of this inheritance also bears the name "Aurum Solis."

According to Plato, the world may be described using the image of a cave, wherein we are enchained in the darkness of illusion. The only reminder of the light of the outer world is the presence of a fire on a hill. This light is the representation of the real sun, which shines in the real world outside the cave.

As always, Iamblichus succeeded in associating Platonic and Chaldaean theology, which are the roots of the Western Theurgic system. The first world (the Noetic) is the realm of Good. "Aion," the invisible sun, emanates from the first father (the Supreme Principle, the Great Architect), and rules over the Noetic Gods.

In the second and intermediate world (the Noeric), the real sun, the God Helios is considered to be the Demiurge by Iamblichus. He rules over the Noeric Gods and creates the visible sun in the visible world.

The visible sun (the third ruler) rules the visible Gods by the continuous power given to him by Helios. His visible light shines upon the visible world and gives it life.

According to the Emperor Julian, who explained Iamblichus's theology, Helios also creates the "angels of the sun," which are situated in the Aether. They guide the divine rays to human souls.

As we can see, the whole universe is emanated from the Supreme Good and enlightened by the benevolent rays of the God Helios. From its birth, the Soul maintains a vertical and inner contact to that which is above. The Emperor Julian followed this path by studying this system, which fit his own belief system so well. After learning this system from a disciple of Iamblichus, he summarized this solar theology in a famous text entitled, "Hymn to the King Helios." As he wrote: "For I am a follower of King Helios.... But this at least I am permitted to say without sacrilege, that from my childhood an extraordinary longing for the rays of the God penetrated deep into my soul; and from my earliest years my mind was so completely swayed by the light that illumines the heavens that not only did I desire to gaze intently at the sun, but whenever I walked abroad in the night season, when the firmament was clear and cloudless, I abandoned all else without exception and gave myself up to the beauties of the heavens; nor did I understand what anyone might say to me, nor heed what I was doing myself." [44]

Aurum Solis, the "Gold of the Sun" witnesses the key role of Helios in Theurgy. "Aurum Solis" is not just a fancy name. It is a statement, a dedication to that which is uppermost, a full commitment to an honorable Theurgic tradition!

After its purification, the Soul will welcome the rays of the sun that are guided to it by the angels of the sun. These rays carry the power of attraction to the visible Gods. With the help of the energy that comes from Helios, our Soul will be filled with this light and will begin to ascend. This is the process of purification. At the same time this is a benevolent ascension, helping us rise toward our specific divinity. This is the time when our Soul is progressively liberated from its fate.

Here begins the third phase, during which we will be united with the Gods. As we can see, the sun's rays are, and continue to be central during the whole process of ascension. They are our guides and protectors. Of course, as you remember, we are still in the cave of the material world. As such we are still surrounded by the spheres of the visible Gods we descended through during our descent. We will have to go back through them again in this ascent, with the help of Theurgic rituals.

---

44. "Hymn to King Helios" by Julian, translated by Emily Wilmer Cave Wright in 1913.

The cosmic harmony of the universe is full of symbols that are linked together by mysterious bonds called "signatures." Theurgy, astrology, and alchemy use these correspondences in their rituals. Thus the universe is not empty. On the contrary, it is full of Gods and of the archetypes that are associated directly with us. Consequently, we can use them in Theurgic rituals to undertake this return with perfect success. We will use the "gold of the sun" as the primary energy and perform the rituals that help us to rise from one planet to the next. As Plato said in the myth of the cave, this return cannot be accomplished by us alone. A guide, an initiator, is needed. The help of someone who really knows the path is paramount. Authentic rituals can sometimes be considered to be an initiator. They were prepared by initiates and they retain those footprints. But they have to be organized in a traditional and balanced way. They must carry a direct and full power coming from a real lineage.

We will begin this spiritual journey by working with the elements, and then being reunited with the planetary Gods. I am not talking here about a fusion with these divinities, but a strong and useful relationship. This connection allows us to progress from one sphere to the next. Eventually we will reach the level of the starry sky and be able to rise from the Ogdoad to the Ennead. In order to do that, training is necessary. We have to learn the passwords (words of power), signs, sacred words, and sounds. We have to connect with the planetary divinities in order to have balance in our current life. From this contact will emerge a deep understanding of the cosmos rooted in love, not fear. This is a very practical approach. The use of the Theurgic rituals should never be disconnected from our daily life. On the contrary, the feeling that we are starting to separate from this world would be the manifestation of a false work. These relationships with the visible Gods of the planets, and later the Noetic Gods, are not an intellectual game. They are a reality; a powerful relationship manifested by friendship and love. We should never become exclusive or intolerant, because we know of the existence of this hierarchy. This Theurgic work will totally change the way you see and live in the world. The liberation of fate is a consequence of the establishment of these relationships. If an astrologer says to you that there is a bad aspect in Mars in your natal chart, you will be able to answer: "Don't worry; I know Mars and I have already solved that problem." The goal we are trying to reach is to purify and elevate our Soul in order to be consciously aware when we die. We can do this now if we undertake this inner transformation.

Remember that this is not a miracle. The ritual practices have to be received from a clear source and repeated very regularly over a long period of time. These rituals act as drops of water regularly falling on a hard stone. At the end, the stone will be pierced. That requires time and persistence. Each ritual practice helps us to acquire a better understanding of the universe, of the Immortal Divinities, as well as giving us a more balanced life and reducing our anxiety.

These rituals, which enable us to achieve this ascent, are not magical formulas. The Theurgic school as taught by the Platonists and Neoplatonicians requires a moral attitude. Of course, anyone can perform magic rituals, Goetia, and other kinds of magic. Nevertheless, the Theurgic way can be used safely only with this commitment to an inner purity, fraternity, and love. The Platonic philosophy teaches that we can progress safely only if we associate a pure moral life with a philosophical (and Theurgic) work. This ascent to the Good must associate the cult of beauty in the visible world, as well as our actions, with our inner self. When we cultivate this beauty in our Body, in our surroundings, and in our rituals, we must also think beautiful thoughts. When we perform these exercises, beauty will become a reality, not something that exists only in our most secret Soul. As a result, our whole life will manifest reliability and trust.

It would be useless to attempt to understand the final consequences of this ascent. This is a liberation and a total purification of our Soul. According to the Theurgic teachings, we can eventually reach this level. Perhaps it will not be completed in this life, but it will be completed in a forthcoming one. This should not be an issue for us. As you remember, all the work you are doing now is not lost. If we can cross the boundary of death while remaining even partially aware, we will keep part, or all of our memory. This is an absolute key for the rest of the destiny of our Soul. Eventually, the Souls that have become pure will be totally liberated from fate and from the necessity to reincarnate. Even so, Plato taught about the concern of the pure Souls, for the human Souls that remain in the darkness of the cave. They use the power of the sun to descend, not for themselves, but for the good of everyone. As in Alexandria, the rays of the sun have never failed to provide the power that the human Soul needs. Helios and Hermes, who are the tutelary divinities of this tradition, are not buried in a sandy desert. They are still alive, helping the Souls that are beginning their path of purification. This is the Sacred Way of Return, and you can begin this path right now.

Exercise Six—The Theurgic Calyx

In the Theurgic Qabalistic system, the Aurum Solis uses a version of the calyx that is focused on the intensification of the Qabalistic cross, which is formed by touching various Sephirotic centers. Even if the invisible process is quite different from that used by the Golden Dawn, most of the steps of this exercise are the same as those used in this tradition.

In this formula, the process is deeply rooted in the occult structure of your being and related to Book Four of the *Corpus Hermeticum* called "The Cup or Monad."

The calyx is used to align the practitioner with the forces of the cosmos, as well as to bring to awareness the counterparts of those cosmic forces that are active in you.

It establishes a balance of forces at every level of your being.

It is a powerful invocation of the different parts of your occult structure, re-enacting the descent of the highest part of your being into you. This process gives you access to the sacred powers of the triple superstructure.

You can make a daily use of this powerful process.

1. You are standing; your arms are at your sides.
2. Extend your arms in front of you, raised to approximately 70° above the horizontal plane, palms up (supine). Maintain this position, breathe deeply, and direct your aspiration to the

highest, most divine level you can think of. Exhale and (after few seconds) inhale once more, simultaneously visualizing the descent of the spiritual light to the area above the top of your head.

Holding this position, vibrate: Ὁ θεός (Ho theós)

3. Lower your arms and cross them on your chest, right over left. Visualize the light descending into the center of your chest, underneath your crossed arms. Visualize this light creating a shining and radiant golden sphere. The word "shine" used either as an adverb or adjective (depending on the usage) is "shining."

Holding this position, once more, vibrate: Ὁ νοῦς (Ho noûs)

4. Holding this position, once more, vibrate: Ἡ ψυχή (HĒ psyché)

5. Visualize the rays of this inner sun shining from this sphere in your aura.

Then, vibrate: Τὸ ὄχημα (Tò óchēma)

6. Visualize your physical body full of this golden light and vibrate: Τὸ σῶμα (Tò sōma)

7. Extend your arms in front of you, raising them, palms up (supine). Your arms should be wide open and your eyes should be lifted to the heavens. Maintaining this position, now say: Πάντα δὲ ταῦτα διὰ τοῦαἰῶνος [45] (Pànta dè taûta dià toû aiônos).

8. Stand, with your arms hanging naturally at your sides.

Self-Test Six

These questions are intended to help you challenge your knowledge about the subjects you have been studying. You can use them before you read the materials or after. Try to answer the questions before checking the answers in the Appendix.

1. Why is it necessary to avoid a specific interpretation of the universe?

---

45. Translation: "And all these things exist for all Eternity."

2. How many parts compose the occult structure of the human being in the Hermetic tradition?

3. Which symbolic representation is associated with this occult structure?

4. Which part can be identified as "you" and why?

5. How many levels are there in the Theurgic tradition?

6. According to this tradition, do you live one or many lives?

7. What is one the main purposes of the Theurgic rituals?

8. How can the Ordo Aurum Solis be clearly linked to the Theurgic tradition?

The following questions are related to your own experience. It is good to use them as personal meditations. [46]

1. Have you already seen or felt your invisible bodies?

2. Did you experience an out-of-body experience, and, if yes, what were the consequences in your life?

3. Do you believe in reincarnation and for what reasons?

4. Do you fear death? Answer yes or no and explain your reasons.

---

46. You can share your thoughts about these questions on the forums of the Aurum Solis website.

Part 7
The Celestial Ladder: Rituals and Practices

Clear Fundamental Rituals Enable You to Eventually Rise to the Highest Levels of Consciousness

The three cosmic principles: You can now fully begin to practice and use the three cosmic principles: 1) Elements (Theurgic Ritual of the Pentalpha), 2) Planets (Ritual of the Seven Gates) 3) Signs (Ritual of the Celestial Temenos).

The planetary days unveiled: Be aware that this part will clearly unveil ritual principles that have never previously been explained, such as the true way to calculate the planetary days and hours.

This Celestial Ladder provides the clear steps we need to use Theurgy in order to ascend to the highest levels of consciousness we can reach.

Ritual of the Pentalpha

The Origin

The pentagram (also called pentacle, pentalpha, or pentangle) is a five-pointed star (*pentes*: five and *gramma*: letter) drawn from the points of intersection of a pentagon. The word "pentalpha" comes from the association of the Greek words meaning "five" and "alpha" (usually the letter A).

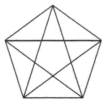

Figure 34: The pentagram is a five-pointed star drawn from the points of intersection of a pentagon.

The representation of the pentagram in the shape of a star is well-known in several cultures and has developed various meanings down through the centuries. In ancient representations you will very often see the six-pointed star and the five-pointed star on magick tools called pentacles or talismans. In European heraldic symbols stars are usually called "estoiles," or "mullets" in old French. In England, these estoiles are composed of six wavy rays. If the rays are straight the star is called a mullet and has five points. In some cases, this symbol has a hole at its center. Thus its origin is linked to the wheel of a spur. In this case, there is no relationship between that symbol and the symbol I am describing.

Without stating any reason or giving his sources, Eliphas Levi explained that a pentagram with the central point at the top is the representation of Good, while a pentagram with the central point at the bottom would be a symbol of Evil. Undoubtedly, this interpretation is personal and comes from the simplified representation of the head of a goat. Numerous rituals and symbols prior to Levi show clearly that the orientation of the pentagram had no specific meaning. For example, this is the case in various Masonic rituals and temples, which have continued to use the original orientations of the pentagram, both point up and point down.

The Meaning of the Pentagram

Scholars Cornelia de Vogel, Beatrice Goff, and Elizabeth Douglas Van Buren explained that the pentagram was used during the reign of Uruk IV (3500 BCE) in ancient Mesopotamia and was the symbol of a "celestial body." During the cuneiform period (2600 BCE) the meaning of the pentagram was "region," "celestial part," or "direction." This symbol's true meaning has remained ambiguous.

In the Hebrew tradition, the five-pointed star was associated with Truth and to the five books of the Pentateuch. In ancient Greece the pentagram was called the "pentalpha." For Pythagoreans the pentagram was a symbol of perfection associated with the human being. This symbol was also linked to the golden ratio and the dodecahedron, which is the fifth Platonic solid having twelve pentagonal sides. For Plato it was associated with the symbol of the sky. Previously I mentioned that the pentagram was used as a password and a secret sign of recognition.

The pentagram was also found on different Egyptian statues and Gallic coins. We can see this sign on a Greek red cup dating from the fifth century BCE. This sign can be found all around the Mediterranean world. For example an Etruscan coin shows a pentagram with the word "pensu," meaning "five" in this language. During the Roman republic, the pentagram was associated with the building trade. The medieval grimoires attributed to Solomon gave a great importance to the pentagram. It was the time when the pentagram became known as "Solomon's seal." Gershom Scholem, a well-known Jewish author, wrote that "in Arabic Magic, the Solomon's seal was largely used, but that its use by Jews was rare. When it was used, the symbols of the hexagram and the pentagram were often considered to be similar and the same name was used for both representations." The Latin version of these medieval texts use the word "pentaculum" for those circular drawings connected with Solomon's seal, even if this is not exactly a representation of the pentagram.

The first time the pentagram appeared in an English text is in the legend of Sir Gawain and the Green Knight, verses 27–28. In this text, the Celtic solar hero wears a "shining shield with the drawing of a pentangle made from pure gold."

The pentagram with the middle point up symbolically represents a human being with his legs and arms spread wide apart. Tycho Brahe in his book *Calendarium Naturale Magicum Perpetuum* (1582), associates the pentagram with the human body. He connected the five Hebrew letters (Yod, He, Shin, Vav, He) to this representation. In a representation attributed to a contemporary of Brahe, Henry Cornelius Agrippa von Nettesheim, we can see the five planets with the moon at the center. Other representations that came from Robert Fludd[47] and Leonardo da Vinci show identical geometrical representations correlating the human body to the universe.

It is now useful to explain the association between the symbol of the pentagram and Christianity. The confusion comes from the presence of the pentagram in the seal of Jerusalem, which is different from the "star of David" you will find on old Jewish shields. Paleochristians associated the pentagram with the five wounds of their savior. But from this time until the medieval period, the pentagram has remained a symbol that was rarely used by Christians. After his conversion to Christianity, the Roman emperor Constantine I included the pentagram in his seal.

Even if several authors tried to associate the pentagram very closely with the Star of Jesus or the "Eastern Star," Christian art is not the best place to find such a symbol. Some Christian esotericists explain that this five-pointed star with the central point up represents the symbol of Christ and the central point down represents his incarnation. You have to remember that the negative aspect of the pentagram (with the central point down) came from Eliphas Levi, who associated this representation with Baphomet.

From this period of time (the nineteenth century), Western magic and the esoteric world began to categorize most of the religious or

---

47. Famous astrologer (1574–1637) who worked extensively on occult philosophy.

spiritual symbols. This duality of the pentagram (positive-up and negative-down) has been overestimated by modern groups under the influence of Christian groups.

The Rite of the Pentagram

Eliphas Levi, MacGregor Mathers, the Kabbalistic Order of the Rose-Cross, and the Golden Dawn were the developers of what is known today as the "ritual of the pentagram." The "minor ritual of the pentagram" and the "major ritual of the pentagram" share the same structure. The difference is simply defined by what happens in the ritual.

There are various parts in this ritual, but all these parts were devised by considering two aspects:

1. The symbolic correspondences of the pentagram;
2. The invocations of the sacred words (Hebrew or Greek essentially) that are linked to the different steps of the ritual.

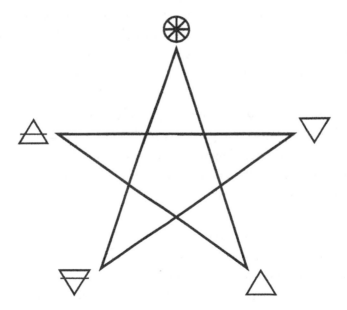

Figure 35: The pentagram and the elements.

My goal here is not to provide an analysis of the ritual of the pentagram as practiced in the Golden Dawn, but to provide a clear presentation of the essential aspects of this magical practice.[48]

In the representation in Figure 35, you will find the traditional elements and their position on the pentagram. Understanding this model is essential. It is used in all the different ritual exercises.

It is interesting to know what happens during the magical use of this symbol. When you draw this symbol of the pentagram in the air in front of you, something special happens on the invisible planes. The energy present in your aura and all around you is activated consistent with this special design. As a matter of fact, this is more than a simple activation. A specific level of energy is specified and selected. You can draw this using various tools: your forefinger, a stick, a dagger, a sword, etc.

It is useful to know that the tool you use to draw this symbol has an impact on the nature of the energy that is created. This means there are two things to consider: the activation of the subtle energy around us, and the energy associated with the magical tool itself. Thus the choice is not arbitrary, because it will have consequences that affect the ultimate result of our actions. It is surprising to find very few indications about the tools used for drawing the pentagram. Most of the time, individual practitioners who have read books from other contemporary magical traditions use a dagger. If they are cautious, they will use a new dagger that has been especially devoted to this purpose. I believe it is more useful to think about the reason we would use that tool to draw these magical figures. Of course we can find deep Hebrew interpretations about the connection of the dagger to various Sephirot or words of power. This is informative, but misses the real reason from a practical point of view. It is correct to assume that we are better off choosing brand-new tools to perform our rituals. The reason is easy to understand: everything that surrounds us, everything we touch, whether it is alive or not, absorbs a part of our specific energy and constructs a memory of the artifact. If we are able to see the aura of such an "in-

---

48. If you are interested in the pentagram as it was used by the Christian Qabalists during the Renaissance, you can go to the website of the famous "Kabbalistic Order of the Rose-Cross" (www.okrc.org).

animate" artifact, we will be surprised to see that something very specific exists.

I remember a Brazilian companion of the Aurum Solis showing me a sword forged from scratch by a blacksmith who was initiated in magick. This sword had been used in several magical rituals. The sword was not beautiful from an aesthetic point of view, but the feeling was completely amazing. Up to this moment in my life, this sword is one of the most powerful magical tools I have ever touched or used. Such a magical tool has a real individuality. Its memory gives a distinctive life to it, and its use is very delicate. In fact, such a magical tool can use us for its own purpose, rather than we using it for our purpose. This is why authentic Theurgic Orders always recommend the use of new tools.

Perhaps you noticed that I am using the word "magical tool" instead of "magical weapon." This is intentional and must be underlined. It is easy to understand that a word like "weapon" is not neutral. It is associated with a specific purpose, either an attack or a defense. It is uncomfortable seeing this word used for art or love. Remember that in Theurgy we are working on our inner being in order to elevate our Soul and to be in harmony with the cosmos. The thoughtless use of a weapon for magical purposes is not recommended. It is true that a magical weapon such as a sword can be used in a very precise way in specific rituals. The most consistent use of these tools is to draw the invisible into manifest reality, by which I mean a manipulation of the invisible energies in a specific way. Therefore the Aurum Solis prefers today to use the word "magical tool" or "Theurgic tool" instead of "weapon."

In order to draw on the invisible level, different tools are used in Theurgy, including daggers, swords, spears, specific stones, medals (lamens), fingers, etc. I must also emphasize that the shape, the material, the text written on it, the colors, etc., of these Theurgic tools are not arbitrary. All these aspects play a role and are unveiled progressively during the initiatic process. Specific rituals of consecration will be used for these tools. You can read elements about the first step of these consecrations in the books published by the Aurum Solis. It is interesting to note that specific initiatic consecrations are needed in order to continue the process of these consecrations and achieve their full completion. For all these reasons, if you are working alone, I recommend that you use your forefinger to draw the symbols used in the rituals of this book. You will not be disappointed if you do.

As you read previously in the excerpt from the *Corpus Hermeticum*, this subtle energy is associated with the five elements and consequently has the potential to have an effect on the physical level. You also remember that these elements are used in the first steps of the ascension of the soul in the following sequence: Earth, Water, Air, Fire, and Aether.

Once the symbolic attributions of the elements have been explained and the recommendations provided, you have to know how to activate these specific energies. The pentagrams are used in two different ways depending on the tradition. The first tradition is the Golden Dawn and the other is the Ogdoadic tradition. Because of the practical inner research that has been performed over many years, the Aurum Solis has unveiled a very effective way to use this powerful symbol. In the *Golden Dawn* we are told to invoke an element by drawing the pentagram in a specific way. "The invoking pentagram of Air commenceth from Water, and that of Water commenceth from the angle of Air. Those of Fire and Earth begin from the angle of Spirit. [. . .] The banishing signs are the reversing of the current." If you are following these rules, you are making an invocation from an element which is different and you never consider the movement of the drawing. Consequently sometimes you invoke drawing counterclockwise and sometimes you banish when drawing clockwise. I have to admit that I never read anything convincing about the reason for proceeding in such a way. More importantly it is difficult to imagine how we can activate the energy of an element by doing that.

The Grand Officers of the Aurum Solis, with the help of advanced members of the Order, are always testing magical processes. To be effective, such experimentations require practitioners from various ethnic origins and cultural backgrounds to work simultaneously. With initiates from all around the world, the Aurum Solis continues this essential work, which was started by its founders. This is the only way for a tradition to avoid dogmatism and keep a real critical point of view active. This is why we experimented with the ritual of the pentagram.

In the Aurum Solis, we draw the pentagram starting from the point associated with that element. To invoke, the logical movement consists of drawing the pentagram clockwise from this point. You can see the diagrams associated with the "activation" and "deactivation" of the elements on the following page.

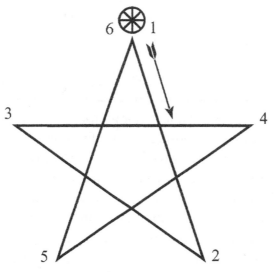

Figure 36: Pentagram of "activation/invocation."

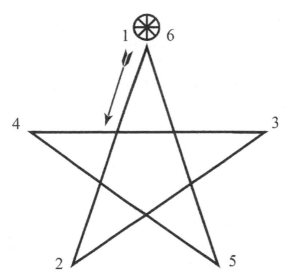

Figure 37: Pentagram of "deactivation/blessing."

The principle at work here is very simple: when we are activating the element, we take the energy of the element and we spread it all around the pentagram by moving clockwise. This is the same thing we would do if we had put our hand in a pot full of dirt to spread it all around this drawing. It is good to remember that logic exists even in the magical arts! This pentagram example is a good illustration of this fact. This movement has two specific effects that are associated, and which occur at the same time on the invisible level: one of the five elements is selected and activated.

If we watch what happens on the astral level, we will see two steps occurring. At the beginning, the power of the five elements is present directly in front of us as radiant vibrations. Then, when we begin to draw the pentagram according to the directions provided by the Aurum Solis, a precise energy is selected in that area of the drawing. As we draw the pentagram clockwise from that point, this specific energy is intensified and activated. Consequently, the four other elements are set aside momentarily. When the work with the element is done, we reverse the process. From the point of the specified element we draw the pentagram counterclockwise. As we do this, we are deactivating that element, and the other elements will return to a balanced state.

The ritual of the pentagram is commonly associated with sacred names that are invoked as we draw the pentagram. In this case the result is different than simply drawing the pentagram without saying any names. I would say a ritual without invocations is the most neutral kind of ritual we can perform. When we choose the sacred names we will be using, we add another power, which could be good, but that power is connected to a specific egregore. It is important to keep that in mind.

Some versions use Hebrew names, others use Enochian names, Greek names, Latin names, etc. As I have just said, undoubtedly the results will vary, depending upon our choice. Even more importantly, it is paramount that the sacred name we chose be the right one, therefore we must consider the element and the direction. If we look at the energy while we are drawing a pentagram that is associated with a sacred name, we will notice a difference during the intensification of the power of the element. If the name is correct, we will see and feel a power coming from the direction we are facing, which is attracted by the symbol we are drawing. Depending on our level of mastery, the power of this name may or may not have any specific shape. In the first case, the shape is generally ovoid and it stands just behind the pentagram, shining at two thirds of the height of the ovoid. This presence will keep the pentagram more active and present throughout the entire ritual. If the name used is not accurately associated with the element, the energy selected by the pentagram and the presence we have invoked will be inadequate. The energy that is intensified will be disturbed and unbalanced.

As you now understand, the direction we use for drawing the pentagrams is essential. This is what is generally called "invocation" and "banishment." As I explained before, the old idea is that any clockwise rotation or circumambulation is "activation" and the contrary "banishment." As you read in a previous chapter of this book, nature and our body are neither good nor evil. We never have to banish any of the five elements that are a part of our physical and occult structure. We have nothing to exorcize. The goal of a Theurgist is to purify, just as we would wash a cloth that has become dirty through use. This is not evil, but sometimes things we use get dirty. There is a real moral and theological difference here. We have to hold onto what is ours and balance all our different physical and energetic bodies. Consequently, this ritual will help us to ascend spiritually. So we have to remember that drawing a pentagram in the same direction that the sun moves across the sky activates, and working against the movement of the sun deactivates. When we invoke a sacred presence while we draw the pentagram, we can use the equivalent phrases of "pentagram of invocation" or a "pentagram of blessing."

The pentagram will help us to balance our inner self. If our personality has too much of the air element in it, we may experience a conscious or unconscious lack of reality in our surroundings; therefore we have two choices: 1) to intensify the element of earth with the use of a pentagram of "activation/invocation"; or 2) to reduce the quantity of air by the use of a pentagram of "deactivation/blessing."

It is also interesting to ask ourselves how we can know whether we have to intensify or reduce the quantity of the element present around us. Several different methods may be used.

The first and most spontaneous method is to attentively examine ourselves in order to evaluate the state of our psychological and physiological being. Of course, it is difficult to get a clear view of ourselves but this is essential. It is a step that is required by every serious initiatic Order.

The second method is the use of our natal chart (or our annual chart) to learn the elements that are present in excess, or those that are lacking. Using astrology will give us good information about which elements we have to increase or reduce. The next step is to find the right moment to perform the ritual. Below I have provided a figure which summarizes the wheel of the year according the Aurum Solis Tradition. You can use the correspondences between the signs and the elements for planning your ritual. Using this table you can easily check the moment of the year that is propitious for working with an element.

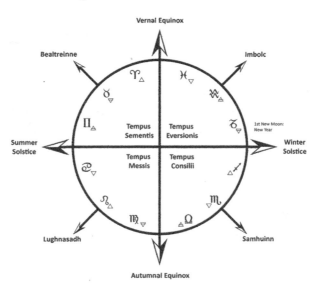

Figure 38: The wheel of the year according to the Aurum Solis Tradition.
Each year the calendar is updated in real time
and provided on the Aurum Solis website.

The number of rituals to perform depends upon the quantity of work needed, when you evaluate the level of your imbalance. Usually the sequences of ritual work involve sets of seven, fourteen, or twenty-eight days. The rituals are performed daily.

If you don't know which element you have to work on, or if you just want to balance the different elements in your being, you will have to perform four series of the "pentagram of invocation," one for each element.

It is good to associate the lunar cycle with these rituals. To do so, we would perform the "deactivation/blessing" during the waxing moon and the "activation/invocation" during the waning moon.

As you can see, at this juncture I am not referring to the uppermost point of the pentagram (Aether-Spirit). In an excerpt of the *Corpus Hermeticum*, the Aether is described as the final step, the moment of the invocation of the divine powers (inward or outward to our psyche). It would be irrational to "banish" these powers instead of welcoming them with gratitude. This is another reason to use the most appropriate words "invocation" and "blessing" when we are working at this level. This pentagram (for the Aether) can be used at any time of the year, because this "element" is above the four levels of the elements linked to the zodiacal signs. It will be used to invoke the upper powers in our aura in order to help us in the process of getting balanced. In this precise case it is useful to only use the "activation pentagram" (beginning by the uppermost point and moving clockwise), without using the "deactivation pentagram" thereafter. This is the case when we are increasing the positive and supernal powers in our aura.

We can find different writings about the use of the pentagram to challenge psychic attacks, dissolve obsessions, or reject negative presences in our aura. I think it is better in these cases to use the power linked to precise divinities (Mars in these situations) and a planetary ritual. Nevertheless, if you have already used the pentagram ritual, you can also use it to solve such situations. In order to do that, it is good to use the following principles:

- Look for the elemental nature of what you plan to eliminate (the character that is associated with Earth, Water, Air, or Fire);

- Draw a circle on the floor (the circle can be drawn on the floor or you can use a cord to delimit the circle—the diameter will be somewhere between 1.5 and 2 feet);

- At the center of this circle visualize the presence of what you want to eliminate (see the examples above);

- Draw an "activation-pentagram" of Spirit in the four directions around this circle (east, south, west, and north) visualizing an increase of celestial light illuminating the presence you want to eliminate, which is still at the center of this circle;

- Draw a "deactivation pentagram" of the nature of the element you are banishing in the four directions of the circle, as follows: north, west, south, and east. At the same time, visualize the elimination (dematerialization) of this presence from the center of the circle;

- Open the circle;

- Draw a "pentagram of invocation" of the Spirit in the four directions around you, facing each one of the directions in the following sequence: east, south, west, and north. At the same time, visualize an increase of light in your own aura. The color of the light is not important, but if you want to use a specific color, choose a golden light.

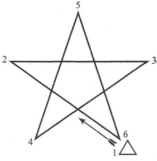

Figure 39: Activation of Fire.

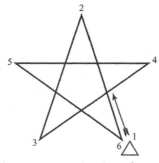

Figure 40: Deactivation of Fire.

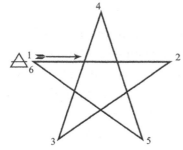

Figure 41: Activation of Air.

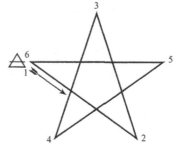

Figure 42: Deactivation of Air.

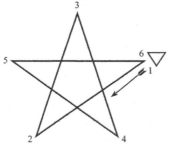

Figure 43: Activation of Water.

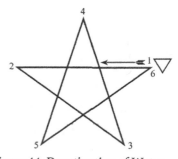

Figure 44: Deactivation of Water.

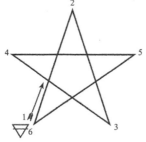

Figure 45: Activation of Earth.

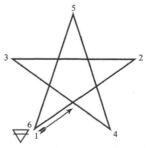

Figure 46: Deactivation of Earth.

Ritual of the Pentalpha (Balancing the Four Elements)

This ritual can be used to balance the four elements in your aura. In order to be consistent with the Hermetic tradition, the vibrations are provided in Greek. In this way, the divine powers you have welcomed will be associated with our origins.

Place a candle (sacred fire) on your altar. Light the candle.

Facing east, perform the calyx as indicated below.

CALYX

1. You are standing; your arms are at your sides.

2. Extend your arms in front of you, raised to approximately 70° above the horizontal plane, palms up (supine). Maintain this position, breathe deeply, and direct your aspiration to the highest, most divine level you can think of. Exhale and (after few seconds) inhale once more, simultaneously visualizing the descent of the spiritual light above the top of your head.

   Holding this position, vibrate: Ὁ θεός *(HO theós)*

3. Lower your arms and cross them on your chest, right over left. Visualize the light descending in the center of your chest, under the cross of your arms. Visualize this light creating a shining and radiant golden sphere.

   Holding this position, once more, vibrate: Ὁ νοῦς *(HO noûs)*

4. Holding this position, once more, vibrate: Ἡ ψυχή *(HĒ psyché)*

5. Visualize the rays of this inner sun shining from this sphere in your aura.

   Then, vibrate: Τὸ ὄχημα *(Tò óchēma)*

6. Visualize your physical body full of this golden light and vibrate: Τὸ σῶμα *(Tò sôma)*

7. Extend your arms in front of you, raising them, palms up (supine). Your arms should be wide open and your eyes should be lifted to the heavens. Maintaining this position, now say:

Πάντα δὲ ταῦτα διὰ τοῦαἰῶνος [49] (Pànta dè taûta dià toû aiônos).

8. Stand, with your arms hanging naturally at your sides.

THE POWERS

Turn your palms down and lower your arms. Point the fingers forward so that your palms are level with your hips and parallel to the floor. Vibrate the following sentence:

Εἰμὶ ὁ παῖς τῆς Γῆς καὶ τοῦ ἀστερίου Οὐρανοῦ.[50] (Eimì ho paîs tês Gês kaì toû asteríou Ouranoû.)

Continue, saying:

Isis said to her son Horus:
    All things in this world are shaped by words and actions; the source of everything is in the ideal world, which emanates to us, through the principles of order and measure, all of manifest reality. Everything in existence came from above, and everything in existence will rise, and then come down once again.

Pause

May the four elements that comprise our physical being be balanced by the ritual I perform!

Still facing east, extend your right arm in front of you, pointing forward with your forefinger, and say:

I now invoke the power of Air!

---

49. Translation: "And all these things exist for Eternity."
50. Translation: "I am the child (as son) of the earth and of the starry heaven."

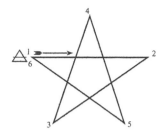

Figure 47: Activation of Air.

Trace the pentagram of the Air clockwise according to the directions provided in Figure 47.

Pronounce the sacred name ὁ Ἀήρ (ho Aḗr)[51] while drawing the presigillum[52] at the center of the pentagram from left to right.

Figure 48: Presigillum of Air.

Cross your arms on your chest, left over right. Hold this position and say:

May you manifest your presence in the various bodies of which I am comprised.

Lower your arms, allowing them to hang naturally at your sides. Remaining in the same place, turn to your right and face south.

Still facing this direction, extend your right arm in front of you, pointing forward with your forefinger, and say:

I now invoke the power of Fire!

---

51. According to the *Corpus Hermeticum*, the elements are considered as real spiritual powers and they are used as such in Theurgy.
52. See Glossary for the definition of a presigillum.

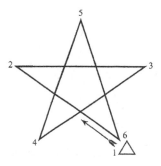

Figure 49: Activation of Fire.

Trace the pentagram of Fire according to the directions provided in the representation in Figure 49. Draw this figure clockwise.

Pronounce the sacred name τò Πῦρ (tò Pŷr) while drawing the presigillum at the center of the pentagram from left to right.

Figure 50: Presigillum of Fire.

Cross your arms on your chest, left over right. Hold this position and say:

May you manifest your presence in the various bodies of which I am comprised.

Lower your arms, allowing them to hang naturally at your sides. Remaining in the same place, turn right and face west.

Still facing this direction, extend your right arm in front of you, pointing forward with your forefinger, and say:

I now invoke the power of Water!

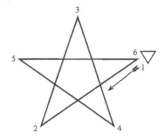

Figure 51: Activation of Water.

Trace the pentagram of Water according to the directions provided in Figure 51. Draw this figure clockwise.

Pronounce the sacred name τὸ Ὕδωρ (tò Hýdōr) while drawing the presigillum at the center of the pentagram from top to bottom.

Figure 52: Presigillum of Water.

Cross your arms on your chest, left over right. Hold this position and say:

May you manifest your presence in the various bodies of which I am comprised.

Lower your arms, allowing them to hang naturally at your sides.

Remaining in the same place, turn right and face North.

Still facing this direction, extend your right arm in front of you, pointing forward with your forefinger, and say:

I now invoke the power of Earth!

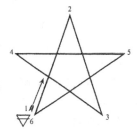

Figure 53: Activation of Earth.

Trace the pentagram of Earth according to the directions provided in Figure 53. Draw this figure clockwise.

Pronounce the sacred name ἡ Γῆ (hē Gê) while drawing the presigillum at the center of the pentagram from left to right.

Figure 54: Presigillum of Earth.

Cross your arms on your chest, left over right. Hold this position and say:

May you manifest your presence in the various bodies of which I am comprised.

Lower your arms, allowing them to hang naturally at your sides. Remaining in the same place, turn right and face east.

Cross your arms on your chest, left over right. Hold this position and say:

May the whole world hear the words of one who, in order and balance, has crossed Fire, Air, Water, and Earth, and who now stands at the center of the Word and the Aether:

(Pronounce the following invocation in English or Greek)

O powers within me, Sing the One and the All. Chant in harmony with my will, All ye Powers within me! Holy Gnosis, illuminated by thee, Through thee I sing the light of thought, I rejoice in the joy of mind. All ye Powers, chant with me!	Αἱ δυνάμεις αἱ ἐν ἐμοί ὑμνεῖτε τὸ ἕν καὶ τὸ πᾶν · Συνᾴσατε τῷ θελήματί μου πᾶσαι αἱ ἐν ἐμοὶ δυνάμεις. γνῶσις ἁγια, φωτισθεὶς ἀπὸ σοῦ, διὰ σοῦ τὸ νοητὸν φῶς ὑμνῶν χαίρω ἐν χαρᾷ νοῦ.**	Hai dynámeis hai en emoí hymneîte tò hèn kaì tò pân : Synáisate tôi thelématí mou pâsai hai en emoì dynámeis. gnôsis hagia, phōtistheìs apò soû, dià soû tò noētòn phôs hymnôn chaírō en charâi noû.
** *Corpus Hermeticum*, Book 13:18.		

Lower your arms, allowing them to hang naturally at your sides.

INVOCATION

Raise your left hand in front of you (with your elbow flexed, so that the upper arm is held forward in an almost horizontal position, slightly out from the side if necessary, the forearm and hand being raised vertically, the palm forward along the axis of your body). Bring your right hand in front of you in order to hold your hand at the height of your hips. Your hand is parallel to the ground, palm down, along the axis of your body and below your left hand.

Visualize in the east (in front of you) a concentration of subtle energy. You can clearly feel its power and the coming of this divine presence.

Maintain this position and vibrate the divine name: Οὐράνος (Oûrános).

Figure 55: Ouranos.

Maintaining the same position of your arms, turn right and face south.

Visualize in front of you a concentration of subtle energy. You can clearly feel its power and the coming of this divine presence.

Maintain this position and vibrate the divine name: Ἔρως (Érōs).

Figure 56: Eros.

Maintaining the same position of your arms, turn right and face west.

Visualize in front of you a concentration of subtle energy. You can clearly feel its power and the coming of this divine presence.

Maintain this position and vibrate the divine name: Πόντος (Póntos).

Figure 57: Pontos.

Maintaining the same position of your arms, turn right and face north.

Visualize in front of you a concentration of subtle energy. You can clearly feel its power and the coming of this divine presence.

Maintain this position and vibrate the divine name: Γαῖα (Gaîa).

Figure 58: Gaia.

Maintaining the same position of your arms, turn right and face east.

Relax your arms for a few moments.

Raise your arms in front of you, palms up (toward the heavens) and, maintaining this position, declaim:

May Beauty, Truth, and Righteousness be manifested in me!
    May Order be established over chaos!
    May Harmony express itself in me and in all aspects of my life!

Lower your arms so they hang relaxed at your sides.

So mote it be!

You may now be seated. You may now write some notes about the ritual, your feelings, and thoughts. You may also meditate for a while.

When you are finished, stand up and perform the calyx in the same way you did at the beginning of the ritual.

Extinguish the candle.

The Planetary Days Unveiled
The Lost History of Planetary Days and Hours
PRINCIPLES AND CALCULATIONS

Anyone who is interested in the Western tradition and its magical heritage will know sooner or later about the existence of planetary days and planetary hours. This concept is very ancient and it is essential from a symbolic and Theurgic perspective.

The principles of these planetary correspondences are simple and easy to explain.

The first principle is the association between the days of the week and the planets. Even today, in many Western countries, the name of the day itself marks this ancient connection. Aurum Solis has written about that in different books published by Llewellyn Publications (see bibliography) and I offer a general presentation about this topic in *The Divine Arcana of the Aurum Solis*. To quote: "The system was adopted by the Romans in the first century BCE. Like the Greeks, they named the five planets after their own Gods: Mars, Mercury, Jove (Jupiter), Venus, and Saturn. The days of the week in Latin were: Dies Solis (Sunday), Dies Lunae (Monday), Dies Martis (Tuesday), Dies Mercurii (Wednesday), Dies Jovis (Thursday), Dies Veneris (Friday) and Dies Saturni (Saturday). In the Germanic languages, roughly similar Germanic Gods were later substituted for the Roman ones, namely Tiu (Twia) for Mars, Woden for Mercury, Thor for Jupiter, and Freya (Fria) for Venus. Only Saturn was retained from the Roman pantheon. When the Germanic Gods were introduced, the symbolic link with the planets was broken, since the Germanic languages did not name the planets after their Gods. The English words Tuesday, Wednesday, Thursday, and Friday have lost their original relationship with the planets Mars, Mercury, Jupiter, and Venus, something which did not happen with Roman languages such as French, Italian, and Spanish. On the other hand, in English the word Sunday does have a link to the sun, while the association has been lost in French, Italian, and Spanish."

To summarize, below I have provided you with the associations among the days of the week, the divinities, and the planets.

DAYS	PLANETS	SYMBOLS	GREEK DIVINITIES
Saturday	Saturn	♄	Kronos
Sunday	Sun	☉	Helios
Monday	Moon	☽	Selene
Tuesday	Mars	♂	Ares
Wednesday	Mercury	☿	Hermes
Thursday	Jupiter	♃	Zeus
Friday	Venus	♀	Aphrodite

The second principle is the association between the hours of the day and the planets. In this system, which has been part of the Theurgic teachings from the earliest time of the Western tradition, the day is divided into twenty-four parts (hours). Twelve hours are associated with the first twelve hours of the day, and the remaining twelve are associated with the night. The first hour of the day is the same as the planet of the day itself. For example the first planetary hour of Sunday is associated with the Sun, the first hour of Monday with the Moon, and so on. As you will see in the following table, the seven days of the week form a contiguous arrangement, which works like a circle. The last hour of Saturday night (the hour of Mars) precedes the first hour of Sunday (the hour of the sun), the last hour of Sunday night (the hour of Saturn) precedes the first hour of Monday (the hour of the Moon), and so on. This sequence was chosen according to the distance of the planets from Earth.

		Saturday	Sunday	Monday	Tuesday	Wednes-day	Thurs-day	Friday
Day Hours	1	Saturn	Sun	Moon	Mars	Mercury	Jupiter	Venus
	2	Jupiter	Venus	Saturn	Sun	Moon	Mars	Mercury
	3	Mars	Mercury	Jupiter	Venus	Saturn	Sun	Moon
	4	Sun	Moon	Mars	Mercury	Jupiter	Venus	Saturn
	5	Venus	Saturn	Sun	Moon	Mars	Mercury	Jupiter
	6	Mercury	Jupiter	Venus	Saturn	Sun	Moon	Mars
	7	Moon	Mars	Mercury	Jupiter	Venus	Saturn	Sun
	8	Saturn	Sun	Moon	Mars	Mercury	Jupiter	Venus
	9	Jupiter	Venus	Saturn	Sun	Moon	Mars	Mercury
	10	Mars	Mercury	Jupiter	Venus	Saturn	Sun	Moon
	11	Sun	Moon	Mars	Mercury	Jupiter	Venus	Saturn
	12	Venus	Saturn	Sun	Moon	Mars	Mercury	Jupiter
Night hours	1	Mercury	Jupiter	Venus	Saturn	Sun	Moon	Mars
	2	Moon	Mars	Mercury	Jupiter	Venus	Saturn	Sun
	3	Saturn	Sun	Moon	Mars	Mercury	Jupiter	Venus
	4	Jupiter	Venus	Saturn	Sun	Moon	Mars	Mercury
	5	Mars	Mercury	Jupiter	Venus	Saturn	Sun	Moon
	6	Sun	Moon	Mars	Mercury	Jupiter	Venus	Saturn
	7	Venus	Saturn	Sun	Moon	Mars	Mercury	Jupiter
	8	Mercury	Jupiter	Venus	Saturn	Sun	Moon	Mars
	9	Moon	Mars	Mercury	Jupiter	Venus	Saturn	Sun
	10	Saturn	Sun	Moon	Mars	Mercury	Jupiter	Venus
	11	Jupiter	Venus	Saturn	Sun	Moon	Mars	Mercury
	12	Mars	Mercury	Jupiter	Venus	Saturn	Sun	Moon

Don't be fooled by the above table. The two divisions of twelve-hour intervals are not identical. In fact, the duration of each hour varies every day. The reason is simple to understand. When I use the expression of "day hours" and "night hours," I am talking about the real duration of the day between sunrise and sunset. It is the same for the night hours that are between sunset and sunrise. In order to know the real duration of each planetary hour and when it begins, you must know the precise, current time of sunrise at your location. This information can easily be found on the Internet; you can go to any weather website to get this information.

Let us illustrate this with an example.[53] Let us assume that you live in Los Angeles (USA), and you want to perform a ritual on August 1, 2010. If you go to a website such as http://www.sunrisesunset.com/usa/ (or if you can find applications for your cell phone or tablet) you will find that the exact time of sunrise at your place is 6:04 a.m. The time for sunset is 7:55 p.m. A simple calculation will reveal that the duration of the day is 13h 51min (831 minutes). Now if you divide this number by twelve, you will find that, on this specific day, each hour of the day had a duration of 1 hour and 09 minutes. Consequently, the first planetary hour of this day (Sunday, August 1), which is the hour of the sun, begins at 6:04 a.m., and the second planetary hour (which is the hour of the moon) begins 1h 09 min later at 7:13 a.m., and so on. The process is the same for the calculation of the night hours. In this case you have to calculate the duration of the night (between sunrise and sunset) and proceed in the same way.

Now that you understand the theory of this process, which enables you to do these calculations manually, you can simply use the Internet to easily calculate these planetary hours with much less effort. You will find web addresses for convenient automatic calculators on the Aurum Solis website.

THE FORGOTTEN PRINCIPLES

The previous explanations are not original. This is what is generally taught to anyone who wanted to learn the Western tradition and be able to perform planetary rituals. But even if these explanations seem clear and obvious, unfortunately they are still incomplete. The hidden principles you are about to learn have been used by a very few initiates (such as those who are initiates of Aurum Solis). They could radically change the way you use the planetary powers.

---

53. You will find more details about the calculations related to this example in the
   Appendix.

Let's begin by asking a simple question: How do we know that Sunday is Sunday? Are we just looking at our calendar, or are we using a more sophisticated system to find out the real essence of the day?

As a matter of fact, nothing can justify assuming that the day we find on a calendar is really associated with a specific planet. If our calendar says that today is "Tuesday" we can be sure that Tuesday is associated with Mars, but we have no idea if "Tuesday" is really "Tuesday." The days printed on our calendar are totally arbitrary and therefore cannot be used to calculate our planetary days and planetary hours. Consequently, even if the first two principles are traditional and correct, the calculations we are using have absolutely no basis in fact.

I have previously explained the interrelations between astrology, Theurgy, and magick. A real Theurgic work and initiatic progression is always closely associated with astrology. The divine and invisible powers we are using in Theurgy are real. They are not simple creations of our mind. They are not merely symbols. When we plan to use a specific planetary day, we don't want to use a pure symbol that has no basis in reality. We want to use a real planetary power and consequently we need to know whether or not the day we are about to choose is the correct one. Right now there is no way for us to know, so we have no guarantee that we are performing our ritual of Mars on the real day of Mars. We are just using an arbitrary day called Tuesday on our calendar. This is most certainly not the way a real Theurgic tradition must teach and work. As you can imagine, the result of performing a ritual of Mars on the wrong day will have very different results than hoped for.

Therefore, in order to perform effective rituals, it is essential that you learn how you can find the "real days" of the week. Fortunately, astrology was not totally destroyed by the opponents of the Theurgic tradition, and some useful ancient books survived. These elements, when associated with the understanding of the initiates, were enough to keep this heritage intact. The time has come to give you the keys that will enable you to access the real powers of the planets.

Figure 59: The Roman calendar of 354, showing the first two days of the week, beginning with Saturday (Saturn). (Bibliothèque Ausonius-Bordeaux)

Figure 60: Small bronze boat from the Roman Epoch, discovered in France, shows the traditional sequence of the days, beginning with Kronos (on the right of the boat).

The seven days of the week were named in Alexandria during the Ptolemaic period (the second century BCE). It is clear that this planetary week is a creation of the astrologers who were living in Alexandria. Before this time, a sequential division of seven days was known and used, but was very often simply numbered. In his books, the Roman historian Cassius Dio provided this information along with the correspondences between the days of the week and the divinities I previously indicated. It is in his writings that we first learn the first hour of the day reveals the planetary identity of the day itself. If Sunday begins with the hour of the Sun, then, as a consequence, Sunday is associated with the Sun. In order to obtain perfect correlations between the days and hours, we would need to have seven days of twenty-four hours. Now you must remember that the sequence of the planets according to the masters of this tradition is ascending: Moon, Mercury, Venus, Sun, Mars, Jupiter, and Saturn. It has been clear from ancient to modern times what the order of the planets is, but the first part of the key is to know what day is actually the first day of the week.

Such a question might seem trivial to you. Whether you say that the week begins on Sunday or Monday doesn't seem to have any consequences for the calculation of the planetary hours, but this is not the case. Cassius Dio clearly states that the first day of the week is Saturn, which is followed by the Sun, and so on.

A Roman manuscript, which was discovered in 1620, is an astrological almanac that was written in 354 CE. This text provides us with essential keys for the understanding of these principles. This Roman manuscript also says that the first day of the week is Saturday. Several ancient artifacts (See the representations in Figures 59, 60, and 61) agree with this sequence. It was only toward the end of the fourth century that the beginning of the planetary week was modified so that Sunday was assigned as the first day. It seems obvious that this modification was the result of the influence of Christianity and Mithraism, both using the Sun as their central symbol. Christianity attempted to supplant all the major religions that were present in the Western Empire. One of the best solutions they often used was to recycle major symbols from Pagan religions and classical philosophy in their own theology, sometimes twisting essential parts of the symbol's meanings. In this case, the purpose was twofold: 1) to appropriate the major Mythraic symbol of the Sun and combine it with the representation of Christ; 2) to modify the structure of the Pagan calendar by using the figure of Christ, ruler of the universal order of the cosmos. As you can see, the Roman manuscript used the traditional Pagan sequence, with the first day as *Dies Saturni*.

*Figure 61: Roman octagonal golden bracelet found in Syria
with the divinities of the week in their original sequence.*

TYXH TYCHĒ	APHC ARĒS
KPONOC KRONOS	EPMHC ERMĒS
HΛIOC ĒLIOS	ZEYC ZEUS
CEΛHNH SELĒNĒ	AΦPOΔITH APHRODITĒ

*Figure 62: Sequence of the divinities on the Syrian bracelet.
As you can see, the first divinity is Tyche (fate-luck).*

Now I must explain why knowing the first day is paramount. The creation of this planetary sequence was accomplished by astrologers, essentially for use in astrology and rituals. Consequently, this sequence has to be related to real astrological phenomena and cannot be totally arbitrary, as it is today. If we refer to the ancient writings, we will see that there is a correspondence between the first day of the week and the New Moon. The consequence of this correspondence is totally astonishing when we think about its ramifications. Theurgy, like astrology, uses a lunisolar calendar. The moon and the sun are the primary references we need to use in our calculation and rituals. When we know that the first day of the week is Saturday, and that the beginning of a cycle is the New Moon, we can determinate the exact planetary days without any arbitrariness. The day of the New Moon is the day of Saturn (Saturday), the day following the New Moon is the day of the Sun (Sunday), and so on. At the end of the week, a second week will continue in the same way. At the next New Moon we will have to reset our calculation in order to once again have Saturn (Saturday) as the first day of the week. If there are days remaining between the end of the fourth week (of the moon) and the next New Moon, they are considered to be "intermediate days" without planetary attributions. In this case, the Theurgist associates these days with the eighth sphere, which is symbolized by the Aether. You can see an example for the months of August and September 2011 in Figure 63.

Now you understand why the first day of the astrological week (Saturn–Saturday) is found on a different, common, and arbitrary day on our calendar. Don't be embarrassed. Now you know that the real planetary days must be calculated using the lunar calendar and not taken directly from a common calendar.

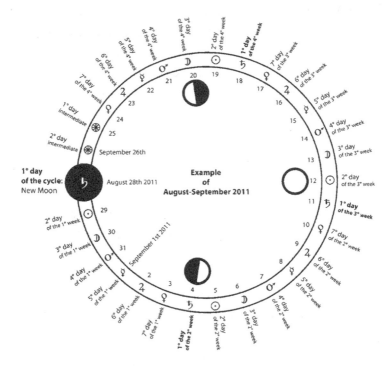

Figure 63: The planetary days and the cycle of the Moon.

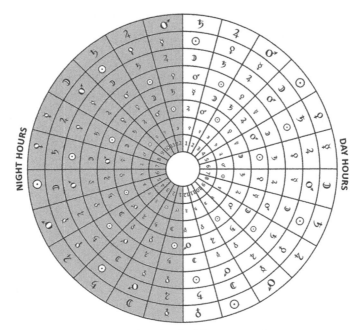

Figure 64: The wheel of the magical hours.

Another important element for precise calculations is to know when the day actually begins. For practical reasons, a consensus has arisen that midnight is the end of the day, with the next second after midnight defining the beginning of a new day. There was no such consensus in ancient times, when there were many different ways of marking the beginning of a day. For the Babylonians the day began at sunrise. You will find contradictory information regarding the determination of the beginning of the day in ancient Egypt. It seems that the confusion began with the Roman historian Marcus Terentius Varro, who associated the Egyptian days with the Roman days without any verification. The most reliable sources show that the Egyptians, like the Babylonians, considered sunrise to be the beginning of the day. The most important rituals in ancient Egypt were performed during the first hour of the day. The Roman calendar of 354 CE presents what we might call the "astrological day" as beginning at sunset. It was the same for the Hebrews and the Athenians. At the same time, the Romans used a civil day, which began at midnight.

Following the Babylonian and Egyptian tradition, Theurgists use sunrise as the beginning of the day. Therefore, after finding the correct day after the New Moon, we can use the chart previously provided. Another way to present this perfect organization of the astrological day is the circular diagram you will find in Figure 65.

Knowing these principles and the best way to use them, we are now able to calculate the correct beginning of the astrological week, determine the planetary days, and consequently we are able to use the planetary hours.

Figure 65: The sequence of the seven planets
according to the most famous ancient Greek astronomers (circle)
and the seven days of the week (heptagram).

The Ritual of the Seven Gates

Principles

The second important principle of the Hermetic hierarchy has to do with the set of planets associated with the seven planetary divinities.

The ritual of the seven gates is rooted in the practice of harmonization, which will enable us to progressively create an inner contact with the divine powers that rule each day. More than this, this set of rituals helps us to focus on the qualities of each sphere in a progressive and balanced way. These rituals are a very good example of a Theurgic practice that is both simple and very effective. You will be surprised by the power of such well-balanced rituals. Repeating these rituals is the only way to get more deeply into this living connection you are about to create.

Preliminaries

TIME

These rituals can be performed at any time of year. As far as possible, perform the rituals at the same time each day. It is better to associate the days with their planets, using the rules I have previously described.

CLOTHING

Wear a white robe with nothing underneath. (If you don't have a robe, you may wear loose-fitting, comfortable clothing that won't restrict your movements.)

BOMOS (ALTAR)

Cover the bomos with a white linen fabric. On the bomos, place the equipment given in the diagram and list below.

ORIENTATION

This rite must be carried out facing the west (unless we give you specific directions otherwise). This position is explained by the fact that the major statue in an ancient temple was placed in the west and had to face the rising sun, when the first rays of the sun entered through the open entrance door that stood in the east.

ELEMENTS ON THE BOMOS

West side of the room		
	1	
	2	
3a-b		4a-b
5	6	7

1. Statue or representation of the divinity. (If you work with the Aurum Solis Tarot, place the Major Arcana of the divinity just in front of the statue.)
2. Sacred fire (candle without any specific color).

3. a) A cup filled with a beverage; b) Empty cup to pour the libation into.

4. a) Plate with food; b) Empty plate to put the offerings on.

5. Olive oil (optionally, you may use the incense of the planets).

6. Censer and incense.

7. Bell (optional).

OFFERINGS

The different offerings are indicated in each ritual. If, for any reason, you cannot use real offerings, you can visualize them and make the real offering later when you have it.

BATTERY

Some rituals call for batteries. A battery is a specified series of knocks, sounded either with the knuckles on a hard surface such as the bomos, a small bell, or any other instrument with which it is possible to make a series of distinct sounds.

The number of knocks in a battery can be represented as follows: "Battery: 3-6-1." That means you should sound three consecutive knocks followed by a moment of silence, then six consecutive knocks followed by another moment of silence, followed by another knock.

WAND POSTURE

In this posture you will stand with your arms hanging naturally at your sides. Your feet are close together, but not in contact.

GENERAL INDICATIONS

The first ritual is dedicated to Saturn. As you will see, several parts of the ritual (parts 1 to 5) are the same for the other planets, whereas others are specific to the Sun. The parts that are used in the other ritual are not written out again for each subsequent ritual. You will have to come back to the first ritual provided (for Helios) to use these parts. I will remind you of this detail in the ritual itself.

This ritual is comprised of eight parts, but you may consider parts 2, 3, and 4 to be optional. You are free to decide if you want to use them daily, or on the days you prefer to choose, such as your birthday, the phases of the moon, etc.

Figure 66: Saturn—Kronos.

Sacred Ritual of Saturn—Kronos

Astrology: Day of Saturn (Saturday as determined from the New Moon of the month).

Offerings (beverage): alcoholic—cognac, brandy, chocolate stout beer, or Trappist beer; non-alcoholic—black coffee or spring water.

Offerings (food): hazelnut or dark chocolate.

1. Opening

Stand facing west. Light the flame of the sacred fire.

Bell: If you have a bell, strike it a few times.

Perform the gesture of the calyx as indicated in the Ritual of the Pentalpha.

Pause for a few moments, then make the double Ave gesture (the arms are raised with the elbows flexed, so that the upper arms are held forward in an almost horizontal position, slightly out from the sides if necessary, the forearms and hands being raised vertically, the palms forward).

Holding this position declaim:

Hearken O Powerful divinities as I call to you!
    O Luminous Beings, may this ritual be in perfect harmony with your will.

Lower your arms, letting them hang naturally at your sides.

2. The Elements

Bell: If you have a bell, strike it a few times.

Visualize your aura becoming more and more luminous.

Extend your arms in front of you in order to hold your hands at the height of your hips. Your hands are parallel to the ground, palms down. Look to the ground and increase your awareness of the presence of the earth on which you stand. Extend this feeling to the whole planet on which you stand. Hold this position while you invoke Gaia with the declamation of her hymn.

Ô Gaia, most honored Goddess. Mother of all blessed immortals and of all of mortal beings, please hear my hymn.
    We feel you in the heart of everything that is, and we feel the pulse of your life when our feet touch your skin, the earth on which we walk and stand.
    Ô Gaia, you who nourish all life, you cause everything living to be born, to grow into maturity, then to blossom and fade; we ask you to come forward in your luxurious attire, spreading your flowers everywhere to sweeten the air and brighten the day with ten thousand wondrous colors.

We envision you as a young woman who exhales beauty with her every breath. To us, you are the source of everything in the cosmos.

You are eternal. We worship you, whose rich and vibrant breath carries the scent of those perfumes that awaken our senses. Please come forth here at this very moment!

The sweet grasses, the soft rain, the gentle breezes and bright flowers, everything that surrounds us, sings to us of your presence; this is the real manifestation of your immediate contact with each of us here today.

The divine wheel of the stars rotates around us, demonstrating the cosmic ebb and flow of all that is.

Ô Gaia, may you ensure that we receive your blessings in each season, the caresses of your body; may all the gifts that you possess be bestowed generously on each and every one of us.

Still facing this direction, extend your right arm in front of you, pointing forward with your forefinger, and say:

I now invoke the power of Water!

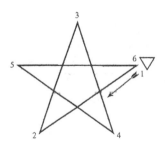

Figure 67: Activation of Water.

Trace the pentagram of Water according to the directions provided in the diagram above. Draw this figure clockwise.

Pronounce the sacred name τὸ Ὕδωρ (tò Hýdōr) while drawing the presigillum at the center of the pentagram from top to bottom.

Figure 68: Presigillum of Water.

Cross your arms on your chest, left over right. Hold this position and say:

> May you manifest your presence in the various bodies of which I am comprised.

Lower your arms, allowing them to hang naturally at your sides. Remaining in the same place, turn right to face north.

Still facing this direction, extend your right arm in front of you, pointing forward with your forefinger, and say:

> I now invoke the power of Earth!

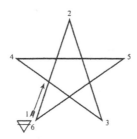

Figure 69: Activation of Earth.

Trace the pentagram of Earth according to the directions provided in the diagram above. Draw this figure clockwise.

Figure 70: Presigillum of Earth.

Pronounce the sacred name ἡ Γῆ (hē Gê) while drawing the presigillum at the center of the pentagram from left to right.

Cross your arms on your chest, left over right. Hold this position and say:

> May you manifest your presence in the various bodies of which
> I am comprised.

Lower your arms, allowing them to hang naturally at your sides.
Remaining in the same place, turn right and face east.
Still facing this direction, extend your right arm in front of you, pointing forward with your forefinger, and say:

> I now invoke the power of Air!

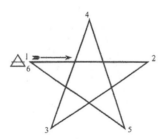

Figure 71: Activation of Air.

Trace the pentagram of Air clockwise according to the directions provided in the diagram above.

Figure 72: Presigillum of Air.

Pronounce the sacred name ὁ Ἀήρ (ho Aḗr) while drawing the presigillum at the center of the pentagram from left to right.

Cross your arms on your chest, left over right. Hold this position and say:

> May you manifest your presence in the various bodies of which I am comprised.

Lower your arms, allowing them to hang naturally at your sides. Remaining in the same place, turn right and face south.

Still facing this direction, extend your right arm in front of you, pointing forward with your forefinger, and say:

> I now invoke the power of Fire!

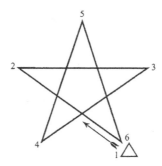

Figure 73: Activation of Fire.

Trace the pentagram of Fire according to the directions provided in the diagram above. Draw this figure clockwise.

Figure 74: Presigillum of Fire.

Pronounce the sacred name τὸ Πῦρ (tò Pŷr) while drawing the pre-sigillum at the center of the pentagram from left to right.

Cross your arms on your chest, left over right. Hold this position and say:

May you manifest your presence in the various bodies of which I am comprised.

Lower your arms, allowing them to hang naturally at your sides.
Turn to your right and face west.
Bell: If you have a bell, strike it a few times.

3. Invocation

Raise your left hand in front of you (with the elbow flexed, so that the upper arm is held forward in an almost horizontal position, slightly out from the sides if necessary, the forearm and hand being raised vertically, the palm forward along the axis of your body). Bring your right hand in front of you in order to hold your hand at the height of your hips. Your hand is parallel to the ground, palm down, on the axis of your body and below your left hand.

Close your eyes during this sequence.
Breathe deeply and regularly.

Maintaining the same position of your arms, turn right and face west.

Visualize in front of you a concentration of subtle energy. You can clearly feel its power and the arrival of this divine presence.

Maintain this position and vibrate the divine name: Πόντος (Póntos).

Continue to breathe deeply and regularly.

Maintaining the same position of your arms, turn right and face north.

Visualize in front of you a concentration of subtle energy. You can clearly feel its power and the arrival of this divine presence.

Maintain this position and vibrate the divine name: Γαῖα (Gaîa).

Continue to breathe deeply and regularly.

Maintaining the same position of your arms, turn right and face east.

Visualize in front of you a concentration of subtle energy. You can clearly feel its power and the arrival of this divine presence.

Maintain this position and vibrate the divine name: Οὐράνος (Oûrános).

Continue to breathe deeply and regularly.

Maintaining the same position of your arms, turn right and face south.

Visualize in front of you a concentration of subtle energy. You can clearly feel its power and the arrival of this divine presence.

Maintain this position and vibrate the divine name: Ἔρως (Érōs).

Continue to breathe deeply and regularly.

Maintaining the same position of your arms, turn right and face west.

Lower your arms, so they hang naturally at your sides.

Bell: If you have a bell, strike it a few times.

4. Dedication

Pause for a few moments, then make the double-gesture Ave and declaim:

From the portal of Earth to the portal of Fire,
From the portal of Air to the portal of Water,

May this bomos be placed under the protection of the three powers who balance the cosmos.

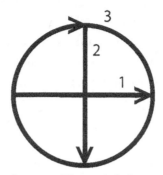

Figure 75: The encircled cross.

With the forefinger of your right hand in front of you (on a vertical plane), draw the encircled cross. You will visualize this symbol in golden light.

During the drawing of the horizontal line (left to right) you will pronounce the sacred name:

Ἡ Λευκοθέα (He Leukothéa)

During the drawing of the vertical line (above to below) you will pronounce the sacred name:

Ὁ Μελανοθεός (Ho Melanotheós)

During the drawing of the circle surrounding the cross (clockwise beginning at the top) you will pronounce the sacred name:

Ὁ Ἀγαθοδαίμων (Ho Agathodaímōn)

Lower your arms, allowing them to hang naturally at your sides.

Bell: If you have a bell, strike it a few times.

5. Invocation of the Divine Powers

Turn your thoughts toward the Divine Powers and light your incense.

While the smoke of your incense is rising, declaim the invocation to the Gods Lares:

Ô you, Lares, Gods of my fathers, you who have taken such good care of everything that concerns my home;

You who nourished me, when, as a little baby, I played in your sight, please hear my voice!

Do not blush if you are made from old wood or old stones, because you are as you were when you lived in the ancient homes of my ancestors, and it is in this form that our descendants will find you again.

Oh great Gods Lares, shield me from the pains and difficulties that might afflict me!

Bring peace and security to my home, and for all these blessings I shall offer you the hymns and offerings which most please you.

O you, the genius who protects my home, I also direct this prayer to you!

You who dwell invisibly within these walls, you, Agathodaimon who brings me all the riches of life, be praised and honored!

O you, my ancestors, to whom I owe my ability to stand here today, may your memory always be a living presence with me. May you be honored by this incense I offer in your memory!

Turn your thoughts to the upper Divine Powers and declaim:

O Mighty Divinities hear my voice as it rises up to you.

Turn your eyes toward me when I call unto you.

O Mysterious Goddesses of Fate, daughters of the blackest night, Goddesses of the earth and starry sky, accept this perfume as my offering to you this day.

Direct toward me your protection and power so that I may manifest in my life your beauty and your eternal glory.

Bell: If you have a bell, strike it a few times.

6. Invocation of the Specific Divinity
OFFERINGS

Turn your thoughts toward the divinity of the day, (in this instance, Kronos) and raise the incense toward the statue (or any other representation you have chosen for the divinity).

Visualize an intense light coming from the representation of Kronos and spreading all around the space in which you stand. Keep this visualization in mind while you declaim:

> On this particular day, I speak to you, divine Kronos, master of Saturn.
>
> O most mighty Kronos, thou most revered, thou who art awesome in exaltation, thou who yet art known, praised, and loved in the worlds of life!
>
> Those who make and create, they know thee when they hearken Inwardly to the voice of inspiration. Children and sages are drawn to thee, and in candor of spirit they praise thee: to them time is not an enemy, nor eternity a stranger. But they of the Mysteries love thee, and spiritual beings immense in power give thee all their allegiance; for to these it belongs to raise their gaze above the many-jeweled border of thy vesture and to behold the inaccessible glory of thy countenance. O dark one, O silent one, with this love and devotion do I invoke thee![54]

Contemplate the representation of Kronos while breathing deeply; return the censer to its place on the bomos, close your eyes, and create a mental representation of the divinity in front of you.

Elevate the cup toward the divinity and say:

> O divine Kronos, accept now this offering of beverage that I am presenting to you!

---

54. Melita Denning and Osborne Phillips, *Planetary Magick: Invoking and Directing the Powers of the Planets* (Woodbury, MN: Llewellyn Publications, 2011), 228–229.

For your libation, pour a small quantity of the beverage into the empty cup. Raise the cup again, saying:

May this beverage create the strong link that unites me to Kronos.

Drink part or all of the beverage, and replace the cup on the bomos. Elevate the plate toward the divinity and say:

O divine Kronos, accept now this offering of food that I am presenting to you!

For your libation, place a small quantity of food on the empty plate. Raise the plate again saying:

May this food create the strong link that unites me to Kronos.

Eat part or all of the food and replace the plate on the bomos.
(All the offerings will be put outside after the ritual. If it is not possible to put them outside, you will have to wait for one hour before throwing them in the trash.)
(If you are using the Aurum Solis Tarot, pick up the Arcana of the divinity in your hands.)
Feel more precisely the presence of the divinity in front of you and declaim his hymn while you create a strong mental link to him:

Hearken, O Kronos, son of the green Gaia and of starry Ouranos, father of the Gods, and of mortals!
   You who order the rhythm of time, you who are born, grow, and decline, hear my words!
   You who foresees everything, hear my words!
   You who resides in each and every element of the universe, hear my words!
   You who destroys and builds anew, you whose laws govern all, hear my words!

You, O Kronos, the ancestor of every living being, you the pure, the robust, the courageous, hear my words praising and invoking you!

Give heed to my call as well as to those who never forgot you, and bestow upon us, when the moment comes, a joyful and pure end.

Be seated and keep the divine presence in your mind. Breathe regularly while deeply feeling the divine power and joy flowing into all the levels of your being.

REQUEST

Stand up. (If you have the Arcana of the Aurum Solis Tarot in your hands, return it to its initial position on the bomos.)

If you want to ask something special of Kronos, put your right hand in contact with the statue (or the representation) and explain your request as precisely as you can. This request cannot be a mental declaration. You must speak it aloud, even if you speak softly. You must really speak to him. This request must begin with the words:

O Kronos, I . . . *say your name* . . . in union with the power of all your worshippers, ask you . . . *continue with your request.*

When this is done, remove your hand, keeping in mind the visualization, and pronounce his divine name: Kronos.

UNCTION

If you are using oil and a statue, place a few drops of oil on the top of your right thumb and anoint a part of the statue, declaiming:

May this perfumed oil be the visible and invisible manifestation of my love for you!

Draw the symbol of the planet on your forehead declaiming:

May this perfumed oil be the visible and invisible manifestation of the link that unites us!

Be seated so that you can meditate in silence.
Release the visualizations.
Bell: If you have a bell, strike it a few times.
Stand up.

7. Ascending the Spheres

Open your mind to the other celestial spheres below and then above you. Feel and imagine a sphere of fixed stars in deepest blue above you that is studded with twinkling golden stars. Elevate your censer with the burning incense, which honors all the divinities; declaim the "Hymn to the Gods"[55] from Proclus:

> Hear me, O Gods, you who hold the rudder of sacred wisdom. Lead us mortals back among the immortals as you light in our souls the flame of return. May the ineffable initiations of your hymns give us the power to escape the dark cave of our lives and purify ourselves.
>
> Hearken, powerful liberators!
>
> Dispel the surrounding obscurity, and grant me the power to understand the holy books; replace the darkness with a pure and holy light. Thus may I truly know the incorruptible God that I am.
>
> May a wicked spirit never keep me, overwhelmed by ills, submerged in the waters of forgetfulness and far away from the Gods and Goddesses.
>
> May my soul not be fettered in the jails of life where I am left to suffer a terrifying atonement in the icy cycles of generation. I do not want to wander anymore.
>
> O you, sovereign Gods of the radiant wisdom, hear me! Reveal to one who hastens on the Path of Return the holy

---

55. This hymn is the central prayer of the Ecclesia Ogdoadica.

ecstasies and the initiations held in the depth of your sacred words!

Replace the censer on the bomos.

Close your eyes and imagine that your body grows larger and larger until your head is among the stars. Open your arms slightly, with the palms of your hands turned upward, while you intone:

> I invoke you, the sacred flame that lives in the luminous and holy silence!
>> May beauty, truth, and goodness be manifested in me!
>> May order be established over chaos!
> By the powers that come from you, may harmony be established in my soul, my body, and in all aspects of my life!

8. Return to Your Physical Body

Turn your mind toward your physical body, which is below you.

Turn the palms of your hands toward your physical body and declaim the intention of the ritual you used earlier.

Begin with:

> May ... *state your first and last name* ... manifest fully ... *continue with your previous intention.*

Hold this position for a while, just acting as the channel of the divine powers that are flowing through your hands.

Cross your arms, left over right. Imagine that your size decreases until you return to your normal height, as you return to your physical body. Breathe peacefully. Lower your head slightly and declaim:

> May all that I have requested of Kronos in presence of the powerful Divinities be mine, now and forever!

Be silent for a few moments, then declaim:

So mote it be!

Bell: If you have a bell, strike it a few times.

You can now open your eyes, extinguish the candle, and if necessary put out the incense.

You may now be seated. Write some notes about the ritual, your feelings, and thoughts. You may also meditate for a while.

Figure 76: Sun—Helios.

Sacred Ritual of the Sun—Helios

Astrology: Day of the Sun (Sunday as determined from the New Moon of the month).

Offerings (beverage): alcoholic—white wine, champagne, harvest ale beer, seasonal beer; non alcoholic—spring water.

Offerings (food): honey or honey spread on a piece of bread.

Note: From part 1 through part 5 of the ritual, proceed as you did for the Sacred Ritual of Saturn.

6. Invocation of the Specific Divinity
OFFERINGS

Turn your thoughts toward the divinity of the day (in this instance, Helios), and raise the incense toward the statue (or any other representation you have chosen for the divinity).

Visualize an intense light coming from the representation of Helios and spreading all around the space in which you stand. Keep this visualization in mind while you declaim:

> On this particular day, I speak to you, divine King Helios, master of the Sun.
>
> Triumphant chieftain of the shining and many-colored days, O divine exemplar of heroes and princes, thou most benign in jubilation, most peaceable in sovereignty!
>
> Numberless as the rays of thy peerless crown are the noble and glorious beings who surround thee. These thou sendest forth to bestow thy royal bounties, scattered at large or as particular gifts: all precious beyond reckoning. In thy power thy radiant emissaries endow with joy of spirit, and with that perception of beauty which is life's purest gold. To thee, life-giving, all seeing, all beneficent, to thee I make this invocation.[56]

Contemplate the representation of Helios while breathing deeply; return the censer to its place on the bomos, close your eyes, and create a mental representation of the divinity in front of you.

Elevate the cup toward the divinity and say:

> O divine Helios, accept now this offering of beverage that I am presenting to you!

For your libation, pour a small quantity of the beverage into the empty cup. Raise the cup again saying:

---

56. Denning and Phillips, *Planetary Magick*, 217.

May this beverage create the strong link that unites me to King Helios.

Drink part or all of the beverage, and replace the cup on the bomos. Elevate the plate toward the divinity and say:

O divine Helios, accept now this offering of food that I am presenting to you!

For your libation, place a small quantity of food on the empty plate. Raise the plate again, saying:

May this food create the strong link that unites me to King Helios.

Eat part or all of the food and replace the plate on the bomos.
(All the offerings will be put outside after the ritual. If it is not possible to put them outside, you will have to wait for one hour before throwing them in the trash.)
(If you are using the Aurum Solis Tarot, pick up the Arcana of the divinity in your hands.)
Feel more precisely the presence of the divinity in front of you and declaim his hymn while you create a strong mental link to him:

Hearken, O blessed one, you whose eternal eye sees all.
   Titan whose golden radiance shines on Earth, celestial light,
   Self-born, untiring, sweet sight to the living,
   Hear my words!
   On the right you beget dawn, on the left, night.
   As you ride dancing horses across the heavens, you temper the seasons.
   O fiery and bright-faced charioteer, you press your course in endless whirl; guiding the pious toward the Good.
   O golden lyre leading harmoniously the cosmos!

You who commands noble deeds and nurture the seasons,
Piping lord of the universe, your course is a fiery circle of
light.

O Paian, light-bearer, giver of life and of the fruits of the
Earth, listen to my hymn!

As immortal Helios, you are pure, eternal, and the father of
time.

Circling eye of the cosmos shining forth light and beauty,
Water-loving lord of the world, ever higher paragon of
justice, your goodness reaches all.

Eye of justice, light of life driving with your screaming
whip the four-horsed chariot,

Hear my words, and grant the longed-for sweetness of life
to your initiates!

Be seated and keep the divine presence in your mind. Breathe regularly while deeply feeling the divine power and joy flowing into all the levels of your being.

Request

Stand up. (If you have the Arcana of the Aurum Solis Tarot in your hands, return it to its initial position on the bomos.)

If you want to ask something special of Helios, put your right hand in contact with the statue (or the representation) and explain your request as precisely as you can. This request cannot be a mental declaration. You must speak it aloud, even if you speak softly. You must really speak to him. This request must begin with the words:

O Helios, I... *say your name*... in union with the power of all your worshippers, ask you... *continue with your request.*

When this is done, remove your hand, keeping in mind the visualization, and pronounce his divine name: HELIOS.

Unction

If you are using oil and a statue, place a few drops of oil on the top of your right thumb and anoint a part of the statue, declaiming:

> May this perfumed oil be the visible and invisible manifestation of my love for you!

Draw the symbol of the planet on your forehead declaiming:

> May this perfumed oil be the visible and invisible manifestation of the link which unites us!

Be seated so that you can meditate in silence.
Release the visualizations.
Bell: If you have a bell, strike it a few times.
Stand up.

Note: Proceed to parts 7 and 8, as you did for the first rite of Saturn.

Figure 77: Moon—Selene.

Sacred Ritual of the Moon—Selene

Astrology: Day of the Moon (Monday as determined from the New Moon of the month).

Offerings (beverage): alcoholic—cocktail of cocoa milk and rum, wheat beer (weizen); non alcoholic—spring water.

Offerings (food): almond or leafs of laurel.

Note: From part 1 through part 5 of the ritual, proceed as you did for the Sacred Ritual of Saturn.

6. Invocation of the Specific Divinity

OFFERINGS

Turn your thoughts toward the divinity of the day (in this instance, Selene), and raise the incense toward the statue (or any other representation you have chosen for the divinity).

Visualize an intense light coming from the representation of Selene and spreading all around the space in which you stand. Keep this visualization in mind while you declaim:

On this particular day, I speak to you, divine Selene, Lady of the Moon.

Thou radiant ecstasy, manifest glory of the night!—far-riding maker of enchantment, stooping low above Earth to fulfill thy purposes!

Thou whisperest to hidden seeds in dark of earth, that they burst forth to life.

Thou criest aloud to the hearts of humankind, that they cry response to thee: the soul cries in yearning for its own greater life, in response to thee.

Ever swift thou art to guard all young beings, and to keep safe the ardent following whose hands are raised to thee. Over all these watch thy gentle and mighty ones with unsleeping eyes of light, the tall-winged and vigorous flashings forth of thy pure brilliance. To thee O nurturing, to thee most widely potent, O sovereign of threefold empire, I make my invocation.[57]

Contemplate the representation of Selene while breathing deeply; return the censer to its place on the bomos, close your eyes, and create a mental representation of the divinity in front of you.

Elevate the cup toward the divinity and say:

O divine Selene, accept now this offering of beverage that I am presenting to you!

For your libation, pour a small quantity of the beverage into the empty cup. Raise the cup again saying:

May this beverage create the strong link that unites me to Selene.

Drink part or all of the beverage, and replace the cup on the bomos. Elevate the plate toward the divinity and say:

O divine Selene, accept now this offering of food that I am presenting to you!

For your libation, place a small quantity of food on the empty plate. Raise the plate again, saying:

May this food create the strong link which unites me to Selene.

Eat part or all of the food and replace the plate on the bomos.

(All the offerings will be put outside after the ritual. If it is not possible to put them outside, you will have to wait for one hour before throwing them in the trash.)

---

57. Denning and Phillips, *Planetary Magick,* 219.

(If you are using the Aurum Solis Tarot, pick up the Arcana of the divinity in your hands.)

Feel more precisely the presence of the divinity in front of you and declaim her hymn while you create a strong mental link to her:

Hearken, O Divine Queen!
> Powerful Selene, shine forth on this place!
> You who circles the night and manifest your presence in the surrounding air, be among us!
> You, maiden of the night, torch-bearer, magnificent star, waxing and waning, male and female, mother of time,
> You, glittering silver light of the night, turn your gaze on us and our works.
> Splendid vestment of night, bestow upon us your grace and perfection.
> May your celestial course guide you toward us, O wise maiden.
> Come, you the most joyful of all, and be propitious and in three ways shine your lights on this new initiate.

Be seated and keep the divine presence in your mind. Breathe regularly while deeply feeling the divine power and joy flowing into all the levels of your being.

REQUEST

Stand up. (If you have the Arcana of the Aurum Solis Tarot in your hands, return it to its initial position on the bomos.)

If you want to ask something special of Selene, put your right hand in contact with the statue (or the representation) and explain your request as precisely as you can. This request cannot be a mental declaration. You must speak it aloud, even if you speak softly. You must really speak to her. This request must begin with the words:

O Selene, I ... *say your name* ... in union with the power of all your worshippers, ask you ... continue with your request.

When this is done, remove your hand, keeping in mind the visualization, and pronounce her divine name: SELENE.

UNCTION

If you are using oil and a statue, place a few drops of oil on the top of your right thumb and anoint a part of the statue, declaiming:

> May this perfumed oil be the visible and invisible manifestation of my love for you!

Draw the symbol of the planet on your forehead declaiming:

> May this perfumed oil be the visible and invisible manifestation of the link which unites us!

Be seated so that you can meditate in silence.
Release the visualizations.
Bell: If you have a bell, strike it a few times.
Stand up.

Note: Proceed to parts 7 and 8, as you did for the first rite of Saturn.

Figure 78: Mars—Ares.

Sacred Ritual of Mars—Ares

Astrology: Day of Mars (Tuesday as determined from the New Moon of the month).

Offerings (beverage): alcoholic—red wine, red IPA beer, Double Bock beer; non alcoholic—tomato juice with few drops of Tabasco.

Offerings (food): red peppers.

Note: From part 1 through part 5 of the ritual, proceed as you did for the Sacred Ritual of Saturn.

6. Invocation of the Specific Divinity

OFFERINGS

Turn your thoughts toward the divinity of the day (in this instance, Ares), and raise the incense toward the statue (or any other representation you have chosen for the divinity).

Visualize an intense light coming from the representation of Ares and spreading all around the space in which you stand. Keep this visualization in mind while you declaim:

> On this particular day, I speak to you, divine Ares, master of Mars.
>
> O most mighty Ares, thou glory of valor, who dost enkindle within the soul the fires of energy and of daring! The heart leaps in eager emulation of thy hardihood, the pulse of thy measured tread sings in the blood. Not the warrior only, not alone the seeker-out of bold exploit, wins thine all-powerful assistance. For thou sendest forth thy flashing cohorts, lithe and sinuous flames of thine own living effulgence: theirs it is to give enthusiasm and inspiration, and to quicken the fierce innocency of the will to go forward, to prosper and to attain. With the ardent fire of the heart and the steel of the mind, and the high-soaring shafts of quenchless resolve, thus do I invoke thee. [58]

---

58. Denning and Phillips, *Planetary Magick,* 221.

Contemplate the representation of Ares while breathing deeply; return the censer to its place on the bomos, close your eyes, and create a mental representation of the divinity in front of you.

Elevate the cup toward the divinity and say:

O divine Ares, accept now this offering of beverage that I am presenting to you!

For your libation, pour a small quantity of the beverage into the empty cup. Raise the cup again, saying:

May this beverage create the strong link which unites me to Ares.

Drink part or all of the beverage, and replace the cup on the bomos. Elevate the plate toward the divinity and say:

O divine Ares, accept now this offering of food that I am presenting to you!

For your libation, place a small quantity of food on the empty plate. Raise the plate again, saying:

May this food create the strong link which unites me to Ares.

Eat part or all of the food and replace the plate on the bomos.

(All the offerings will be put outside after the ritual. If it is not possible to put them outside, you will have to wait for one hour before throwing them in the trash.)

(If you are using the Aurum Solis Tarot, pick up the Arcana of the divinity in your hands.)

Feel more precisely the presence of the divinity in front of you and declaim his hymn while you create a strong mental link to him:

Hail to you, Ares! Indestructible and dauntless-hearted Daimon.

You the valorous, the robust, hear my words!

Weapons, wars, and the destruction of cities are all manifestations of your power and passions.

O terrifying God, human blood and the clash of battles are your delights; the shock of swords and spears gladden your ears.

Most terrible God, you are also the one ending conflicts and discords, establishing peace and bestowing riches.

I praise you, take away from me any ills, and sweep aside any difficulties and conflicts appearing on my path.

O Ares, may the slanders, calumnies, and attacks I suffered and might still be a victim of be definitely brushed aside of my life. Send them back to those who acted malevolently so that balance be restored!

It is thus that beauty and divine intoxication will flow in my life, increasing the qualities and the strength I possess.

Be seated and keep the divine presence in your mind. Breathe regularly while deeply feeling the divine power and joy flowing into all the levels of your being.

REQUEST

Stand up. (If you have the Arcana of the Aurum Solis Tarot in your hands, return it to its initial position on the bomos.)

If you want to ask something special of Ares, put your right hand in contact with the statue (or the representation) and explain your request as precisely as you can. This request cannot be a mental declaration. You must speak it aloud, even if you speak softly. You must really speak to him. This request must begin with the words:

O Ares, I... *say your name*... in union with the power of all your worshippers, ask you... *continue with your request.*

When this is done, remove your hand, keeping in mind the visualization, and pronounce his divine name: ARES.

UNCTION

If you are using oil and a statue, place a few drops of oil on the top of your right thumb and anoint a part of the statue, declaiming:

> May this perfumed oil be the visible and invisible manifestation of my love for you!

Draw the symbol of the planet on your forehead, declaiming:

> May this perfumed oil be the visible and invisible manifestation of the link which unites us!

Be seated so that you can meditate in silence.
Release the visualizations.
Bell: If you have a bell, strike it a few times.
Stand up.
Note: Proceed to parts 7 and 8, as you did for the first rite of Saturn.

Figure 79: Mercury—Hermes.

Sacred Ritual of Mercury—Hermes

Astrology: Day of Mercury (Wednesday as determined from the New Moon of the month).

Offerings (beverage): alcoholic—Armagnac, Belgian blonde beer, or amber ale beer; non alcoholic—sparkling water.

Offerings (food): goat cheese (feta).

Note: From part 1 through part 5 of the ritual, proceed as you did for the Sacred Ritual of Saturn.

6. Invocation of the Specific Divinity

OFFERINGS

Turn your thoughts toward the divinity of the day (in this instance, Hermes), and raise the incense toward the statue (or any other representation you have chosen for the divinity).

Visualize an intense light coming from the representation of Hermes and spreading all around the space in which you stand. Keep this visualization in mind while you declaim:

> On this particular day, I speak to you, divine Hermes, master of Mercury.
>
> O most mighty Hermes, thou swift and self-luminous, whose aspect is refreshing as welcome news: far-seeing friend, sure guide, true counselor! The fore of herb and gem is in thy gift, words and the charm of words, and the magical might of number. Thine are the bright Ethereal messengers, gladsome as flashing waves of the sea, ever eager and youthful! Leader and chief art thou also, potent and subtle, among the children of High Magick: for the hidden ways of life and death, and of every mystery, are alike thy free approaches, and thou movest scintillant but unseen between Earth and the heavens.

Here I invoke thee, I who love and venerate thee: O giver of knowledge, giver of power, thou immortal Energy bathed in dew of light divine! [59]

Contemplate the representation of Hermes while breathing deeply; return the censer to its place on the bomos, close your eyes, and create a mental representation of the divinity in front of you.

Elevate the cup toward the divinity and say:

O divine Hermes, accept now this offering of beverage that I am presenting to you!

For your libation, pour a small quantity of the beverage into the empty cup. Raise the cup again saying:

May this beverage create the strong link which unites me to Hermes.

Drink part or all of the beverage, and replace the cup on the bomos. Elevate the plate toward the divinity and say:

O divine Hermes, accept now this offering of food that I am presenting to you!

For your libation, place a small quantity of food on the empty plate. Raise the plate again saying:

May this food create the strong link which unites me to Hermes.

Eat part or all of the food and replace the plate on the bomos.

(All the offerings will be put outside after the ritual. If it is not possible to put them outside, you will have to wait for one hour before throwing them in the trash.)

---

59. Denning and Phillips, *Planetary Magick*, 222-223.

(If you are using the Aurum Solis Tarot, pick up the Arcana of the divinity in your hands.)

Feel more precisely the presence of the divinity in front of you and declaim his hymn while you create a strong mental link to him:

> Hear my voice, O Hermes, son of powerful Zeus.
> You, the inspired prophet I listen to in the breathing wind,
> You, swift herald moved by your winged sandals from
> Gods to mortals, be attentive to my voice as I sing your praises.
> You are the one who solves conflicts, the one guiding those
> who reach the gates of death, but you are also the cunning
> God who loves profit.
> You brandish the caduceus, symbol of peace and power.
> You, Lord of Korykos, who possesses the terrible and
> venerable power of language, come here and now before me.
> Hear my words and grant me the gift of speech, of memory
> and, overall, a happy end at your side.

Be seated and keep the divine presence in your mind. Breathe regularly while deeply feeling the divine power and joy flowing into all the levels of your being.

REQUEST

Stand up. (If you have the Arcana of the Aurum Solis Tarot in your hands, return it to its initial position on the bomos.)

If you want to ask something special of Hermes, put your right hand in contact with the statue (or the representation) and explain your request as precisely as you can. This request cannot be a mental declaration. You must speak it aloud, even if you speak softly. You must really speak to him. This request must begin with the words:

> O Hermes, ... *say your name* ... in union with the power of all
> your worshippers, ask you ... *continue with your request.*

When this is done, remove your hand, keeping in mind the visualization, and pronounce his divine name: HERMES.

UNCTION

If you are using oil and a statue, place a few drops of oil on the top of your right thumb and anoint a part of the statue, declaiming:

May this perfumed oil be the visible and invisible manifestation of my love for you!

Draw the symbol of the planet on your forehead declaiming:

May this perfumed oil be the visible and invisible manifestation of the link which unites us!

Be seated so that you can meditate in silence.
Release the visualizations.
Bell: If you have a bell, strike it a few times.
Stand up.
Note: Proceed to parts 7 and 8, as you did for the first rite of Saturn.

Figure 80: Jupiter—Zeus.

Sacred Ritual of Jupiter—Zeus

Astrology: Day of Jupiter (Thursday as determined from the New Moon of the month).

Offerings (beverage): alcoholic—whisky, scotch, scotch ale beer, or oak-aged beers; non-alcoholic—spring water.

Offerings (food): citrus.

Note: From part 1 through part 5 of the ritual, proceed as you did for the Sacred Ritual of Saturn.

6. Invocation of the Specific Divinity

OFFERINGS

Turn your thoughts toward the divinity of the day (in this instance, Zeus), and raise the incense toward the statue (or any other representation you have chosen for the divinity).

Visualize an intense light coming from the representation of Zeus and spreading all around the space in which you stand. Keep this visualization in mind while you declaim:

On this particular day, I speak to you, divine Zeus, master of Jupiter.

O most mighty Zeus, thou who dost direct the illimitable powers of the heavens, thou who out of the frenzy of the elements bringest sustenance for the earth! O thou most magnificent the lightnings are thine to impel, and to do thy bidding thou dost summon a multitude more swift, more refulgent, more vital than thy lightnings. The minds of humankind, contemplating thy majestic splendor, are illuminated and empowered with the freedom of new visions: at thy hands thy children receive wondrous gifts.

Royal arbiter of justice, paternal lavisher of mercy, by thine ancient titles—Father of the Heavens, best and greatest—do I invoke thee.[60]

---

60. Denning and Phillips, *Planetary Magick,* 224–225.

Contemplate the representation of Zeus while breathing deeply; return the censer to its place on the bomos, close your eyes, and create a mental representation of the divinity in front of you.

Elevate the cup toward the divinity and say:

O divine Zeus, accept now this offering of beverage that I am presenting to you!

For your libation, pour a small quantity of the beverage into the empty cup. Raise the cup again saying:

May this beverage create the strong link which unites me to Zeus.

Drink part or all of the beverage, and replace the cup on the bomos. Elevate the plate toward the divinity and say:

O divine Zeus, accept now this offering of food that I am presenting to you!

For your libation, place a small quantity of food on the empty plate. Raise the plate again, saying:

May this food create the strong link which unites me to Zeus.

Eat part or all of the food and replace the plate on the bomos.

(All the offerings will be put outside after the ritual. If it is not possible to put them outside, you will have to wait for one hour before throwing them in the trash.)

(If you are using the Aurum Solis Tarot, pick up the Arcana of the divinity in your hands.)

Feel more precisely the presence of the divinity in front of you and declaim his hymn while you create a strong mental link to him:

Hail to you, O Zeus, my Father. Hearken as I call you with confidence.

You are the one leading the courses of the stars with order and beauty.

You are the one shooting from the celestial arch the resounding and shining lightning.

Your resonant voice shakes the hall of the happy and your fire lights up the multitudes treading our world.

Tempests and storms go forth on your command as you brandish your luminous and swift thunderbolt, striking the Earth.

Your fiery arrows terrorize the mortal failing to recognize your paternal power.

Fleeing your vivacious traits falling around him, his hair stands on end, frightened.

Wild creatures also hide and flee from your divine power.

Troubled, the divinities look up to your radiant face as the deepest folds of the Aether reverberate your vibrant breath.

However, O Zeus my Father, your strength is the manifestation of life.

I recognize in your light, your voice, and your breath the manifestation of your power and of your love for your sons and daughters.

In this hour when your roar surrounds me, I offer you this libation.

Grant me your power, your shining beauty, your dazzling health, and your countless riches.

May your peace dwell in me and generate order and strength!

Be seated and keep the divine presence in your mind. Breathe regularly while deeply feeling the divine power and joy flowing into all the levels of your being.

REQUEST

Stand up. (If you have the Arcana of the Aurum Solis Tarot in your hands, return it to its initial position on the bomos.)

If you want to ask something special of Hermes, put your right hand in contact with the statue (or the representation) and explain your request as precisely as you can. This request cannot be a mental declaration. You must speak it aloud, even if you speak softly. You must really speak to him. This request must begin with the words:

O Zeus, I . . . *say your name* . . . in union with the power of all your worshippers, ask you . . . *continue with your request.*

When this is done, remove your hand, keeping in mind the visualization, and pronounce his divine name: ZEUS.

UNCTION

If you are using oil and a statue, place a few drops of oil on the top of your right thumb and anoint a part of the statue, declaiming:

May this perfumed oil be the visible and invisible manifestation of my love for you!

Draw the symbol of the planet on your forehead, declaiming:

May this perfumed oil be the visible and invisible manifestation of the link which unites us!

Be seated so that you can meditate in silence.
Release the visualizations.
Bell: If you have a bell, strike it a few times.
Stand up.
Note: Proceed to parts 7 and 8, as you did for the first rite of Saturn.

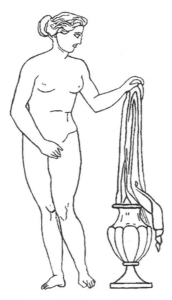

Figure 81: Venus—Aphrodite.

Sacred Ritual of Venus–Aphrodite

Astrology: Day of Venus (Friday as determined from the New Moon of the month).

Offerings (beverage): alcoholic—white wine, pale ale beer, or blonde beer; non alcoholic—apple or mango juice.

Offerings (food): yellow roses, cakes with essence of rose.

Note: From part 1 through part 5 of the ritual, proceed as you did for the Sacred Ritual of Saturn.

6. Invocation of the Specific Divinity

OFFERINGS

Turn your thoughts toward the divinity of the day (in this instance, Aphrodite), and raise the incense toward the statue (or any other representation you have chosen for the divinity).

Visualize an intense light coming from the representation of Aphrodite and spreading all around the space in which you stand. Keep this visualization in mind while you declaim:

On this particular day, I speak to you, divine Aphrodite, Lady of Venus.

O most mighty Aphrodite, thou beauteous, thou golden, who dost awaken the heart with inward song. Of thy giving is the love which draws us to all loveliness, whether of spirit, soul, or earthly frame. Thine is the deep unity which binds all that is, the bond that lovers need no wisdom but love to discern, uniting them in the universal joyousness of thy presence. Most wonderful thou art, and wonderful are those celestial ones who, excelling in strength and beauty, show forth through the worlds thy victorious power alike with thy compassion. Thou art ruler and bestower of the gifts of Fortune. To thee who movest all the forces of life, who dost decree all concord and fruitful interplay of force and force. I make invocation.[61]

Contemplate the representation of Aphrodite while breathing deeply; return the censer to its place on the bomos, close your eyes, and create a mental representation of the divinity in front of you.

Elevate the cup toward the divinity and say:

O divine Aphrodite, accept now this offering of beverage that I am presenting to you!

For your libation, pour a small quantity of the beverage into the empty cup. Raise the cup again, saying:

May this beverage create the strong link which unites me to Aphrodite.

Drink part or all of the beverage, and replace the cup on the bomos. Elevate the plate toward the divinity and say:

O divine Aphrodite, accept now this offering of food that I am presenting to you!

---

61. Denning and Phillips, *Planetary Magick,* 226–227.

For your libation, place a small quantity of food on the empty plate. Raise the plate again, saying:

May this food create the strong link which unites me to Aphrodite.

Eat part or all of the food and replace the plate on the bomos.

(All the offerings will be put outside after the ritual. If it is not possible to put them outside, you will have to wait for one hour before throwing them in the trash.)

(If you are using the Aurum Solis Tarot, pick up the Arcana of the divinity in your hands.)

Feel more precisely the presence of the divinity in front of you and declaim her hymn while you create a strong mental link to her:

Aphrodite, O smiling Goddess born of the sea, lover of the long celebrations of the night, source of generation, O you holy mother, hear my words!

You are the one from where everything proceeds; the one who gave us life.

The three kingdoms, the sky, the earth, and the sea obey you.

As you sit at the sides of Bacchus, you preside to the feasts, thread the ties leading to marriage, and spread your mysterious grace in the lover's bed.

You are the secret Goddess slipping in the desire of men and women, silent she-wolf treading the night.

You are who all men desire, the image stemming from their soul, the Magic philtre of their love and of the sacred ecstasies.

You who were born in Cyprus and put your foot on the pebbles of the shore, come close to me. Feel my desire to contemplate your perfect face, your perfect body.

You wander through the lands of Syria and sacred Egypt, and cross the seas on your immaculate chariot pulled by swans.

O most happy and voluptuous Goddess, I invoke you and desire you. Ride the seas and come to me. Driven by the Nymphs' songs, come on the foam of the waves.

O desirable Goddess, may you manifest yourself to me at this instant. May I contemplate your naked beauty.

May these sacred words be pleasant to you as I hope my purest desire can reach the most inward folds of your being.

O Aphrodite, I invoke you!

Be seated and keep the divine presence in your mind. Breathe regularly while deeply feeling the divine power and joy flowing into all the levels of your being.

REQUEST

Stand up. (If you have the Arcana of the Aurum Solis Tarot in your hands, return it to its initial position on the bomos.)

If you want to ask something special of Aphrodite, put your right hand in contact with the statue (or the representation) and explain your request as precisely as you can. This request cannot be a mental declaration. You must speak it aloud, even if you speak softly. You must really speak to her. This request must begin with the words:

O Aphrodite, I . . . *say your name* . . . in union with the power of all your worshippers, ask you . . . *continue with your request.*

When this is done, remove your hand, keeping in mind the visualization, and pronounce her divine name: APHRODITE.

UNCTION

If you are using oil and a statue, place a few drops of oil on the top of your right thumb and anoint a part of the statue, declaiming:

May this perfumed oil be the visible and invisible manifestation of my love for you!

Draw the symbol of the planet on your forehead, declaiming:

May this perfumed oil be the visible and invisible manifestation of the link which unites us!

Be seated so that you can meditate in silence.
Release the visualizations.
Bell: If you have a bell, strike it a few times.
Stand up.
Note: Proceed to parts 7 and 8, as you did for the first rite of Saturn.

Ritual of the Celestial Temenos

A temenos is the name given to a temple in ancient Greece. As you can imagine there were several type of temples. I want to make things simple here without any complicated architectural notions, therefore, I want to distinguish between two important types of sacred space: the first one is called a "temenos" and the second a "Telesterion."

Figure 82: A temenos.

The temenos was a place of worship where believers were able to go, make their offerings, and pray to their divinities. The Telesterion was a place that was restricted to initiates and closed to the public. For example, the Telesterion of Eleusis was a large, square temple in which initiations were performed.

For this reason, a temple in the Aurum Solis is called a Telesterion.

I previously explained the organization of the worlds in the Theurgic tradition and the existence of archetypes. Plato called those archetypes "ideas." What was true for the symbols that were associated with spiritual principles is also true for the temenos linked to an archetypal temple called the "Celestial Temenos." This is the astral archetype of every temenos. In order to be effective and efficient a ritual must be performed simultaneously on the physical level and the celestial level. A Theurgic tradition like Aurum Solis consciously uses these principles. The initiation itself is a powerful help in this ascension. Every initiate or non-initiate who works in this temenos increases the power of this place. If you practice this ritual regularly, your connection with this place of light will begin to be more and more effective. Consequently, your other rituals will benefit from this contact.

I recommend using this ritual at a specific time of the year. Your birthday, the full moon, solstices, and equinoxes are powerful times to connect easily with the powers of the Celestial Temenos. It is also good to first create a strong connection with the Celestial Temenos. In this case, I recommend performing a complete cycle of the Moon, from the day of the New Moon to the day preceding the next New Moon.

Undoubtedly you will progressively feel a very close connection to this place. In fact, it is not unusual to feel the presence of other people working in this place.[62]

Preliminaries

TIME

This ritual can be performed at any time of year.

---

62. You can share your experiences on the public forums of the Aurum Solis website (http://www.aurumsolis.info).

CLOTHING

Wear a white robe with nothing underneath. (If you don't have a robe, you may wear loose-fitting, comfortable clothing that won't restrict your movements.)

BOMOS (ALTAR)

Cover the bomos with a white linen fabric. On the bomos, place the elements indicated in the representation and listed below.

ORIENTATION

This rite must be carried out facing the west (unless special directions are given).

ELEMENTS ON THE BOMOS

West side of the room
1
2
3

1. Sacred fire (candle without any specific color)
2. Golden cup with white wine or spring water
3. Censer and incense

THE WALLS

It is possible, but not obligatory, to hang representations of the twelve Olympian divinities upon the walls of the temple for this occasion, using the positions indicated hereafter. You can also use the Arcana of the Aurum Solis Tarot instead, if you choose.

Ritual

PREPARATION

Light the sacred lamp and then light the incense.

Walk to the eastern side of the bomos, facing the west.

The Ascension Toward the Temenos

Battery: 1.

Visualize that you are outside. Above your head you will see a great blue sky. The place in which you find yourself is surrounded by pines, which are moving gently in a slight breeze. The scents of the warmth of summer and of aromatic herbs surround you. You are in front of a Greek temple. The temple is surrounded by a colonnade in Doric style. These columns, which are resting upon the plinth of the temple, are located at the third of three steps.

Visualize yourself advancing to the foot of the first step, where you come to a halt in front of it. Your breathing is slow and deep.

Physically perform the calyx (in the same way you did previously) while visualizing yourself standing in front of the Celestial Temenos.

Entering the Temenos

Visualize yourself mounting the three steps so that you stand under the colonnade facing the double-door entrance, which is currently closed. This door is made of wood. The Glorious Star in golden metal is seen to be encrusted thereon.

Perform the calyx again, in exactly the same way.

Visualize yourself knocking on this door eight times, then waiting in silence for a while. Visualize yourself opening the doors and walking in, so that you are one step inside the temple.

Perform the calyx again, for the third time.

Figure 83: Official seal of the Aurum Solis.

Visualize the sacred bomos directly in front of you, at the center of the Celestial Temenos. It is made of stone. Upon each of its vertical faces, the four traditional representations of Hermes (upon the southern face Anubis, upon the northern face the Serpent Agathodaimon, upon the eastern face the ibis, and upon the western face the ape) are found in relief. Against the western wall you see a great banner bearing the same glorious Star you saw on the entrance door. All around the temple you see twelve magnificent, gigantic statues of the Olympian divinities. Beginning on your right (in the northwest), completing a circular clockwise movement, you will successively pass by the statues of: Athena, Aphrodite, Apollo, Hermes, Zeus, Demeter, Hephaestus, Ares, Artemis, Hestia, Hera, and Poseidon. The first six are located on the northern side and the other six on the southern side. Before each statue you will see a perfume burner, from which is billowing an aromatic smoke. At their feet there are also small tablets in which are placed various offerings.

Take a few minutes to become conscious of the sacred power in this place and to feel the divine presences.

You may close your eyes for a few moments if you wish, in order to re-center yourself, and place yourself once again in the Celestial Temenos.

Approach the bomos and kneel, maintaining this respectful position for a while. At the same time, imagine that you accomplish the same gesture simultaneously upon the bomos of the Celestial Temenos.

Battery: 1

THE CELEBRATION

Make the double Ave gesture.

Silent pause; continue by saying:

En Giro Torte Sol Ciclos Et Rotor Igne![63]
Such are the Words, such are the Greetings!

Silent pause.
You can return to the Wand posture.
Battery: 1

Raise your arms toward the bomos, the palms of the hands directed toward the bomos, and declaim:

O Supreme Guardians of our Mysteries, behold me and hear me!

I ask you to aid me in accomplishing my work this day in the Celestial Temenos.

May this rite be performed in union with the Golden Chain of the Initiates.

May this rite simultaneously honor the eternal protective divinities of the Ogdoadic tradition on the invisible and the visible planes!

---

63. This sentence can be found in a floor mosaic of the Baptistery of Florence. The text mixing old Italian and Latin can be approximately translated as followed: "I am the Sun, I am the wheel moved by the fire which makes the spheres turn." This text is used as a mantra in several rituals and individual practices of the Aurum Solis.

Through this spiritual communion, may the ancient Mysteries regain life in me and the world around me!

Silent pause.

May the powerful divinities be honored now!

Battery: 1
Declaim:

Grant this to me, O Gods, you who hold the rudder of sacred wisdom, and who, by lighting in the souls of men the flame of return, lead them back amongst the Immortals, whilst giving them, by the ineffable initiations of the hymns, the power to escape the dark cave and to purify themselves.

Grant this to me, powerful liberators.

Grant me, by knowledge of the divine books and by dissipating the darkness which surrounds me, a pure and holy light, so that I may know exactly the incorruptible God and the man/woman that I am.

May a wicked Genius never, whilst overwhelming me by ills, retain me indefinitely captive under the rivers of oblivion and far from the Gods!

May a terrifying expiation never enchain, in the prisons of life, my soul fallen into the icy rivers of generation, and which wants not to wander there too long!

So, O Gods, sovereigns of radiant wisdom, grant me, and reveal to one who hastens upon the ascending path of return, the holy ecstasies and the initiations which are at the heart of the sacred words!

Pick up the censer (or light another cone of incense). Maintain this position and say:

May all the powerful and immortal divinities be invoked now.

O powerful divinities, may this incense rise toward you as the testimony of my love and of my attachment to you!

O Goddesses and Gods who have always been present in this Celestial Temenos, grant me the power to work effectively!

Walk to the place where the statue of Athena is located in the temple, hence to the northwest, raise the incense, and say:

O Athena, be honored!

Walk around the temple in a clockwise direction and halt before each of the statues that you are visualizing. Proceed in the same way for each divinity whilst saying the same phrases. Raise the censer and say successively:

O Aphrodite, be honored!
Observe a moment of silence.

Walk to the right, stand in front of the next statue, raise the censer and say:

O Apollo, be honored!
Observe a moment of silence.

Walk to the right, stand in front of the next statue, raise the censer and say:

O Hermes, be honored!
Observe a moment of silence.

Walk to the right, stand in front of the next statue, raise the censer and say:

O Zeus, be honored!
Observe a moment of silence.

Walk to the right, stand in front of the next statue, raise the censer and say:

O Demeter, be honored!
Observe a moment of silence.

Walk to the right, stand in front of the next statue, raise the censer and say:

O Hephaestus, be honored!
Observe a moment of silence.

Walk to the right, stand in front of the next statue, raise the censer and say:

O Ares, be honored!
Observe a moment of silence.

Walk to the right, stand in front of the next statue, raise the censer and say:

O Artemis, be honored!
Observe a moment of silence.

Walk to the right, stand in front of the next statue, raise the censer and say:

O Hestia, be honored!
Observe a moment of silence.

Walk to the right, stand in front of the next statue, raise the censer and say:

O Hera, be honored!
Observe a moment of silence.

Walk to the right, stand in front of the next statue (southwest), raise the censer and say:

O Poseidon, be honored!
Observe a moment of silence.

Walk to the eastern side of the bomos, facing west. Raise the incense above the bomos in silence for a few seconds. Return the censer to its place on the bomos.

Raise both hands toward the sky and say:

Light and Life shall be born of the radiance of the Star and that Star shall mount the summits to illuminate forever.
I invoke the divine powers which are present in this sacred place!
All you Powers that are within me, chant in unison with my will and participate in the work that I accomplish this day!

Direct your palms at the great banner you previously visualized in the West and continue by saying:

May the Sacred Mysteries be celebrated once more!

Visualize the cup upon the center of the bomos surrounded by a bright golden light. When this visualization is definitely present, continue by saying:

I invoke the power of the Sun, Father of all things, animator of the world and of all beings, heart of the Theurgic and Hermetic traditions, so that he showers me with his benefits, now and for each moment of my life!
You, glorious dispensator of light and life, master of inner visions and the flash of prophecy, whose standard streaks the heavens with lines of golden fire! Divine holder of recovery

and of hope, you who confers the insuperable joy, omniscient Lord of Day, may your power be with me!

Pick up the cup with your hands and raise it toward the sky. Then say:

O incomparable Hélios, toward you I raise this cup, symbol of my aspiration!

I pray you, O Resplendent One, to receive this witness of my rite in the light of your presence, so that this liquid will be charged with your living power!

May it thus become a veritable alchemical ferment, vivified by your blessing!

Partaking of this mystery, may the rays of the sun elevate my soul, leading me step by step upon the sacred way of return!

So mote it be!

Replace the cup upon the bomos.

Make four circumambulations around the bomos while visualizing the intensification of the solar light in the temple. During each of the circumambulations vibrate the phrase of the Ogdoadic Catena under your breath:

En Giro Torte Sol Ciclos Et Rotor Igne!

At the end of these four circumambulations, remain at the eastern side of the bomos, facing west. Direct your palms toward the cup. Visualize rays of golden light coming from the sky and surrounding you and the bomos.

Observe a silent pause. Lower your arms, hanging naturally on each side of your body.

Battery: 1
Raise the cup in both hands and proclaim:

Behold the visible presence of the Sun!
    May his power purify my being and raise my soul toward
the sacred temple!

Drink part of the liquid that is in the cup. Replace the cup upon the
bomos. Be aware of this energetic liquid flowing into your energetic
body.

Once this is done, sit and meditate for a little while.
    Thereafter, rise, make the double Ave gesture and intone the Latin
invocation of the Eternal, while maintaining this gesture:

Ave ortus omnium, tu ipse sine ortu;
    Ave finis omnium, tu ipse fine;
    Ave vita omnium, tu ipse ultra omnes mundos.[64]

Resume the Wand Posture.
    Invoke the presence and protection of thrice-great Hermes, Father
and founder of the Hermetic tradition.
    Visualize his glorious presence at the western side of the temple.
    Place your right hand flat upon your chest and say:

Thrice-great Hermes, Father and founder of the Ogdoadic tradition, I invoke you!
    May your power protect me during my Theurgic rites, and
in my daily life!
    May I always render myself worthy of your protection!

Observe a moment of silence.

---

64. Translation: Hail, Beginning of all things, Thou thyself without beginning;
    Hail, End of all things, Thou thyself without end;
    Hail, Life of all things, Thou thyself beyond all worlds.

Battery: 8
Resume the Wand Posture.

Thus I, . . . *say your name* . . . , have acted as a true worshipper of
the old ways.

May the light which was revealed to me remain in my
being, accomplishing the Mysteries of the Hermetic tradition.

Exiting the Temenos

Kneel in silence facing the west.

Stand up.

Battery: 1

Make the double Ave gesture facing west and maintain this gesture
as you say:

We give thee grace, thou the Most High, who infinitely surpasses
all things. It is by thy grace that we have received the infinite light
that permits us to know thee.

O thou, the only One, whom we invoke under many
names, thou who givest to all beings thy paternal affection,
thy vigilant care, thy love, and whatsoever virtue there is that
is sweeter than these, hear our grateful voices! Thou hast
endowed us, as thou hast endowed all humanity, with the
intellect to know thee; the mind to accomplish our quest; the
knowledge that we may take joy in knowing thee.

Let us rejoice, for thou hast shown thyself to us in all thy
fullness. Let us rejoice, for thou hast deigned to place in our
mortal flesh an immortal substance—for the sole means of
rendering grace unto thee is to know thy majesty by using the
gifts that thou hast given us.

O Eternal Constancy, we have known thy light supreme,
which can be seen only by the spirit. We have understood thee,
O Life of Life, O Thou who bringest all into being.

We have known in thee the eternal permanence of all nature. O God, let this hymn, this whole-hearted adoration, be an expression of our love.

We ask of thee only one favor, O Eternal One: that Thou wilt keep us constant in our love of knowing thee, and that we will never be far from this kind of life.[65]

Close your eyes for some moments and visualize that you exit the temenos and close its doors.

Perform the calyx as you did at the beginning and visualize descending the three steps of the Celestial Temenos.

Efface the visualization and regain complete awareness of your physical chamber of art.

You may then extinguish the flame upon the bomos, return everything to a state of order, and write some notes about the ritual.

Self-Test Seven

1. What is the difference between the use of the pentagram symbol in the Golden Dawn and the Aurum Solis?

2. Is the tool used to draw a magical symbol important?

3. Is there anything you need to banish from the world you live in?

4. Is there any difference between drawing a pentagram while vibrating a sacred name, or drawing it without the sacred name?

5. How many planetary hours are there in a day and how do you find the first one of a specific day?

6. Are the durations of the magical hours all equivalent?

7. How can you be sure of finding the correct planetary day?

8. When does the day begin in the Theurgic tradition?

---

65. Asclepias XIV–41

The following questions are related to your own experience. It is good to use them as personal meditations.[66]

1. Write a few lines to explain the difference between magic and Theurgy.
2. Which element (among Earth, Water, Air, and Fire) seems for you the most important when you want to express your real personality and why?
3. Calculate the "real" day of your birth and see if you can find any connection with your personality.
4. After using the ritual of the Celestial Temenos, what divinity around the Temple is the most easy to visualize? Do you know why?

---

66. You can share your thoughts about these questions on the Aurum Solis website.

Appendix

Pletho and the Creed of the Ecclesia Ogdoadica

A short text will introduce the eight principles written by the master Pletho during the Renaissance. You can read these principles below:

Figure 84: Official symbol of the Ecclesia Ogdoadica.

Here are the Ogdoadic Principles of the Creed, which are the most essential to everyone who wishes to live as a wise human being.

1. I believe that the Goddesses and the Gods really exist.

2. I believe that, by their providence, the Goddesses and the Gods sustain and guide human destiny for the good. They accomplish this directly, by themselves, or through the divinities of the lower planes, but always in accordance with the divine laws.

3. I believe that the Goddesses and the Gods are never the origin of any evil, neither for us, nor for any being. On the contrary, they are, by their essence, the origin of every good.

4. I believe that the Goddesses and Gods act to bring about the best possible result, according to the laws of an immutable fate, which is inflexible and emanates from the supreme divine principle.

5. I believe that the universe is eternal. It did not begin at some point in the past and it will never end. It is composed of many parts that are organized together and harmonized into a unique whole. It was created to be the most perfect it can be and there is nothing to add that would make it more perfect. It always remains steadily the same—in its original state—and it continues to be eternally immutable.

6. I believe that our Soul shares the same essence as the divinities; it is immortal and eternal. The Immortal Divinities direct the Soul, sometimes in one Body, sometimes in another, according to the laws of universal harmony and from the perspective of what is needed for that being to ascend to the Divine. This union between the mortal and the immortal contributes to the unity of everything.

7. I believe that, in order to be in harmony with our divine nature, we must consider Beauty and Goodness to be the most essential aspects of what exists, and the highest aspirations of our lives.

8. I believe that, in determining the laws that govern our existence, the Immortal Divinities have put our happiness into the immortal part of our being, which is also the most important part of us.

Calculations of the Magical Hours

The time used for the calculations below is from the example explained in Part 7 of this book (Planetary Days Unveiled).

Once the time of sunrise and sunset are known, you must calculate the number of hours and minutes in a day hour and a night hour, which vary with your distance from the equator. The first step is to convert the night hours to military or twenty-four-hour time. If sunrise is at 6:04 a.m. and sunset is at 7:55 p.m., you would convert 7:55 to 19:55 by adding 12:00, and then you would subtract the sunrise time from that number. This yields 13:51, or 13 hours and 51 minutes. Convert hours to minutes before continuing. We have 13 hours and 51 minutes; 13 hours = 780 minutes; then we add the 51 minutes to get 831. To calculate the number of minutes in a planetary hour, the number of minutes in a day hour is calculated by dividing the number of minutes from sunrise to sunset by 12. In this instance, 831 minutes divided by 12 yields 69.25 minutes, or 1 hour, 9 minutes, and 25 seconds. This result is the number of minutes in one day hour. When you change this back to hours and minutes, and add the resultant number to the time of sunrise, you will have the time of the beginning and end of the first magical hour of the day. In this example, sunrise is at 6:04, and we add one hour and nine minutes to that, which tells us that the first magical hour ends at 7:13.

If you continue in this way, you will easily be able to determine when each magical hour starts and ends. After sunset, the length of these magical hours varies. The easiest way to calculate the length of a night hour is to subtract the length of the day hour (converted to minutes) from 120 minutes (or two standard hours). This always yields the correct number of minutes in a night hour, and you can proceed as you did for day hours to determine the start and end of each magical hour for ritual use.

Timeline of the Hermetist and Theurgic Traditions

A beautifully crafted timeline that is easy and intuitive to use is available on the Aurum Solis website. You have just to follow the link (http://goo.gl/pCAcs) or scan the QR code provided.

Figure 85: QR code of the timeline.

Bibliography

Recommended Readings

Sacred Books

Chaldean Oracles

Corpus Hermeticum: The Way of Hermes: New Translations of The Corpus Hermeticum and The Definitions of Hermes Trismegistus to Asclepius, translated by Clement Salaman, Dorine Van Oyen, William D. Wharton, and Jean-Pierre Mahé. Rochester, VT: Inner Traditions, 2004.

Magic and the Mysteries

Graf, Fritz. *Magic in the Ancient World.* Cambridge, MA: Harvard University Press, 1997.

Price, Simon. *Religions of the Ancient Greeks.* Cambridge, MA: Cambridge University Press, 1999.

Dignas, Beate and Kai Trampedach. *Practitioners of the Divine: Greek Priests and Religious Officials from Homer to Heliodorus.* Washington, DC: Center for Hellenic Studies, 2008.

Renaissance Hermetism

Voss, Angela, and Marsilio Ficino. Berkeley, CA: North Atlantic Books, 2006.

Walker, D.P. *Spiritual and Demonic Magic: From Ficino to Campanella.* University Park, PA: The Pennsylvania University Press, 2000.

Astrology

Holden, James H. *A History of Horoscopic Astrology: From the Babylonian Period to the Modern Age.* Tempe, AZ: American Federation of Astrologers, 2006.

Mythology

Graves, Robert. *Greek Myths.* London: Penguin Books, 1981.

Mclean, Adam. *The Triple Goddess: An Exploration of the Triple Feminine.* Grand Rapids, MI: Phanes Press, 1989.

Philosophy

Apuleius. *The Golden Ass.*

Marcus Aurelius. *Meditations.*

Seneca. *On Tranquility of Mind.*

Platonism—Primary Texts

Plato. (1997) *Plato: Complete Works,* ed. John Cooper and D.S. Hutchinson. Indianapolis, IN: Hackett Publishing Company, 1997.

Neoplatonism—Primary Texts

Iamblichus. *The Theology of Arithmetics,* translated by R. Waterfield. Grand Rapids, MI: Phanes Press, 1998.

Iamblichus. *De Anima,* translated by John F. Finamore & John M. Dillon. Atlanta, GA: Society of Biblical Literature, 2002.

Iamblichus of Chalcis. *The Letters,* translated by John M. Dillon and Wolfgang Polleichtner. Atlanta: Society of Biblical Literature, 2009.

Iamblichus. *De Mysteriis*, translated by Emma C. Clarke, John M. Dillon, and Jackson P. Hershbell. Atlanta, GA: Society of Biblical Literature, 2003.

Ovid. *The Metamorphoses*. Biblioteca Universale Rizzoli, 1994.

Proclus. *Platonic Theology*. Milan, Italy: Bompiani, 2005.

Proclus. *Proclus' Metaphysical Elements* translated by T.M. Johnson. Osceola, MO: 1909.

Van den Berg, R.M. *Proclus' Hymns: Essays, Translation, Commentaries*. Leiden, Netherlands: Koninklijke Brill NV, 2000.

Proclus. Commentary on Plato's Timeus—Book I: Proclus on the Socratic State and Atlantis, edited and translated by H. Tarrant. Cambridge, UK: Cambridge University Press, 2007.

The Greek Magical Papyri in Translation Including the Demotic Spells: Volume One, ed. Hans Dieter Betz. Chicago: The University of Chicago Press, 1996.

Neoplatonism—Secondary Texts

Corrigan K. *Reading Plotinus—A Practical Introduction to Neoplatonism.* West Lafayette, IN: Purdue University Press, 2004.

Dillon, John. *The Middle Platonists: 80 B.C. to A.D. 220.* Ithaca, NY: Cornell University Press, 1996.

Finamore John F. *Iamblichus and the Theory of the Vehicle of the Soul.* Oxford: Oxford University Press, American Classical Studies 14, 1985.

Fowden, Garth. *The Egyptian Hermes: A Historical Approach to the Late Pagan Mind.* Princeton: Princeton University Press, 1986.

Shaw, Gregory. *Theurgy and the Soul: the Neoplatonism of Iamblichus.* University Park: The Pennsylvania State University Press, 1995.

Uždavinys, Algis. *Philosophy and Theurgy in Late Antiquity.* Sophia Perennis, 2010.

Note

An extended bibliography, which is regularly updated, can be found on the website of the Aurum Solis, along with a large number of books you can download for free.

Answers to the Self-Tests

Self-Test One

1. The God Thoth and the Goddess Isis are considered to be the founders of this specific lineage of initiates. It might seem strange to suggest that a God and a Goddess could be the founders of a human lineage. Nevertheless, you must remember that Theurgists did not consider contact between divinities and humans to be an exceptional occurrence.

2. Yes, and no; a myth is a specific kind of discourse that describes how ancient people saw and understood the world. It would be better to think of a myth as a story that is trying to answer to the question: "Why?" instead of the question "How?" Science answers the latter question and mythology answers the former. Myth and spirituality search for an understanding of values and beliefs.

3. The Egyptian Ogdoad is composed of four pairs of personified deities. Each pair is composed of a male and female God (a couple). These deities are named: Nun and Naunet, Kuk and Kauket, Hu and Hauhet, and Amun and Amaunet. Each deity has a human body. The Gods have frog heads, and the Goddesses have the heads of snakes.

4. Djehuti (or Tehuti) is the Egyptian God usually known as Thoth. He is the founder of the magical (Theurgic) tradition. He is also known as the Thrice Great (Trismegistos).

5. No, they are not. The Greek Hermes is the symbolic successor of Thoth. We might describe him as Thoth's cousin. Perhaps this is the reason that there is very little connection between their iconographies. It is interesting to remember that even if Gods share several characteristics they are rarely identical. Furthermore, on the Theurgic level, you must understand that divinities are dependent on their temples, clergy, initiates, and Mysteries.

6. Homer was the first to mention the "Golden Chain of the Initiates." In *The Iliad* (Book 8) this famous author describes a golden chain suspended from heaven with all the Gods and Goddesses attached to this chain. Later this symbolic image was used to represent the transmission of teaching and power from a master to his successor in the Theurgic and Hermetic lineage.

7. Even though the cities of Hermopolis and Alexandria were essential to the development of the Theurgic tradition, it was in Apamea, Syria, that Iamblichus founded the Theurgic tradition per se, and unified its rituals and philosophy.

8. The most significant Masonic rituals that can be associated with the transmission of the Theurgic tradition are the ceremonies used by the "Academy of the Sublime Masters of the Luminous Ring" (Académie des Sublimes Maîtres de l'Anneau Lumineux). The full constitutions and rituals were written in 1788 and a copy is currently held in the archives of the Ordo Aurum Solis.

Self-Test Two

1. The word "philosophy" means: "the love of wisdom." It is interesting to remember that this word was first used by Pythagoras to express the difference between someone looking for the truth and someone who has the truth: a wise man. The teachings of this latter type of person can easily foster dogmatic

religious beliefs in others. When you are always searching for wisdom, you must hold onto your ability to reason critically, which is very helpful in magick and Theurgy.

2. Classical philosophy is interesting in many ways. We should keep two main aspects in mind: 1) we must learn how to die symbolically (how to spiritualize your life in order to ascend to the divine); 2) we must learn how to enjoy the life we are living.

3. Even if some Neoplatonists emphasized the influence of the body, which is opposed to the liberation/ascension of the soul, Iamblichus, who was the founder of the Theurgic tradition, clearly emphasized the importance of the body. Everything we experience in life is important and the *Corpus Hermeticum* explains very well that you can be optimistic about life.

4. No; the concept of "original sin" is a Christian invention from the second century, which was first used in the war between two Christian factions. Eventually this concept (which was rooted in biblical texts) constituted a tremendous power that was used by Christians to impose their political power. Hermetists believe that the soul descends into the body in order to have an experience before returning to its celestial origin, and then being re-born (the concept of reincarnation). There is no malediction in this cosmic law.

5. "High Magick" is another way to speak about "Theurgy," as opposed to "low magic."

6. "Goetic Magic" can be dangerous if you use it without a clear understanding of the laws involved. In the same way, your intent plays an important role in determining the consequences of your magical actions. Someone whose work is totally egotistical will necessarily have negative personal results.

7. The goal of Theurgy is to use symbols and rituals to ascend to the divine. This ascension is accompanied with a better understanding of the cosmos and positive consequences in your life.

8. No, but the contrary is true. See the diagram in Part 2.

Self-Test Three

1. Not completely; according to the anthropologist Mircea Eliade, for example, we can be seen as "Homo Religious." This term means that everyone has a part of their being that needs to express itself through rituals performed in a sacred world. Myths are as real as matter but cannot be analyzed with the same tools. Theurgists think that we also have the ability to use our rational minds to help us stay balanced in our inner life. These strategies are the safest solution to prevent becoming dogmatic, intolerant, and mentally ill.

2. In Paganism and in the Theurgic tradition, there is a Unique Principle: the Good we cannot conceive of, express, or even pray to. However, there are also many Gods and Goddesses with whom we can establish a relationship. Each of us might think that their Gods and Goddesses are unique, but that doesn't mean there is only one God or Goddess.

3. Yes, and you can choose more than one divinity. During our lifetime, we may even change the divinity we worship several times. Theurgists use these beliefs from both the religious and the ritual perspectives, which are slightly different.

4. Yes they are. Because the Gods and Goddesses are immortal, it is clear that a monotheist who believes in only one God cannot have any rational reason for rejecting the existence of all the other divinities. Consequently, all the classical divinities still exist today: Egyptian, Hellenistic, Roman, Celtic, etc.

5. They are two main methods: 1) to use the astrological associations between the stars and the divinities; 2) to think about the life of the divinities as it is related in legends and myths.

6. Religion is a human organization generally based on dogmas the believer is not allowed to challenge. Religion has a hierarchical structure; in monotheism (and even more obviously in Catholicism) the priest is set as an intermediary between the believer and God. Spirituality is an individual and inner relationship with the spiritual world. In this case we do not

need a human intermediary. We can use rituals and the ascension to the divine to establish that relationship.

7. Curiosity is a powerful virtue that helps us open our minds to people who have different beliefs. That doesn't mean we will tolerate intolerable behaviors.

8. "In every action, harm no one. For all the rest, you are free to do as you wish."

Self-Test Four

1. The "religions of the book" are Judaism, Christianity, and Islam. They all stem from the Bible but the latter two also developed their own sacred book: for Christianity there is the New Testament and, for Islam, the Koran. The corpus of the current Bible is the result of a strong and continuous selection of texts in which thousands of pages were eliminated in order to calibrate a precise belief and dogma and then impose this belief system and dogmatism on its adherents.

2. Yes, several books are considered to be sacred in the Theurgic tradition. They are: 1) the *Chaldaean Oracles*; 2) the *Corpus Hermeticum*; 3) a book written by a prophet (priest) named Bitys (no copies exist today). Other texts that have been discovered in recent years are associated with this corpus; this includes various Hermetic texts that were discovered in Nag Hammadi (Egypt).

3. The *Chaldaean Oracles* is a book received from the divinities by adepts referred to as the Julians: Julian the Chaldaean and his son Julian. The Theurgists used Theurgic rituals to obtain these revelations.

4. Most of the *Corpus Hermeticum* has been preserved, even if a few translators changed the meaning of a few parts. Today we only have excerpts from the *Chaldaean Oracles*. The original text was destroyed. The third text was a book written by a prophet (priest) named Bitys. Very often the destructions of

such sacred texts were intentional and were the result of partisans of the new proselyte religious zeal against the old religions.

5. If a book contains an injunction that advocates violence, cruelty, or murder we cannot consider it to be sacred. These behaviors are radically opposed to the principle of a divine essence. This is true even in symbolic and metaphorical terms. There are no valid reasons to use violent words or symbols in sacred writings, which may be taken literally by the adherents of that belief system. It is for this reason that the Hermetic and Theurgic sacred texts have never encouraged violent actions, even in symbolic terms.

6. No; a divine principle cannot be reduced to a specific gender. It is for this reason that we read in the first book of the *Corpus Hermeticum*: "The Nous God, which is both male and female, life and light . . ." Every human being also has these two genders, which originally existed in them and still exist in them in different proportions.

7. It teaches us the first principle, which is that, as human beings we have a dual nature: mortal and immortal bodies. As such, the Theurgic tradition teaches that both the mortal and immortal bodies require the fulfillment of certain needs in order to be healthy and satisfied. Fulfilling these needs can be a source of pleasure and joy.

8. "That which is below is like that which is above, and that which is above is like that which is below."

Self-Test Five

1. Like any other method of interpreting what we see in the cosmos, Qabalah can be considered to be both a specific tool and a map. When we are travelling in a new country, we may need a map or a GPS. As you know, there are several makers and brands of GPS equipment. Each one has their own way of presenting information; each uses different symbols, etc. It is natural to check, test, and compare them against each other, in order to see which one

seems the best to you. It would be strange to say that our map is the only one that has the truth. The same must be said for Qabalah, Christianity, Rose-Cross, Hermetism, etc., even though we often see that companies spend a lot of money and time trying to stop or even destroy their opponents.

2. Astrology uses celestial bodies to explain human behavior and the events of life. It is not clear whether stars and planets can have a real and material effect on our lives. However, the planets and signs were associated with divinities. As such they can be considered to be divine. These Gods and Goddesses can also be seen as archetypes, which are symbolic elements that are also present in our inner being and in the Universe.

3. If you consider that you have two different parts in your being, a spiritual and a physical part, you can begin the work of balancing their needs. A healthy life must involve a well-balanced diet for the physical body, as well as the opportunity to have the spiritual life of your choice without any threats from dogmatic religions.

4. The form of astrology that is used in High Magick (Theurgy) represents the cosmos using symbols of the following principles: the four elements, the seven planets, the Aether, and the twelve astrological signs.

5. Earth is related to the lower part of the body, water to the belly, air to the lungs, and fire to the brain.

6. The Greek letters are: Earth—Gamma; Water—Delta; Air—Rho; Fire—Pi; Aether—Theta. The Hebrew Letters are: Earth—none assigned; Water—Mem; Air—Aleph; Fire—Shin; Aether—none assigned. As we can see the Traditional Qabalistic system is strangely incomplete.

7. Saturn (♄); Jupiter (♃); Mars (♂); Sun (☉); Venus (♀); Mercury (☿); Moon (☽).

8. The signs are divided into *three quadruplicities,* which are: cardinal, fixed, and mutable. In astrology these three groups are alternated, beginning with cardinal and followed with fixed and mutable. Here is the list:

Aries: Cardinal   *Libra:* Cardinal
Taurus: Fixed   *Scorpio:* Fixed
Gemini: Mutable   *Sagittarius:* Mutable
Cancer: Cardinal   *Capricorn:* Cardinal
Leo: Fixed   *Aquarius:* Fixed
Virgo: Mutable   *Pisces:* Mutable

(The *cardinal signs* are considered to be starting points. The *fixed signs* are considered to indicate the stabilization of situations or things in general. The *mutable signs* are indications of situations in evolution or transformation.) The signs are also classified according to a symbolic gender aspect:

Aries: Male   *Libra:* Male
Taurus: Female   *Scorpio:* Female
Gemini: Male   *Sagittarius:* Male
Cancer: Female   *Capricorn:* Female
Leo: Male   *Aquarius:* Male
Virgo: Female   *Pisces:* Female

Self-Test Six

1. When trying to understand the world as it is, you are always using your brain and senses. The senses are rarely objective and the brain is influenced by education. One of the best solutions, in order to avoid or reduce illusions, is to be aware that we are under these influences. We have to develop a larger point of view and a critical mind.

2. We may realize that we have more than one body: one visible and material, the other one immaterial and spiritual. Furthermore, we can look into the Theurgic tradition in order to be more precise. There we will find the five essential parts, which are: the Body, the Body of Light, the Soul, the Spirit, and the Divine.

3. The symbolic representation of a temenos summarizes the five principles of our occult being with two columns (the Body and

the Body of Light) plus an upper triangle placed at the top of these columns (the Soul, the Spirit, and the Divine).

4. Each part can be considered to be a real part of us, but like the astrological signs some are cardinal, or mutable, while others are stable. The Soul (Psuche) can be seen as a spiritual, individual, and immortal part, which maintains who we are.

5. As with any map, every tradition has a specific way of representing the cosmos and classifying its manifestations. The Theurgic tradition defines three main levels of manifestation (sometimes with other sub-levels): the Empyrean or Noetic (the highest level), the Ethereal or Noeric (the median level), and the Hylic or Visible (the lowest level). Theurgic rituals and the philosophy of the Western High Magick are rooted in this map.

6. Hermetism, Neoplatonism, and Theurgy consider the Soul to be immortal. Consequently, when the spiritual parts of your being are embodied at your birth, you can understand that they return to their origin after your death and come back in a new body. This is called "metempsychosis" or "reincarnation." From the Theurgic point of view these consecutive lives offer each of us an opportunity to continually make progress.

7. Theurgic rituals are used as tools to ascend to the Divine following what is called "the path of the return." It is easy to understand that there is a precise progression that can be taught to you by people who have already completed or experienced this journey. As with any physical expedition, training is essential to avoid any injuries and to approach the ascent safely. Many occult societies keep advanced techniques secret. Their goal is not to retain a special power for themselves, but to be careful about what is provided to the neophyte. It is easy to understand that you do not give the keys of a race car to a neophyte driver.

8. "Aurum Solis," the "Gold of the Sun" is a witness to the key role of Helios in Theurgy. From the beginning of the Western magick tradition, the sun has been considered to be the perfect representation of "the Good." We cannot really address our prayers

to this divine principle, but the sun is clearly associated with it. Even the rays of the sun are considered as living and spiritual manifestations that can help us in our Theurgic rituals. As Plato explained, fire is the lower manifestation of the sun and consequently of "the Good." This is also the reason why fire has a precise role to play in the rituals and visualizations.

Self-Test Seven

1. The pentagram is a geometric figure with five points. As you can see in Part 7 of this book, each one is associated with a specific element. The pentagrams are used in two different ways depending on the tradition. In the Golden Dawn a pentagram is drawn by facing the direction of this element. The same "logic" is used for banishing an element. In the Aurum Solis, the pentagram is drawn starting from the point associated with that element. To invoke, the logical movement consists of drawing the pentagram clockwise from this point.

2. Yes, the tool used to draw a magical figure is very important. The goal is to concentrate a specific energy and activate it in a specific figure created on the invisible plane. The result is very different depending on whether you use your finger, a metallic blade, a knife that has already cut meat, or a piece of wood. If you have some doubt about what you can use in your individual rituals, just use your index finger. It is safer and easy to carry with you.

3. Yes and no; the Theurgic tradition believes that the physical world is good and there is nothing to banish from it. Consequently, there is no need of any kind of exorcism. However, just as you might be dirty after engaging in outdoor activities, there are some situations in which your invisible bodies need a substantial scrubbing. In this case you can use the pentagram as a cleaning tool. In the same way it is sometimes useful to protect ourselves and to balance our inner energies.

4. Yes; when we draw a pentagram without any vibration of sacred names we activate (or deactivate) the element we chose. When we vibrate a specific word, a new level of magical work is added; we are invoking an individual power that is related to the element we chose.

5. Each day has twenty-four planetary hours, twelve during the daylight, and twelve during the night. The first planetary hour of the day corresponds to the planet of the day. That means, for example, that the first planetary hour of Sunday (day of the Sun) is the hour of the Sun. You can find the chart of the days, planets, and their divinities in Part 7, "Planetary Days Unveiled." The sequence of the planets is: Saturn, Jupiter, Mars, Sun, Venus, Mercury, and Moon. You will understand this sequence if you look at the diagram at the end of the section in Part 7 entitled "The Forgotten Principles."

6. No; the duration of the hours varies according the time of the year and the duration of the night and day. To summarize, the duration of a day hour is the duration between sunrise and sunset divided by twelve. This is the same for the calculation of the night hours, using sunset and the sunrise of the following day.

7. If you just use a standard calendar there is no way to be sure. In this case the days are totally arbitrary and have no correspondence to any astronomical, astrological, or magical principle. This is precisely why High Magick and Theurgy used the ancient magick and astrologic lunisolar calendar to obtain a real and precise determination. The first day of the week, which is a Saturday, corresponds to the day of the New Moon. The following day is the day of the Sun, and so on. This sequence is recalculated at each New Moon. You can find a chart that explains this calculation in the section in Part 7 entitled "The Forgotten Principles." Planetary powers cannot be used arbitrarily with any success.

8. In the magical and Theurgic traditions, the day begins at sunset, which is the moment that determines the planetary character of the day.

Glossary

Aether

The definition of the term "Aether" has varied with the period of time and the philosophers who defined it. In the *Corpus Hermeticum*, "Aether" is generally considered to be equivalent to the element of Air. This is "the vehicle of the vital breath, which has been mixed with Nature." Sometimes the Aether is considered to be a fifth element and is placed at the top of the figure of the pentagram.

When you consider the situation in its spiritual context, as you continue with your Theurgic ascent, the Aether is situated between the planets and the stars. The initiate Proclus discussed this aspect of the Aether extensively in his book *Commentary on the Timaeus*.

Consequently, in High Magick, the Aether is used as the vital energy that you can activate, for example, with the pentagram. The Aether is also the celestial place you must ascend through in order to reach the level of the fixed stars.

Alchemy

Alchemy can be seen as the origin of modern chemistry. However, the purpose of the alchemists was (and is) not just a study of chemical reactions. For them, everything in the universe is connected. Your body is a representation of the cosmos. The long process of working with plants and stones is meant to simultaneously accomplish an inner spiritual work. If you are inwardly pure, you will achieve a connection between the inner life and the outer world that enables you to obtain such results as the alchemical elixir. As a matter of fact, all of the external work is just a representation of the ascension of the soul. Alchemy cannot be understood or practiced independent of the spiritual alchemy that is the real alchemy of the soul. Even if alchemy can be seen as a part of the Western tradition, its practice is not mandatory to practice magick and Theurgy.

Alexandria

Alexandria is the famous city that was founded by Alexander the Great in the Nile Delta in Egypt. The first, and most famous library of Alexandria was built there. It was the central hub of a great cultural network involving all the religions and cultures of that time. This is the place where the Hermetic tradition emerged. It is meaningful that this tradition was the result of interaction between Egyptian priests and the Greek immigrants who were working together in a city founded by a Macedonian. When Hermetism returned to Greece, nationalism always remained an obstacle to the universal point of view of the original tradition.

Altar

At the time of the earliest beginnings of many religious traditions, the central altar (which is called a *bomos* in Greek) was very often a piece of stone that was employed for offerings and sacrifices. Depending on the religion, or philosophical mystery teaching, the altar was placed variously, including: at the center of the temple, in the east, or in front of the eastern wall. There is no set rule for the shape of these altars. They may be: circular, cubic, rectangular, etc. However, despite the variations, it is quite impossible to imagine a temple or church without such an altar.

In the first exercise of this book you will find a description of the bomos as it is generally used in the first degrees of the Aurum Solis.

Angel

See daimon.

Apotheosis

This word means to become divine, to ascend to a divine level. The origins of this concept are found in the historical writings of many ancient religious and Theurgic traditions. In ancient civilizations like Sumer and Egypt, the King was made divine and considered to be the manifestation of God itself. This was also true in Greece. In Theurgy, apotheosis occurs when, as a result of the soul's contemplation, it is raised to the highest level of consciousness. Theurgic rituals are performed in order to enable the ascent of the soul to this divine world.

Astral

This word is often used as a synonym for "invisible level." The astral is a substance considered to be similar to the "starry sky." This is an invisible energy present in the whole cosmos and constitutes part of its structure. Human beings have subtle bodies composed of astral energy. It is possible to use the expression "astral vehicle," even if this word is too general. This vehicle, sometimes called the "ethereal vehicle" or the "heavenly vehicle," is composed of subtle energy.

Astrology

For many centuries, astrologers have believed that a natal chart offers indications about our character, tendencies, psychology, etc. Our psyche still has the marks of these planetary influences, which compose what we are in a specific way. Astrology can also be used to calculate charts for specific periods of our life and to understand how the present astral influences are combined with our natal character.

Theurgy provides us with the opportunity to understand these influences and achieve an inner balance. Theurgists learn astrology in order to associate their rituals with precise moments of the year.

Aura

According to the main spiritual traditions of both the East and West, the physical body is surrounded by a subtle energy field that is usually invisible. This energy is a manifestation of the life force in all living things, and can be found in every living being (plants, humans, etc.). This energy (called Prana in India, and the Aether in the Western tradition) constantly surrounds us and is continually being absorbed by our energetic centers. The "aura" is the invisible body that also surrounds us on a more subtle level than the etheric body. It reflects our inner life, passions, desires, urges, etc. The Theurgic tradition uses the same word: "aura (αὔρα)."

Special spiritual states of consciousness reveal this aura as an intense light surrounding the head or entire body. The aura is seen by clairvoyants as a colored light that is egg shaped, which surrounds the physical body. These colors may reveal interesting information about the person.

Aurum Solis

Aurum Solis is also called the "Ogdoadic tradition." This Order is the modern heir to the Theurgic tradition I have been describing in this book. In our modern age, this initiatic tradition has been given different names, such as the "Societas Rotae Fulgentis" (Society of the Blazing Wheel) and the "Order of the Sacred Word." Eventually this society took the name of Order of the Aurum Solis in 1897, thereby continuing the Golden Chain of the adepts under its various aspects. From the earliest time, as in modern time, the Order has been governed by a Collegium Cathedrarum, which is presided over by the Lifetime Grand Master and the Associate Grand Master. The Aurum Solis is one of the very rare examples of a stable initiatic Order that can be proud of its heritage.

From its inception, the Ordo Aurum Solis has included what is called a "Guild." The Guilds of the Aurum Solis are a very old custom of the Order. They are inner groups of the Order, which gather together as initiated members who have specialized in a particular field of the tradition (i.e. philosophy, divination, alchemy, the ancient Mysteries of a specific divinity, Renaissance magick, etc.). Some of these guilds are dormant, others active. These members are researching, experimenting, and working under the supervision of the Collegium Cathedrarum of the Order.

More at: http://www.aurumsolis.info

Body and Body of Light

See Part 6 of the book.

Cave (Allegory of the Cave)

The philosopher Plato used the allegory of the cave to represent our human condition; the way we live in this material world. Two worlds are considered: 1) the real world outside of the cave, and 2) the world of illusions inside the cave. We live in the latter. There are different levels of delusions that we suffer from as a result of our condition. Most of these delusions are the result of our lack of memory and the influence of our senses. Our goal is to remember the ideal world we inhabited before being enslaved in the cave. When this memory emerges, we will be able to undertake the journey that will enable us to leave the cave.

This allegory also represents the situation of our souls being embodied in a physical body. Leaving the cave (in the allegory) is the same as performing the Theurgic work that liberates our soul from our body.

Centers of Power

The aura is the subtle energy that surrounds us. There are different levels of energy, some closer to our body, others further away and more subtle. The etheric body is believed to be the closest to the physical body. In Platonic theology we would call this etheric body the "thumos (θυμός)."

This subtle body is crisscrossed with a web of energetic waves and currents. Their interconnections constitute hubs we might call "centers of energy." Some of them are minor centers, others are major centers. The major hubs create powerful vortices that create effects not limited to this etheric body. As with hurricanes, the more powerful the vortex is, the higher this energy rises. Consequently, some of the major centers create real channels between the physical body and the highest subtle bodies, such as the "aura" and above. The number of these centers varies depending on which system you are reading. The system of High Magick (Theurgy) uses seven centers that are related to the seven planets, and the seven Greek vowels. This is generally the same number of centers used in the Eastern traditions. The Qabalistic map generally uses five centers, which are located on what is called the "central column" of the Qabalistic Tree.

Daimon

It is essential to make a clear distinction between the terms "demon" or "devil" and daimon. In Classical philosophy, such as the Neoplatonic tradition, a daimon is an intermediary between divinities and humans. Christianity created the word demon to characterize invisible spirits that are evil. If we want to find a modern equivalent to the beings we have called "daimons," they are equivalent to the angels of the Christian theology. Daimons are not limited to their role of messengers. A specific daimon is supposed to be attached to everyone at birth. Plato sometimes described the personal daimon as a "Guardian Angel," sometimes as an intermediary or even as the soul of the incarnated being. The definition of daimon has been hotly debated in the Neoplatonic tradition and is very important in High Magick.

Declamations

There are various kinds of vocalizations during the rituals. One is the "declamation" and the other is the "vibration" (see Glossary). When you make a declamation, an entire text (of whatever length) is vocalized with reverence and a deep conviction. There are two essential aspects to keep in mind if you want to use a declamation in a Theurgic ritual: 1) The declamation must be made out of a deep love (not fear or a sense of superiority); 2) The declamation must be performed on both the subtle and physical levels at the same time. You must receive special training in order to be able to do that correctly.

It is also necessary to mention that the language used in the declamations is important. For example, the results achieved when you use Greek are different than the result you get when you use Hebrew. You may get an unbalanced result if you use a language that is not appropriate to the specific egregore you are utilizing in the ritual. Theurgists must be aware of that if they want to have a safe spiritual journey.

Divination

The Western tradition teaches that everything in the cosmos is connected. Just as the weather affects everyone on our planet, every phenomenon, declamation, and ritual has an impact on us and consequences in our life. Knowing the associations between things that have no apparent association allows us to understand the cause of our current circumstances. The same concept can also be applied to divination. If we know how to identify real signs, we will be able to understand their meanings. Divination is a very important part of the Western tradition, and is commonly used in Theurgic Orders such as Aurum Solis. A theurgist always employs his intellectual mind when he uses divination to analyze the signs so that he will not fall into superstitious behavior. There are various techniques used to divine signs, including: trance, rousing the planes, scrying, reading signs in water, etc.

Divine

Divine is a general term that characterizes the highest spiritual level of something. In the Theurgic tradition, the "Divine World" is the "World of the Ideas," which contains the principles of everything we see in our physical world.

The "divine" can also be understood to be the "ineffable good," the "principle," which is present everywhere in the cosmos.

Divinities

There is no breach in the cosmos. Everything is connected and there is a relationship among all beings. Consequently, there are different levels of divinities between our world and the "divine," the "ineffable good," which may sometimes be referred to with the very limited word "God" without any consideration of gender. The "highest" divinities (hypercosmic) create the essence of other "lower" divinities, the Spirits, and the Souls. The "lower" divinities create the world, provide the harmony between human beings, give us life, and maintain the ultimate harmony. As these divinities are close to us, their shapes have been described (written about, drawn, sculpted) by numerous authors and artists. They have been the subject of a multitude of representations.

Egregore

This is an invisible power that is the result of a group working together ritually. This egregore may progressively become autonomous and independent from its source.

We are composed of two parts: a spiritual (invisible) part and a material (visible) part. Groups are also composed of these two aspects. Any group can be considered to be a meeting of visible and invisible bodies. There is more in a group than the mere sum of its parts. A ritual group (lodge, coven, chapter, etc.) gives birth all throughout its existence, and during each of its ritual practices to a kind of independent psychological creature, which progressively develops its own unique character, thereby becoming more and more effective as an egregore. This identity is bigger than any individual participant and is commonly considered by initiates to be something called an egregore or a "thought-form" (to use the Theosophical expression created by Russian occultist Helena P. Blavatski). Over the years this archetype sometimes becomes autonomous. This may be helpful or not, depending on whether the character of the group (and therefore the egregore) is well-balanced.

Elements

See Part 5, "the Four Elements."

Ennead

The Ennead is a group of nine divinities. As worshipped in Heliopolis (Egypt) the Ennead was composed of the Gods Atum, Shu, Tefnut, Geb, Nut, Osiris, Isis, Set, and Nephthys.

In the Theurgic tradition, the Ennead is also considered to be the Ogdoad (see Glossary) plus Thoth, as well as the level of the cosmos that is reached when the initiate crosses the level of the starry sky.

Exotericism

This word has the opposite meaning of esotericism. The phrase "esoteric teachings" means "teachings from the inside," or "knowledge that is hidden from the public." In the mystery school of Pythagoras, students were divided into non-initiates and initiates. From this separation, came the idea of an inner circle and an outer circle. Thus, exotericism provides the outer (mundane) explanations of private (inner) knowledge.

Geobiology

Geobiology can be seen as an interdisciplinary field that explores interactions between the earth and the heavens. I might say that geobiology is the Western version of feng shui. Even if the word was coined in modern times, this knowledge is ancient and was used by the Egyptian, Greek, and Roman architects. They used their knowledge of cosmo-telluric radiations and geobiology to determine the location on which they would build their cities, homes, any rooms within rooms, etc. They also utilized the services of "water witches." In Theurgy, this knowledge is used to build the temple and choose the place where rituals are performed outside. This ability is part of the training of a Theurgist. In Aurum Solis, this is a major study of the Guild called "The Green Flame of Albion."

Hermes Trismegistus

It is possible that Hermes Trismegistus was the fictional representation of a master. Many teachings and writings (probably by several other authors) were attributed to him. These teachings and writings were developed in Egypt during the Ptolemaic Period and expanded over the first few centuries of that period. The God Hermes was later associated with the divine figure of the Egyptian God Thoth by the Hermetists. The *Corpus Hermeticum* (his surviving collected teachings) is considered by all Hermetic initiates to be a sacred book. If you compare this book with the books of other religions you will find that this text is one of the very rare sacred books that contains no violent writings and no exhortation to intolerance.

Illumination

The meaning of this word is different in the Eastern and Western traditions. In the Mediterranean, pre-Christian, and Western Hermetic traditions, the term "illumination" is used to mean "a contemplation of the Divine." In this spiritual contemplation, the Soul partakes of divine beauty, wisdom, and truth. However, this process does not entail the dissolution of the Soul. Rather, the Soul's own essence is preserved. The Western tradition provides a variety of practices intended to facilitate the ascent to this level, including: prayer, meditation, ritual exercises, Theurgy, etc.

Initiation

An initiation is a specific ceremony that is used in an "initiatic tradition." A special ritual is used to create a special effect in a candidate who generally doesn't know the details of this ceremony. This latter uses various symbols, words, gestures, perfumes, sounds, etc. These kinds of specific ceremonies come from the ancient Mysteries in the Mediterranean world. They are either symbolic or Theurgic. In the first case, their effect will only be psychological. In the latter the ceremony is performed simultaneously on the physical and spiritual levels. This kind of performance requires that the initiators are extremely well-trained. The result for the initiate is a positive effect that is not limited to his human level and that constitutes a very essential aid so that they can progress substantially in their initiatic journey.

Lamen

This word is used to indicate a kind of pendant worn by a Theurgist (or any magician) during a given ritual. Different symbols can be represented (engraved or colored) to distinguish a ritualistic function or any power the Theurgist wishes to associate with his work.

Depending on the purpose of the ritual, the lamen may be blessed or ritually consecrated.

Magic, Magick, Theurgy

See Part 2, "Theurgy, the Divine Magick."

Magnetism

Magnetism is an invisible energy that is present everywhere in the universe. I might describe this energy as electricity, terrestrial magnetism, or as a flux of particles moving throughout the cosmos. According to spiritualists (and those with psychic vision) this astral energy is a fluid that gives life to human cells, providing health by causing a good balance and circulation at the different levels of our being. Initiates from every period in human history, living on every continent, have written about these "Bodies of Light." (See the entry "aura" in this Glossary.)

Meditation

Meditation is an inner process that allows us to create a more balanced life and helps us to develop the spiritual dimension of our lives. The Eastern and Western traditions have evolved different methods for meditating. The fundamental differences in these two systems are the result of the differences in the unique cultural heritages and archetypal subconscious of these two groups of people. There are some similarities and some marked differences in the two systems. As explained earlier, Freemasonry has its own tradition, which provides its adherents with a very interesting and original system for learning to meditate.

Metempsychosis

Also called reincarnation, this word means "the transmigration of souls." According to Western beliefs, souls are immortal and are embodied in order to improve their knowledge and experience. Every life is an opportunity for progress, until the soul reaches the level of the divinities, and eventually becomes divine.

See also Part 6.

Mysteries and Mystery schools

In ancient Greece (approximately 2000 BCE) there were several groups of highly developed initiates. These groups were generally formed around their interest in a particular divine story, such as Orpheus, Demeter, Mithras, Isis, etc. These myths emphasized teachings about the afterlife and personal destiny. Special rituals and initiations allowed the candidates to directly experiment with these teachings in order to achieve an inner knowledge of these "truths." After these ceremonies, personal fears regarding destiny and death were resolved (no longer traumatic) and the initiates were able to prepare for the end of their physical lives and rebirth through reincarnation (metempsychosis).

Myth

A myth is a story that describes the life and mythology surrounding a God, Gods, or Goddesses. Even though some myths may have certain historical events as part of their story line, the fundamental characteristic of myths is that they utilize potent universal symbols to evoke certain states and to teach. Myths are the foundation of the sacred books of every religion, including: Christianity, Hinduism, etc. Other myths gave birth to the various Mystery Schools.

Numerology

In several ancient alphabets (Greek, Hebrew, Latin, etc.) the letters were also used to represent numbers. For example 1=A=Aleph=Alpha, 2=B=Beth=Beta, etc. Thus, a sequence of letters that formed a word might also have a numerical value that would yield further meaning about the word by comparing it to other words that had the same value. This comparison offered valuable information that would otherwise be hidden. Numerology evolved from this characteristic of ancient alphabets. Numerologists attempt to extract hidden meanings from words by comparing words whose numerical value is equivalent. Numerologists also (conversely) use words to find the hidden meaning in numbers that occur in sacred works and other important documents. The main problem with numerology is that it does not have a consistent table of correspondences that can reliably be used to relate the various ancient alphabets. This problem is due to the fact that ancient alphabets do not have an equal number of letters, and Hebrew (and some other ancient languages) has only consonants. Thus, modern numerology has invented correspondences that are not always perfectly logical.

Ogdoad

See Part 1, "Egypt—Birth of the Theurgic Tradition."

Pagan

In the year 356, Constance II, successor to Constantine, forbade the celebration of traditional rituals and ordered that all temples be closed. Christians were looking for a name for the traditional believers of the Immortal Divinities, and they eventually called them "Pagans" (peasants). However, the essence of one religion cannot be legitimately classified by another religion. No belief system is superior or inferior to another. Consequently, the Immortal Divinities continue to be immortal and they still have many followers today. These followers may be called Wiccans, Hermetists, Theurgists, etc. The essence of this religious tradition is tolerance. Pagans consider all non-violent religions to be respectable ways of searching for the divine.

Path of Return

This is the spiritual journey of our soul ascending from the physical world to the spiritual world. It is not necessary to die in order to perform this ascent. Our soul can use meditation and ritual in order to utilize its personal vehicle and accomplish this essential training.

Philosophy

See Part 2, "The Love of Wisdom."

Polytheism

This is a religion that believes in the existence of multiple divinities. Prior to the first century every religion involved several Gods and

Goddesses. Consequently, polytheism is a religion without dogma that allows each person to choose the divinity of his tribe, family, etc. He can also choose his own divinity, or associate several divinities, or even change his choice of divinity more than once during his lifetime. Philosophers and Theurgists believe in the idea of a "Supreme Good," which is situated above everything. In any case this idea does not contradict the concept of the existence of other divinities.

Later in history, a new dogmatic religious tradition called monotheism tried to eliminate other forms of religion in order to impose their unique view of the universe, and their way of reaching the sacred on the world. Ultimately this aggression did not succeed, even though this association among political power, religion, and dogma still dominate the religious panorama worldwide. It is good to remember that we cannot speak about progress in religion. No religious belief system is superior to any another belief system. The exception is this: no one religion has the right to claim they have the unique truth, nor can any one system impose their ideas by using violence on others.

Postures

Postures are movements and positions that are used at a specific moment during a ritual. Your body is composed of energy and surrounded by subtle bodies. Specific physical positions or movements can activate this invisible energy in a specific way. In group rituals, postures can be combined in a precise choreography that intensifies their effect.

Presigillum

In the Aurum Solis tradition the "presigillum" is the first of three parts that comprise a sigil (magical signature).

This symbol intensifies the power that is invoked by drawing on the visible and invisible levels of the symbol used.

The two other parts of the sigil are the sigillic line (with circles) and the terminal. Generally, the sigillic line is constructed using sacred words and names. The letters of the sacred names are organized in a specific way on a magic square. By tracing the name letter by letter on the magic square, you can easily obtain a signature to which you can add the associated presigillum needed to invoke the sacred power. It is difficult to know exactly how the presigillums originated. Their origin could be the result of the rituals of oracles, or deformations of ancient languages.

Qabalah

Qabalah is a set of esoteric teachings about the Torah. This tradition includes several aspects. Some are focused on a kind of spiritual meditation, others on magical practices. However, all of them are founded on texts, such as the Sepher Yetzirah and the Zohar. Qabalists study the texts in order to understand their occult or hidden meanings.

Qabalah is considered to be one map of the world, other maps being (for example) Neoplatonism, Hermetism, Hinduism, etc.

As Qabalah has been used for many centuries in the Western tradition, Theurgists believe that its teachings are important to enable us to understand books that come from the past. Qabalah is also an interesting tool that we may use to explore different levels of consciousness. However, Qabalah remains one particular expression of the Western world, which is associated with monotheism.

Rose-Cross

This term refers to certain esoteric groups that came into being after the publication in Germany (1614–1616) of the fundamental writings of the Rose-Cross by John Valentin Andreae and his "circle" of friends. After these publications, the Rose-Cross was developed along two main lines: one was Masonic, the other one Hermetic. In the twentieth century several other initiatic Rose-Cross orders were created. The Kabbalistic Order of the Rose-Cross was the first one to be unveiled (more at www.okrc.org).

Soul—Spirit

See Part 6 of this book.

Symbol

Symbols are visual images that are considered to be linked to a spiritual reality. They can be found in texts, myths, or rituals. Consequently, using symbols is a very efficient way to learn about spiritual realities. There are ways to ritually animate a symbol in order to use its link with the spiritual reality it represents in order to manifest this higher power.

Talisman

A talisman is a pictorial representation comprised of geometric symbols, sacred characters, magical squares, etc. It is possible for this drawing, engraving, or painting to have an effect on an invisible plane.

Tarot

The Tarot, derived from the Tarot de Marseille, has primarily been used in three ways over the last several centuries:

1. As simple playing cards without other intention or derived meaning;
2. As a system founded on an esoteric basis, for the purpose of divination;
3. The Tarot was created to invoke specific invisible forces, to generate energies present both within you (microcosm) and at universal levels (macrocosm). Each card or Arcanum represents a state of consciousness and a particular energy, which can be invoked and used in a ritual. The Tarot keys that you use in divination are also talismans that are connected to the most ancient archetypes; they are symbols that can generate specific states of consciousness.

The modern Tarot has been copied thousands of times, unfortunately preserving fundamental errors due to its unnatural association with the Hebrew Qabalah. For example, the number of Arcana was reduced to twenty-two in order to correspond to the number of Hebrew letters, even though the original system was composed of twenty-four divine powers. To know more about that and discover the Aurum Solis Tarot, you can read my book: *The Divine Arcana of the Aurum Solis*, from which this definition is partly excerpted.

Temple

A temple is a place separated from the world and consecrated by specific rituals that confer to it a sacred character. In the Western Pagan tradition we make a distinction between two sacred spaces.

The first kind of sacred space is called a "temenos" in Greek. This is the place where the representations of the divinities stand and are worshipped.

The second kind is called a "Telesterion." This is a private space that is restricted to initiates. This is a room (which has no specified size and shape) in which initiations are performed.

Aurum Solis uses the same kind of Egypto-Hellenic temple that the Ogdoadic tradition uses, because they are both derived from that same source. Ultimately, Aurum Solis also use a temple that is directly related to the Egyptian temples.

Thought-form

This is a Theosophical expression invented by Helena P. Blavatski. As an archetype, a thought-form is the result of a conjunction of wills, thoughts, and ritual actions. Over many years, this sort of archetype can sometimes become autonomous.

Vibration

When rituals are performed, different texts are declaimed. Various sacred names are also used and they can be pronounced loudly or vibrated. The note, pitch, and duration of the pronunciation of such names are a secret that is taught orally. Even if you receive an explanation from a book about how to do this, it is worthwhile to receive the complete training from someone who is qualified to teach you how to feel and understand the right way to vibrate the words. This vibration will allow the magician to increase the power that is invoked in a more efficient way. Sometimes "harmonic sounds" can also be used as a vibration.

Visualization

Visualization is the primary key to the effectiveness of any magical and Theurgic rituals. Visualization involves an ability to focus our mind on a specific image or idea. As the purpose is ritual, visualization is not limited to the physical world. The mental representation generates a concentration of energy that gives life to the phenomenon. Training our visualization is paramount.

Vowels

Since the time of the Egyptian temples, pronunciations of combinations of vowels have always been considered to be a powerful and very efficient part of rituals. The seven vowels have been progressively associated with the seven planets. Theurgists and initiates of the Aurum Solis are still using vowels in the same way described in Exercise 5, which is provided in this book. Vowels are not always used individually and they are sometimes used in combination. Rhythmic repetitions are also used during rituals as well as when you are performing a ritual outside.

Weapon

Some Western traditions talk about "magical weapons." According to the Theurgic point of view, no weapons are necessary if you base your ritual work on a principle of ascent to the Light and a good balance of your different energetic bodies. A weapon might be useful if you are working with an attitude of fear and expecting to have to fight something. In High Magick, it seems more appropriate to use the words "magical tool." We can talk about "elemental tools," which are used to invoke the power of the elements or "major tools," such as the spear for example. Each one has its specific attribution and use.

Worlds

The concept of different worlds is very old. The basic idea is to consider two different worlds, one visible and material, and the second invisible and spiritual. Even if this distinction is sufficient to describe most magical work, each tradition explains the cosmos with different maps and consequently uses different models, maps, and teachings.

For Qabalah, there are four different worlds: Assiah (the material plane), Yetzirah (the astral plane), Briah (the mental plane), and Atziluth (the divine plane).

For the Theurgic tradition and the Chaldaean representation of the world, there are three principal worlds, which are: the Empyrean (the highest level), the Ethereal (the median level), and the Hylic (the lowest level). Iamblichus used this description: Noetic (the Intelligible, highest level), the Noeric (the intermediate world), and the Visible (the lowest level).

It is not necessary to try to force correspondences between systems that are markedly different. The most important thing is to use an accurate map that adequately conveys the information of the tradition in which the rituals are performed.

Index

To Write to the Author

If you wish to contact the author or would like more information about this book, please write to the author in care of Llewellyn Worldwide Ltd. and we will forward your request. Both the author and publisher appreciate hearing from you and learning of your enjoyment of this book and how it has helped you. Llewellyn Worldwide Ltd. cannot guarantee that every letter written to the author can be answered, but all will be forwarded. Please write to:

Jean-Louis de Biasi
℅ Llewellyn Worldwide
2143 Wooddale Drive
Woodbury, MN 55125-2989

Please enclose a self-addressed stamped envelope for reply, or $1.00 to cover costs. If outside the U.S.A., enclose an international postal reply coupon.

Many of Llewellyn's authors have websites with additional information and resources. For more information, please visit our website at http://www.llewellyn.com

SECRETS AND PRACTICES OF THE
FREEMASONS

SACRED MYSTERIES, RITUALS, AND SYMBOLS REVEALED

JEAN-LOUIS DE BIASI 32°

Secrets and Practices of the Freemasons
Sacred Mysteries, Rituals and Symbols Revealed
JEAN-LOUIS DE BIASI

Discover the fascinating truth behind Freemasonry with this remarkably detailed and comprehensive insider's guide.

Jean-Louis de Biasi, a 32nd degree Freemason who's been involved in the order for over twenty years, gives readers a rare candid look at the little-known facts and essential aspects of Freemasonry. de Biasi reveals the Masonic tradition's history, the Scottish Rite's degree-based system, and the order's closely held beliefs. He explores Freemasonry's roots in the Ancient Egyptian Mysteries, its hermetic and Qabalistic underpinnings, and the sacred symbolism embedded in the U.S. Capitol and Washington Monument. Also discussed: Masonic temples, power-charged grids hidden in architecture, Albert Pike's teachings, the Rose Cross mysteries, and the Masonic themes in Dan Brown's popular books.

Also featured are practical Masonic meditations and rituals, plus interviews with scientists who lend a modern perspective on Freemasonry.

978-0-7387-2340-2, 312 pp., 7^1/$_2$ x 9^1/$_8$ **$19.95**

THE

DIVINƐ
ΛRCANΛ
OF THE
ΛURUM SΘLIS

Using Tarot Talismans for Ritual & Initiation

JEAN-LOUIS DE BIASI

The Divine Arcana of the Aurum Solis
Using Tarot Talismans for Ritual & Initiation

JEAN-LOUIS DE BIASI

Take the first steps on the path of initiation using the universal power of the tarot. Jean-Louis de Biasi, Grandmaster of the Ordo Aurum Solis, presents the tarot as a complete system of High Magick. He pairs the symbolic components of the Hermetic macrocosm—the five elements, the seven ancient planets, and zodiac signs—with corresponding deities of the classical Greek pantheon, enabling you to channel cosmic energies. Using the tarot images as talismans, you'll connect with and invoke the unique energies of each card to reach higher states of consciousness through rituals that further your inner development.

978-0-7387-2086-9, 384 pp., 6 x 9 $21.95

Mysteria Magica
Fundamental Techniques of High Magick
OSBORNE PHILLIPS AND MELITA DENNING

Mysteria Magica is the classic ritual text of training and development in the Western Mystery Tradition, appearing on countless suggested reading lists. Long out of print, this book has been hard to find and expensive when chanced upon.

A complete system of Magick, *Mysteria Magica* reveals essential and advanced teachings in terms that even newcomers can follow, with a richness of inspiration embraced by experienced mages. *Mysteria Magica* explores the core of Ceremonial Magick-the inner system of symbolism, philosophy, and spiritual technology. It shows how and why ritual acts can lead to their desired result in the "Principles of Ceremonial" section. This comprehensive work also presents a formal traditional education in the key elements of High Magick: sigils; telesmata; consecration; protection; and Enochian rituals and techniques, including proper pronunciation of the Enochian language. Designed for individual or group use, *Mysteria Magica* contains the most vital procedures of High Magick with authentic texts and formulae.

978-0-7387-0169-1, 408 pp., 6 x 9   **$24.95**

ASCENSION
MAGICK

Ritual, Myth & Healing for the New Aeon

CHRISTOPHER PENCZAK

Ascension Magick
Ritual, Myth & Healing for the New Aeon
CHRISTOPHER PENCZAK

Taking a magickal approach to this often misunderstood spirituality, Christopher Penczak explores the fascinating path of ascension. *Ascension Magick* unveils the diverse mystical roots of ascension, and highlights where the beliefs and practices of today's "light workers" intersect with those of modern Pagans, witches, and magick practitioners. It also examines the practical side-various forms of magick, energy healing, meditation, past life regression, channeling, dowsing-and provides helpful meditations, spells, and exercises. From angels and aliens to reincarnation and the Merkaba, Penczak leaves no stone unturned in this remarkably thorough and absorbing examination of ascension spirituality and magick.

978-0-7387-1047-1, 576 pp., 7¹/₂ x 9¹/₈   **$24.99**

BRAIN
magick

exercises in meta-magick and invocation

PHILIP H. FARBER

Brain Magick
Exercises in Meta-Magick and Invocation
Philip H. Farber

Recent discoveries in neuroscience suggest that the magickal practices of evocation and invocation are related to natural brain functions—this book is the first to present a theory of magick based on the new research. The ultimate goal of invocation is to infuse your life with more excitement, meaning, and passion. *Brain Magick* is packed full of exercises that illustrate the principles of neuroscience and magick, and has everything you need to quickly develop skill in the art of invocation.

This easily practiced form of ritual technology is appropriate for beginners and advanced students alike. For those familiar with any kind of magick—Wiccan, Thelemic, Golden Dawn, Goetic, Chaos or Hermetic—this book will provide opportunities to consider their practice in a new light, and take their magical experiences to a new level. Even complete novices will be able to start immediately.

978-0-7387-2926-8, 264 pp., 5 ³/₁₆ x 8   **$15.95**

Revised and Expanded
MODERN MAGICK
TWELVE LESSONS IN THE HIGH MAGICKAL ARTS
DONALD MICHAEL KRAIG

Modern Magick
Twelve Lessons in the High Magickal Arts
DONALD MICHAEL KRAIG

For more than two decades, *Modern Magick* has been the world's most popular instruction manual on how to work real magick. Now, author Donald Michael Kraig, with decades more experience, research, training, and study, has created the ultimate version of this contemporary classic. This expanded edition features an updated design, more personal stories, and a wealth of new information, including more than 175 original images and a completely new chapter on three emerging trends in magick and how readers can put them to use. What hasn't changed: the comprehensive scope and clear, step-by-step ritual instructions that have made this book an indispensable guide for more than 150,000 magicians.

978-0-7387-1578-0, 528 pp., 8¹/₂ x 11 **$29.95**

THE MAGICAL PHILOSOPHY · BOOK IV

Planetary Magick

Invoking and Directing the Powers of the Planets

DENNING & PHILLIPS

Planetary Magick

Invoking and Directing the Powers of the Planets

OSBORNE PHILLIPS AND MELITA DENNING

Llewellyn is pleased to announce the return of *Planetary Magick*, one of the most respected and well-known books on the topic of planetary spell-work, and the fourth book in Denning and Phillips's renowned Magickal Philosophy series.

Planetary magick lies at the root of all astrological, alchemical, and Qabalistic lore. Designed for both the beginner and the established mage, this book teaches how to invoke and direct planetary energies of the seven spheres to empower any magical working. It includes 65 classic magickal rites in full detail and provides the reader with a thorough understanding of the foundation of Western Magick.

978-0-7387-2734-9, 480 pp., 6 x 9   **$24.95**

To order, call 1-877-NEW-WRLD
Prices subject to change without notice
Order at Llewellyn.com 24 hours a day, 7 days a week!